CONTENTS

v

FOREWORD

"Without counsel plans fail, but with many advisors they succeed" (Proverbs 15:22 ESV).

Thus says the ancient Proverb.

For anyone who thirsts to know God and to nourish a well-rooted, deeply anchored, resilient, and joyful faith, very few things could be truer than this.

Left to ourselves, none of us would be able to rightly know God, creation, our neighbor, or even ourselves. Perhaps this is why Jesus told Nicodemus, the Old Testament scholar and teacher of Israel, that not even he can receive even one thing unless it is first given him from heaven (see John 3:27). Perhaps this is also why Paul prayed earnestly for those under his spiritual care, that the Holy Spirit would open the eyes of their hearts to help them hear, discern, experience, and conduct their lives according to the riches of God's truth and grace (see Ephesians 1:18).

We who claim Christ as Lord and Savior ought to thank God every day that He has not left us without a witness. Because He loves us, He has given us the Bible to show us clearly "what man is to believe concerning God, and what duty God requires of man."[1] In the Old and New Testaments, He has given us a

---

1. Westminster Shorter Catechism, Question 3.

sacred treasure. There we learn firsthand from the patriarchs, the prophets, the psalms and poetic writings, the wisdom books, the gospels, the epistles, and the apocalyptic writings.

God has also given us the Holy Spirit, whom Scripture calls the Wonderful Counselor. The Counselor helps us understand, believe, and walk according to the truth that was once for all delivered to the saints. Working by and with the Word of God, he also convicts us of our sin, covers our guilt and shame, comforts us in our sorrows, makes known to us the path of life, and leads us in the way everlasting.

Along the way, God has also given us some specially gifted teachers through whom the same Spirit speaks for our profit. These include our parents, mentors, pastors, peers, some authors, and even a few podcasts. Among these there are also some historic and uniquely anointed teachers—a great cloud of witnesses, as Hebrews calls them—who not only inspire us to persevere in a race that they have already finished but who also continue speaking to us today.

This book, compiled by Susan Hill, a very bright woman who calls me her pastor and who also teaches me much, is a collection of several such voices. Citing works written by the likes of Luther, Calvin, Edwards, Spurgeon, and others, *Captivating Grace* serves up a rich feast in what it means to think, breathe, live, love, and serve according to the five core salvation truths that sparked the Protestant Reformation: Through Scripture Alone, Through Faith Alone, By Grace Alone, In Christ Alone, and To the Glory of God Alone. As you'll soon discover as you engage them, these great truths are as relevant for us today as they were for those who lived centuries ago.

Perhaps after journeying through this rich devotional, you will discover new heroes as well as reconnect with old ones. But even more than this, I pray that this fine and careful work will lead you into the riches of Christ and stir within you the same courage, fervor, and joy that gave birth to a movement that still shakes the world today.

SCOTT SAULS

Senior Pastor of Christ Presbyterian Church and author of *Jesus Outside the Lines* and *Irresistible Faith*

SCRIPTURE
ALONE

THE AUTHOR OF SCRIPTURE

*All Scripture is God-breathed and is
useful for teaching, rebuking, correcting
and training in righteousness.*

2 TIMOTHY 3:16

First, then, concerning this book, who is the author? The text says that it is God. "I have written to him the great things of my law." Here lies my Bible—who wrote it? I open it, and I find it consists of a series of tracts. The first five tracts were written by a man called Moses. I turn on and I find other. Sometimes I see David is the penman, at other times, Solomon. Here I read Micah, then Amos, then Hosea. As I turn further on, to the more luminous pages of the New Testament, I see Matthew, Mark, Luke, and John, Paul, Peter, James, and others, but when I shut up the book, I ask myself, *Who is the author of it? Do these men jointly claim the authorship? Are they the compositors of this massive volume? Do they between themselves divide the honor?* Our holy religion answers, No! This volume is the writing of the living God: each letter was penned with an almighty finger, each word in it dropped from the everlasting lips, each sentence was dictated by the Holy Spirit.

CHARLES SPURGEON

ALL POWER RESTS ON THE WORD

I am not ashamed of the gospel, because it is the power of God that brings salvation to everyone who believes; first the Jew, then to the Gentile.

ROMANS 1:16

This is the kingdom of Christ: it is thus that He reigns, so that all power stands and rests upon the Word of God. And those who hear and believe this Word belong to this kingdom; which Word becomes so powerful, that it affects all things that are necessary for man and brings all good things which might be desired: for it is the power of God which can and may save all who believe on it, as Paul saith.

Wherefore, if thou believe that Christ died to deliver thee from all misery, and if thou cleave to that Word, it is so sure and certain that no creature can overthrow it. And as no creature can subvert the Word, so no one can harm thee, since thou believest on it. And thou wilt with the Word conquer sin, death, the devil, and hell; and thus thou wilt come and be drawn into that state where the Word itself is; that is, into eternal peace, joy, and life. And, to be brief, thou wilt be made partaker of all the blessings that are contained in the Word: this kingdom, therefore, is wonderful.

MARTIN LUTHER

ALL WE HAVE IS FROM GOD

We have this treasure in jars of clay to show that this
all-surpassing power is from God and not from us.

2 CORINTHIANS 4:7

It is of God that the redeemed do receive all their true excellency, wisdom, and holiness; and that two ways, namely as the Holy Ghost, by whom these things are immediately wrought, is from God, proceeds from Him, and is sent by Him; and also as the Holy Ghost Himself is God, by whose operation and indwelling the knowledge of divine things, and a holy disposition, and all grace, are conferred and upheld.

And though means are made use of in conferring grace on men's souls, yet 'tis of God that we have these means of grace, and 'tis God that makes them effectual. 'Tis of God that we have the Holy Scriptures; they are the Word of God. 'Tis of God that we have ordinances, and their efficacy depends on the immediate influence of the Spirit of God. The ministers of the Gospel are sent of God, and all their sufficiency is of Him.

JONATHAN EDWARDS

THE BOOK OF GOD

"I wrote for them the many things of my law."

HOSEA 8:12

This Bible is God's Bible; and when I see it, I seem to hear a voice springing up from it, saying, "I am the Book of God: man, read me. I am God's writing: open my leaf, for I was penned by God; read it, for He is my Author, and you will see Him visible and manifest everywhere."

"I have written to him the great things of my law." How do you know that God wrote the book? That is just what I shall not try to prove to you. I could, if I pleased, do a demonstration, for there are arguments enough, there are reasons enough, did I care to occupy your time in bringing them before you: but I shall do no such thing. I might tell you, if I pleased, that the grandeur of the style is above that of any mortal writing, and that all the poets who have ever existed, could not, with all their works united, give us such sublime poetry and such mighty language as is to be found in the Scriptures.

CHARLES SPURGEON

THE SCHOOL OF THE HOLY SPIRIT

The statutes you have laid down are
righteous; they are fully trustworthy.

PSALM 119:138

In order to keep the legitimate course in this matter, we must return to the Word of God, in which we are furnished with the right rule of understanding. For Scripture is the school of the Holy Spirit, in which as nothing useful and necessary to be known has been omitted, so nothing is taught but what it is of importance to know. Everything therefore delivered in Scripture on the subject of predestination we must beware of keeping from the faithful, lest we seem either maliciously to deprive them of the blessing of God, or to accuse and scoff at the Spirit, as having divulged what ought on any account to be suppressed.

Let us, I say, allow the Christian to unlock his mind and ears to all the words of God which are addressed to him, provided he do it with this moderation—namely that whenever the Lord shuts His sacred mouth, He also desists from inquiry. The best rule of sobriety is not only in learning to follow wherever God leads, but also when He makes an end of teaching, to cease also from wishing to be wise.

JOHN CALVIN

THE SACRED WRIT

Devote yourselves to prayer, being watchful and thankful.

COLOSSIANS 4:2

It is interesting to remark how large a portion of Sacred Writ is occupied with the subject of prayer, either in furnishing examples, enforcing precepts, or pronouncing promises. We scarcely open the Bible before we read, "Then began men to call upon the name of the Lord"; and just as we are about to close the volume, the "Amen" of an earnest supplication meets our ear. Instances are plentiful. Here we find a wrestling Jacob—there a Daniel who prayed three times a day—and a David who with all his heart called upon his God. On the mountain we see Elias, in the dungeon Paul and Silas. We have multitudes of commands, and myriads of promises. What does this teach us but the sacred importance and necessity of prayer?

We may be certain that whatever God has made prominent in His Word, He intended to be conspicuous in our lives. If He has said much about prayer, it is because He knows we have much need of it. So deep are our necessities, that until we are in heaven we must not cease to pray.

CHARLES SPURGEON

GOD'S COUNSEL

You guide me with your counsel, and
afterward you will take me into glory.

PSALM 73:24

B e assured that thy God will be thy Counsellor and Friend; He shall guide thee; He will direct all thy ways. In His written Word thou hast this assurance in part fulfilled, for Holy Scripture is His counsel to thee. Happy are we to have God's Word always to guide us! What were the mariner without his compass? And what were the Christian without the Bible? This is the unerring chart, the map in which every shoal is described, and all the channels from the quicksands of destruction to the haven of salvation mapped and marked by One who knows all the way.

Blessed be Thou, O God, that we may trust Thee to guide us now, and guide us even to the end! After this guidance through life, the psalmist anticipates a divine reception at last: "and afterward receive me to glory." What a thought for thee, believer! God Himself will receive thee to glory—thee! Wandering, erring, straying, yet He will bring thee safe at last to glory! This is thy portion; live on it this day.

CHARLES SPURGEON

THE VOICE OF GOD

*"My sheep listen to my voice; I know
them, and they follow me."*

JOHN 10:27

We ministers can do nothing else than become the mouths and instruments of our Lord Christ, through which He sensibly preaches His Word. He permits the Word to be proclaimed openly, that all may hear it. But for the heart itself to digest it and feel it within, that is the operation of faith, and is the mystical work of Christ; which He works, according to His divine knowledge and good pleasure.

For who is a good shepherd? "A good shepherd," says Christ, "layeth down his life for his sheep; and I also lay down My life for My sheep." In this virtue He comprehends all things at once and sets before us a sweet parable of the sheep. You see that this animal is altogether foolish and is the simplest of all beasts, so that if one would speak of some simple person, he says, "He is a sheep!" Nevertheless the sheep has this characteristic more than any other animal, that it quickly hears the voice of its shepherd; nor will it follow any other than its own shepherd.

MARTIN LUTHER

WRITTEN ON YOUR HEART

"All that belongs to the Father is mine. That is why I said the Spirit will receive from me what he will make known to you."

JOHN 16:15

There are times when all the promises and doctrines of the Bible are of no avail, unless a gracious hand shall apply them to us. We are thirsty, but too faint to crawl to the waterbrook. When a soldier is wounded in battle, it is of little use for him to know that there are those at the hospital who can bind up his wounds, and medicines there to ease all the pains which he now suffers: what he needs is to be carried thither, and to have the remedies applied.

It is thus with our souls, and to meet this need there is one, even the Spirit of truth, who takes of the things of Jesus and applies them to us. Think not that Christ hath placed His joys on heavenly shelves that we may climb up to them for ourselves, but He draws near and sheds His peace abroad in our hearts. O Christian, if thou art tonight labouring under deep distresses, the promises He has written in the Word He will write anew on your heart.

CHARLES SPURGEON

A DOCTRINE OF PIETY

All his precepts are trustworthy.
They are established forever.

PSALM 111:7-8

The Word of God in the beginning, who is Himself God, must be our life, meat, light, and salvation. Therefore we cannot attribute to Christ's human nature the power of making us alive, but the life is in the Word, which dwells in the flesh and makes us alive by the flesh. This interpretation is simple and helpful. Thus Saint Paul is wont to call the doctrine of the Gospel *doctrina pietatis*, a doctrine of piety—a doctrine that makes men rich in grace.

However, the other interpretation which the heathen also have, namely, that all creatures live in God, does indeed make subtle disputants and is obscure and difficult; but it teaches nothing about grace, nor does it make men rich in grace. Wherefore the Scriptures speak of it as "idle." Just as we interpret the words of Christ when He says, "I am the life," so also should we interpret these words, and say nothing philosophically of the life of the creatures in God. On the contrary, we should consider how God lives in us, and makes us partakers of His life, so that we live through Him, of Him, and in Him.

MARTIN LUTHER

MEDITATE ON THE WORD

I meditate on your precepts and consider your ways.

PSALM 119:15

Our bodies are not supported by merely taking food into the mouth, but the process which really supplies the muscle, and the nerve, and the sinew, and the bone, is the process of digestion. It is by digestion that the outward food becomes assimilated with the inner life. Our souls are not nourished merely by listening a while to this, and then to that, and then to the other part of divine truth. Hearing, reading, marking, and learning all require inwardly digesting to complete their usefulness, and the inward digesting of the truth lies for the most part in meditating upon it.

Why is it that some Christians, although they hear many sermons, make but slow advances in the divine life? Because they neglect their closets, and do not thoughtfully meditate on God's Word. They love the wheat, but they do not grind it; they would have the corn, but they will not go forth into the fields to gather it; the fruit hangs upon the tree, but they will not pluck it; the water flows at their feet, but they will not stoop to drink it. From such folly deliver us, O Lord, and be this our resolve this morning, "I will meditate in thy precepts."

CHARLES SPURGEON

EXALT THE WORD

God is no respecter of persons.

ACTS 10:34 KJV

We are talking about the Word of God now, and the truth of the Gospel. That Gospel is more excellent than all apostles. God accepteth no man's person. Paul is quoting Moses: "Thou shalt not respect the person of the poor, nor honor the person of the mighty" (Leviticus 19:15). This quotation from Moses ought to shut the mouths of the false apostles.

"Don't you know that God is no respecter of persons?" cries Paul. The dignity or authority of men means nothing to God. The fact is that God often rejects just such who stand in the odor of sanctity and in the aura of importance. In doing so God seems unjust and harsh. But men need deterring examples. For it is a vice with us to esteem personality more highly than the Word of God. God wants us to exalt His Word and not men.

There must be people in high office, of course. But we are not to deify them. The governor, the mayor, the preacher, the teacher, the scholar, father, mother, are persons whom we are to love and revere, but not to the extent that we forget God.

MARTIN LUTHER

MIGHTY IN THE SCRIPTURES

Let the message of Christ dwell among you richly as you teach and admonish one another with all wisdom.

COLOSSIANS 3:16

Let us be thoroughly well acquainted with the great doctrines of the Word of God, and let us be mighty in expounding the Scriptures. I am sure that no preaching will last so long, or build up a church so well, as the expository. To renounce altogether the hortatory discourse for the expository would be running to a preposterous extreme; but I cannot too earnestly assure you that, if your ministries are to be lastingly useful, you must be expositors.

For this purpose, you must understand the Word yourselves, and be able so to comment upon it that the people may be built up by the Word. Be masters of your Bibles, brethren; whatever other works you have not searched, be at home with the writings of the prophets and apostles. "Let the Word of God dwell in you richly."

Having given that the precedence, neglect no field of knowledge. The presence of Jesus on the earth has sanctified the whole realm of nature; and what He has cleansed, call not you common. All that your Father has made is yours, and you should learn from it.

CHARLES SPURGEON

LOVE FOR THE WORD

How sweet are your words to my taste,
sweeter than honey to my mouth.

PSALM 119:103

Only the acts of a Christian are truly good and acceptable to God, because they are done in faith, with a cheerful heart, out of gratitude to Christ. We ought to have no misgivings about whether the Holy Ghost dwells in us. We are "the temple of the Holy Ghost" (1 Corinthians 3:16).

When we have a love for the Word of God and gladly hear, talk, write, and think of Christ, we are to know that this inclination toward Christ is the gift and work of the Holy Ghost. Where you come across contempt for the Word of God, there is the devil.

We meet with such contempt for the Word of God mostly among the common people. They act as though the Word of God does not concern them. Wherever you find a love for the Word, thank God for the Holy Spirit who infuses this love into the hearts of men. We never come by this love naturally, neither can it be enforced by laws. It is the gift of the Holy Spirit.

MARTIN LUTHER

STUDENTS OF THE WORD

*Ezra had devoted himself to the study and
observance of the Law of the LORD.*

EZRA 7:10

See to it that you have, in a sevenfold degree, light of a
higher kind. You are to be, above all things, students of the
Word of God; this, indeed, is a main point of your avocation.
If we do not study Scripture, and those books that will help
us to understand theology, we are but wasting time while we
pursue other researches. We should judge him to be a foolish
fellow who, while preparing to be a physician, spent all his
time in studying astronomy. There is a connection of some
kind between stars and human bones, but a man could not
learn much of surgery from Arcturus or Orion.

So, there is a connection between every science and religion,
and I would advise you to obtain much general knowledge; but
universal information will be a poor substitute for a special and
prayerful study of the Scriptures, and of the doctrines contained
in the revelation of God.

CHARLES SPURGEON

THE FOUNDATION
OF FAITH

The grass withers and the flowers fall, but
the word of our God endures forever.

ISAIAH 40:8

True faith is ignorant of all division; for "there is," saith the apostle, "one Lord, one faith, one baptism, one God and Father of all." For there remaineth, from the beginning of the world even unto the end thereof, one and the same faith in all the elect of God. God is one and the same forever, the only Well of all goodness, that can never be drawn dry.

The truth of God, from the beginning of the world, is one and the same, set forth to men in the Word of God. Therefore the object and foundation of faith, that is, God and the Word of God, remain forever one and the selfsame. In one and the selfsame faith with us have all the elect ever since the creation of the world believed, that unto us through Christ all good things are freely given, and that all truth necessary to be believed is declared in the Word of the Lord. Wherefore the faithful of the old world always settled their faith on God and His Word, so that now, without all doubt, there cannot be any more than one true faith.

MARTIN LUTHER

THE BALM OF GOD

He sent out his word and healed them;
he rescued them from the grave.

PSALM 107:20

There is no balm in Gilead, but there is balm in God. There is no physician among the creatures, but the Creator is Jehovah-rophi. It is marvellous how one sweet word of God will make whole songs for Christians. One word of God is like a piece of gold, and the Christian is the gold-beater, and can hammer that promise out for whole weeks.

So, then, poor Christian, thou needest not sit down in despair. Go to the Comforter, and ask Him to give thee consolation. Thou art a poor dry well. You have heard it said, that when a pump is dry, you must pour water down it first of all, and then you will get water, and so, Christian, when thou art dry, go to God, ask Him to shed abroad His joy in thy heart, and then thy joy shall be full. Do not go to earthly acquaintances, for you will find them Job's comforters after all; but go first and foremost to thy "God, that comforteth those that are cast down," and you will soon say, "In the multitude of my thoughts within me thy comforts delight my soul."

CHARLES SPURGEON

THE NINEVITES BELIEVED

When God saw what they did . . . he relented.

JONAH 3:10

Long before the time of Moses, God justified men without the Law. He justified many kings of Egypt and Babylonia. He justified Job. Nineveh, that great city, was justified and received the promise of God that He would not destroy the city. Why was Nineveh spared? Not because it fulfilled the Law, but because Nineveh believed the word of God. The prophet Jonah wrote: "So the people of Nineveh believed God, and proclaimed a fast, and put on sackcloth." They repented.

Nowhere in the book of Jonah do you read that the Ninevites received the Law of Moses, or that they were circumcised, or that they offered sacrifices. All this happened long before Christ was born. If the Gentiles were justified without the Law and quietly received the Holy Spirit at a time when the Law was in full force, why should the Law count unto righteousness now, now that Christ has fulfilled the Law? And yet many devote much time and labor to the Law, to the decrees of the fathers, and to the traditions of the pope.

MARTIN LUTHER

OBSERVE THE SCRIPTURES

Do not merely listen to the word, and so
deceive yourselves. Do what it says.

JAMES 1:22

The Scriptures are full of wondrous things. Those histories which are too commonly read as if they were only private concerns of particular persons, such as of Abraham, Isaac, Jacob, and Joseph; of Ruth, Joshua, the Judges, David, and the Israelitish princes, are accounts of vastly greater things, things of greater importance and more extensive concernment, than they who read them are commonly aware of.

The histories of Scripture are but too commonly read, as if they were written only to entertain men's fancies, when the infinitely great things contained in them are passed over without notice.

He that has a Bible and does not observe what it contains is like a man who has a box full of silver and gold, and does not know it, nor observe that it is anything more than a vessel filled with common stones. He will be never the better for his treasure and so might as well be without it. He who has plenty of the choicest food stored up in his house and does not know it will never taste what he has, and will be as likely to starve as if his house were empty.

JONATHAN EDWARDS

THE BOOK OF BOOKS

Everything that was written in the past was
written to teach us, so that through the endurance
taught in the Scriptures and the encouragement
they provide we might have hope.

ROMANS 15:4

My friends, stand over this volume, and admire its authority. This is no Solomon book. It is not the sayings of the sages of Greece; here are not the utterances of philosophers of past ages. If these words were written by man, we might reject them, but oh, let me think the solemn thought—that this Book is God's handwriting, that these words are God's. Let me look at its date: it is dated from the hills of heaven. Let me look at its letters: they flash glory on my eye. Let me read the chapters: they are big with meaning and mysteries unknown. Let me turn over the prophecies: they are pregnant with unthought-of orders.

Oh, Book of books! And wast thou written by my God? Then will I bow before thee. Thou Book of vast authority, thou art a proclamation from the Emperor of heaven; far be it from me to exercise my reason in contradicting thee. Reason! Thy place is to stand and find out what this volume means, not to tell what this book ought to say.

CHARLES SPURGEON

GOD IN YOU

Correct, rebuke and encourage—with
great patience and careful instruction.

2 TIMOTHY 4:2

When you preach the Word of God in its purity and also live accordingly, it is not your own doing, but God's doing. And when people praise you, they really mean to praise God in you. When you understand this—and you should because "what hast thou that thou didst not receive?"—you will not flatter yourself on the one hand and on the other hand you will not carry yourself with the thought of resigning from the ministry when you are insulted, reproached, or persecuted.

It is really kind of God to send so much infamy, reproach, hatred, and cursing our way to keep us from getting proud of the gifts of God in us. The Lord is our glory. Such gifts as we possess we acknowledge to be the gifts of God, given to us for the good of the church of Christ.

Therefore we are not proud because of them. We know that God is no respecter of persons. A plain factory hand who does his work faithfully pleases God just as much as a minister of the Word.

MARTIN LUTHER

TEACH ME YOUR WORD

"Call to me and I will answer you and tell you
great and unsearchable things you do not know."

JEREMIAH 33:3

We should be abler teachers of others, and less liable to be carried about by every wind of doctrine, if we sought to have a more intelligent understanding of the Word of God. As the Holy Ghost, the Author of the Scriptures, is He who alone can enlighten us rightly to understand them, we should constantly ask His teaching, and His guidance into all truth.

When Daniel interpreted Nebuchadnezzar's dream, what did he do? He set himself to earnest prayer that God would open up the vision. The apostle John, in his vision at Patmos, saw a book sealed with seven seals which none was found worthy to open, or so much as to look upon. The book was afterwards opened by the Lion of the tribe of Judah, who had prevailed to open it; but it is written first—"I wept much." The tears of John, which were his liquid prayers, were, so far as he was concerned, the sacred keys by which the folded book was opened.

CHARLES SPURGEON

A STEADY RULE

Many have undertaken to draw up an account
of the things that have been fulfilled among
us, just as they were handed down to us.

LUKE 1:1-2

The written Word of God is the main instrument employed by Christ in order to carry on His work of redemption in all ages. There was a necessity of the Word of God being committed to writing, for a steady rule to God's church. Before this, the church had the Word by tradition, either by immediate tradition from eminent men inspired, that were living, or else by tradition from former generations, which might be had with tolerable certainty in ages preceding this, by reason of men's long lives.

But the distance from the beginning of things was become now so great, and the lives of men become so short—being brought down to the present standard about the time of Moses—and God having now separated a nation to be a peculiar people, to be the keepers of the oracles of God; God saw it to be a convenient time now to commit His Word to writing, to remain henceforward for a steady rule throughout all ages.

JONATHAN EDWARDS

OBJECTS OF LOVE

*Every good and perfect gift is from above, coming
down from the Father of the heavenly lights.*

JAMES 1:17

The Father gives us His promises, the Son signs them in His blood, and the Holy Spirit seals them with His signet. The Father ordains salvation to us, the Son acquires it, and the Holy Spirit applies it. The Father adopts us to be His children, the Son purchases us to be His members, and the Holy Spirit regenerates us to be His temples. So we become objects of the love of these three adorable persons, and as the Father takes particular care of us as His children, the Son and the Holy Spirit give themselves to us with all their graces.

Jesus Christ is our Surety to make satisfaction for us, our Head to give us life, our Prophet to promise us salvation in His Word, our Priest to merit it by His blood, and our King to apply it to us by His power. The Holy Spirit is our Doctor to teach us in our ignorance, our Comforter to gladden us in our afflictions, our Sanctifier to cleanse us of our stains, and our Life to deliver us from our death. In short, we find nothing in the Holy Trinity which is not ours, and which does not work for our good.

FRANCIS TURRETIN

RIGHTLY HANDLE THE WORD

*Do your best to present yourself to God
as one approved . . . who correctly
handles the word of truth.*

2 TIMOTHY 2:15

Let us be warned by [the] mistakes of others never either to add to or take from the Word of God so much as a single jot or tittle. Keep upon the foundation of the Scriptures and you stand safely, and have an answer for those who question you; yea, and an answer which you may render at the bar of God. But once allow your own whim, or fancy, or taste, or your notion of what is proper and right, to rule you, instead of the Word of God, and you have entered upon a dangerous course, and unless the grace of God prevent, boundless mischief may ensue.

The Bible is our standard authority; none may turn from it. The wise man says in Ecclesiastes, "I counsel thee to keep the King's commandment"; we would repeat his advice and add to it the sage precept of the mother of our Lord, at Cana, when she said, "Whatsoever He saith unto you, do it."

CHARLES SPURGEON

THE HIDDEN MYSTERIES OF SCRIPTURE

The words of the LORD are flawless,
like silver purified in a crucible,
like gold refined seven times.

PSALM 12:6

Hitherto our chief object has been to stretch out our hand for the guidance of such as are disposed to learn, not to war with the stubborn and contentious; but now the truth which was calmly demonstrated must be vindicated from the calumnies of the ungodly. Still, however, it will be our principal study to provide a sure footing for those whose ears are open to the Word of God. Here, if anywhere, in considering the hidden mysteries of Scripture, we should speculate soberly and with great moderation, cautiously guarding against allowing either our mind or our tongue to go a step beyond the confines of God's Word.

For how can the human mind, which has not yet been able to ascertain of what the body of the sun consists, though it is daily presented to the eye, bring down the boundless essence of God to its little measure? Nay, how can it, under its own guidance, penetrate to a knowledge of the substance of God while unable to understand its own? Wherefore, let us willingly leave to God the knowledge of Himself.

JOHN CALVIN

HEED THE TEACHER

Beginning with Moses and all the Prophets,
he explained to them what was said in all
the Scriptures concerning himself.

LUKE 24:27

The two disciples on the road to Emmaus had a most profitable journey. Their Companion and Teacher was the best of tutors; the Interpreter one of a thousand, in whom are hid all the treasures of wisdom and knowledge. The Lord Jesus condescended to become a Preacher of the Gospel, and He was not ashamed to exercise His calling before an audience of two persons, neither does He now refuse to become the Teacher of even one. Let us court the company of so excellent an Instructor, for till He is made unto us wisdom we shall never be wise unto salvation.

This unrivalled Tutor used as His class-book the best of books. Although able to reveal fresh truth, He preferred to expound the old. He knew by His omniscience what was the most instructive way of teaching, and by turning at once to Moses and the prophets, He showed us that the surest road to wisdom is not speculation, reasoning, or reading human books, but meditation upon the Word of God.

CHARLES SPURGEON

THE GREAT PROMISER

Remember your word to your servant,
for you have given me hope.

PSALM 119:49

Whatever your especial need may be, you may readily find some promise in the Bible suited to it. Are you faint and feeble because your way is rough and you are weary? Here is the promise: "He giveth power to the faint." When you read such a promise, take it back to the great Promiser, and ask Him to fulfill His own Word.

Are you seeking after Christ, and thirsting for closer communion with Him? This promise shines like a star upon you—"Blessed are they that hunger and thirst after righteousness, for they shall be filled." Take that promise to the throne continually; do not plead anything else, but go to God over and over again with this—"Lord, Thou hast said it, do as Thou hast said." Are you distressed because of sin, and burdened with the heavy load of your iniquities? Listen to these words—"I, even I, am he that blotteth out thy transgressions, and will no more remember thy sins." You have no merit of your own to plead why He should pardon you, but plead His written engagements and He will perform them.

CHARLES SPURGEON

HEAVENLY MANNA

"I am the bread of life."

JOHN 6:35

Let us say again, my brothers, that if God sent His servants the prophets every morning to speak to Jerusalem according to His heart, and to declare His will, He has not withheld from us the same advantage. Is it not true that He sends His servants daily to instruct us in His ways, to show us the way of salvation? As He causes famine to be felt in so many places, not of bread, but of the Word of God, He nourishes us abundantly with His heavenly manna, causing it to fall daily at our doors.

If Jerusalem had honored the presence of the Lord Jesus, who usually stayed there while in the days of His flesh, may we not boast of a similar privilege? I know well that we cannot see Him anymore with our natural eyes, and that He no longer appears visibly on earth since His ascension. But can we doubt that He was, and still is, with us in our midst by the saving effects of His grace present in His Word, present in His sacraments, present in His governing providence and in a thousand other blessings that He heaps upon us every day?

FRANCIS TURRETIN

REVERENCE FOR CHRIST AND HIS WORD

*We do not use deception, nor do we
distort the word of God.*

2 CORINTHIANS 4:2

I trust that we shall always hold Christ as Lord and God. He is to be spoken of and thought upon with deepest reverence of soul. The spirit that trifles with the Word of God, and the things of Christ, is almost more vicious than the action which comes out of it. I have read many things which I have shuddered at; but I have shuddered much more at the state of mind into which a man must have come to be able to write them. Let us cultivate the highest reverence for our Divine Lord, and the surest confidence in His power, and in His ultimate victory. Trust in that hand which He keeps on the helm. Have no shadow of a doubt that His wisdom and might will cause all things to end well.

Go, therefore, and speak in His name. When you have done stating a doctrine, command your hearers, in the name of Jesus, to believe it. Be daring enough for that.

CHARLES SPURGEON

A PRECIOUS TREASURE

This command is a lamp, this teaching is a light,
and correction and instruction are the way to life.

PROVERBS 6:23

What a precious treasure God has committed into our hands, in that He has given us the Bible. How little do most persons consider what a privilege they enjoy in the possession of that holy Book, the Bible, which they have in their hands, and may converse with as they please.

What an excellent book is this, and how far exceeding all human writings! It reveals God to us and gives us a view of the grand design and glorious scheme of Providence from the beginning of the world, either in history or prophecy. It reveals the great Redeemer, His glorious redemption, and the various steps by which God accomplishes it from the first foundation to the top-stone!

Shall we prize a history which gives us a clear account of some great earthly prince or mighty warrior? And shall we not prize the history that God gives us of the glorious kingdom of His Son, Jesus Christ, the Prince and Saviour, and of the great transactions of that King of kings, and Lord of armies, the Lord mighty in battle; and what He has wrought for the redemption of His chosen people?

JONATHAN EDWARDS

DO NOT BE DECEIVED

I meditate on your precepts and consider your ways.

PSALM 119:15

Paul explains how those who had been deceived by false teachers may be restored to spiritual health. The false apostles were amiable fellows. Apparently they surpassed Paul in learning and godliness. The Galatians were easily deceived by outward appearances. They supposed they were being taught by Christ Himself. Paul proved to them that their new doctrine was not of Christ, but of the devil. In this way he succeeded in regaining many.

We also are able to win back many from the errors into which they were seduced by showing that their beliefs are imaginary, wicked, and contrary to the Word of God. The devil is a cunning persuader. He knows how to enlarge the smallest sin into a mountain until we think we have committed the worst crime ever committed on earth. Such stricken consciences must be comforted and set straight as Paul corrected the Galatians: by showing them that their opinion is not of Christ because it runs counter to the Gospel, which describes Christ as a meek and merciful Savior.

MARTIN LUTHER

THE MASTER INSTRUCTS

"Come, follow me," Jesus said.

MATTHEW 4:19

A follower may follow blindly and hear a great deal which he does not understand; but when he becomes a disciple, his Master instructs him, and leads him into truth. To explain, to expound, to solve difficulties, to clear away doubts, and to make truth intelligible is the office of a teacher amongst his disciples.

Now, it was a very blessed thing for the followers to become disciples, but still disciples are not necessarily so intimate with their Master as to sit and eat with Him. My brethren, if Jesus had but called us to be His disciples, and no more we should have had cause for great thankfulness; if we had been allowed to sit at His feet, and had never shared in such an entertainment as that before us, we ought to have been profoundly grateful; but now that He has favoured us with a yet higher place, let us never be unfaithful to our discipleship. Let us daily learn of Jesus, let us search the Bible to see what it was that He taught us, and then by the aid of His Holy Spirit let us scrupulously obey.

CHARLES SPURGEON

TO KNOW CHRIST

I want to know Christ—yes, to know the
power of his resurrection and participation in
his sufferings, becoming like him in his death.

PHILIPPIANS 3:10

We should be wise, that we may learn to know Christ rightly and to know that His kingdom is nothing else than a hospital where lie the sick and languishing, who need to be nursed. But this knowledge very few receive; this wisdom is very deeply hidden; so that, oftentimes, those who are partakers of the Gospel and of the Spirit are very deficient in it. For this is the highest wisdom that can be had.

Wherefore, although men look into the Scriptures and see that those Scriptures extol the kingdom of Christ, and say what a splendid thing it is, yet they do not clearly see what the words really mean, nor do they observe that in this lies the true wisdom, which far surpasses all human wisdom. For our wisdom is not ours in order to deal with the wise, the prudent and clever people, and talk about it and preach it, but to deal with fools and imprudent men and win them to it so that they attain unto righteousness and a sound understanding.

MARTIN LUTHER

SEARCHING FOR TREASURE

*I seek you with all my heart; do not let
me stray from your commands.*

PSALM 119:10

No man who merely skims the Book of God can profit thereby; we must dig and mine until we obtain the hid treasure. The door of the Word only opens to the key of diligence. The Scriptures claim searching. They are the writings of God, bearing the divine stamp and imprimatur—who shall dare to treat them with levity? He who despises them despises the God who wrote them. God forbid that any of us should leave our Bibles to become swift witnesses against us in the great Day of Account. The Word of God will repay searching. God does not bid us sift a mountain of chaff with here and there a grain of wheat in it, but the Bible is winnowed corn—we have but to open the granary door and find it.

Scripture grows upon the student. It is full of surprises. Under the teaching of the Holy Spirit, to the searching eye it glows with splendor of revelation, like a vast temple paved with wrought gold, and roofed with rubies, emeralds, and all manner of gems. No merchandise is like the merchandise of Scripture truth.

CHARLES SPURGEON

SCRIPTURE AS GUIDE

I run in the path of your commands, for you
have broadened my understanding.

PSALM 119:32

In describing the world as a mirror in which we ought to behold God, I would not be understood to assert either that our eyes are sufficiently clear-sighted to discern what the fabric of heaven and earth represents, or that the knowledge to be hence attained is sufficient for salvation. And whereas the Lord invites us to Himself by the means of created things, with no other effect than that of thereby rendering us inexcusable, He has added (as was necessary) a new remedy, or at least by a new aid, He has assisted the ignorance of our mind.

For by the Scripture as our Guide and Teacher He not only makes those things plain which would otherwise escape our notice but almost compels us to behold them, as if He had assisted our dull sight with spectacles. This herald therefore approaches, who excites our attention, in order that we may perceive ourselves to be placed in this scene, for the purpose of beholding the glory of God; not indeed to observe them as mere witnesses but to enjoy all the riches which are here exhibited as the Lord has ordained and subjected them to our use.

JOHN CALVIN

TAUGHT BY THE HOLY SPIRIT

"The Advocate, the Holy Spirit,
whom the Father will send in my
name, will teach you all things."

JOHN 14:26

The Holy Spirit is so given that there is not a truth which you may not understand. You may be led into the deepest mysteries by His teaching. You may be made to know and to comprehend those knotty points in the Word of God which have hitherto puzzled you. You have but humbly to look up to Jesus, and His Spirit will still teach you.

I tell you, though you are poor and ignorant, and perhaps can scarcely read a word in the Bible; for all that, you may be better instructed in the things of God than doctors of divinity, if you go to the Holy Spirit and are taught of Him. Those who go only to books and to the letter, and are taught of men, may be fools in the sight of God; but those who go to Jesus and sit at His feet, and ask to be taught of His Spirit, shall be wise unto salvation. Blessed be God, there are not a few amongst us of this sort. We are not left orphans; we have an Instructor with us still.

CHARLES SPURGEON

FULFILLED PROMISES

No matter how many promises God
has made, they are "Yes" in Christ.

2 CORINTHIANS 1:20

If He is our God, we can say assuredly that His virtues are ours, and that there is nothing in them which does not contribute to our salvation. For example, if God is all-good, it is to do us well. If He is all-wise, it is to guide us. If He is all-powerful, it is to defend us. If He is just, it is to avenge Himself of our enemies. If He is merciful, it is to pardon our crimes. If He is faithful, it is to grant us the fulfillment of His promises.

Finally (not to prevent us from considering His other excellent virtues, for the sake of which both men and angels exult in admiration), if He is all-powerful and sufficient for Himself, it is to assure us that He will also be so for us, and that there is nothing we could desire which we would not find in this inexhaustible spring of good things. On this all those excellent promises are founded, which God gives us in His Word, of which there is none that does not relate to one of these glorious attributes.

FRANCIS TURRETIN

HOLD FAST THE TRUTH

"Sanctify them by the truth; your word is truth."

JOHN 17:17

The passages of Scripture which prove that the instrument of our sanctification is the Word of God are very many. The Spirit of God brings to our minds the precepts and doctrines of truth and applies them with power. These are heard in the ear, and being received in the heart, they work in us to will and to do of God's good pleasure. The truth is the sanctifier, and if we do not hear or read the truth, we shall not grow in sanctification.

We only progress in sound living as we progress in sound understanding. "Thy word is a lamp unto my feet and a light unto my path." Do not say of any error, "It is a mere matter of opinion." No man indulges an error of judgment without sooner or later tolerating an error in practice. Hold fast the truth, for by so holding the truth shall you be sanctified by the Spirit of God.

CHARLES SPURGEON

A WELCOME GUEST

It is for freedom that Christ has set us free.

GALATIANS 5:1

This "liberty" makes us free to heaven's charter—the Bible. Here is a choice passage, believer: "When thou passest through the rivers, I will be with thee." You are free to that. Here is another: "The mountains shall depart, and the hills be removed, but my kindness shall not depart from thee"; you are free to that. You are a welcome guest at the table of the promises.

Scripture is a never-failing treasury filled with boundless stores of grace. It is the bank of heaven; you may draw from it as much as you please, without let or hindrance. Come in faith and you are welcome to all covenant blessings. There is not a promise in the Word which shall be withheld. In the depths of tribulations let this freedom comfort you; amidst waves of distress let it cheer you; when sorrows surround thee let it be thy solace. This is thy Father's love-token; thou art free to it at all times.

CHARLES SPURGEON

THE GOSPEL INVITATION

"Go and make disciples of all nations."

MATTHEW 28:19

This is a Gospel full of consolation, setting forth the Lord Christ in a kind of fertile description—teaching us what His character is, what His works are, and how He is affected toward men. And we cannot better understand it than by setting in contrast light and darkness, day and night; that is, a good and a bad shepherd, for this is what Christ does. You have often heard that God has ordained two kinds of preaching to the world. The one, which sets forth the Word of God—"Thou shalt have no other gods," likewise, "Thou shaft not kill, commit adultery, or steal"—and thereupon threatens that whosoever does not keep these commandments shall die. This teaching, however, does not purify any man's heart; for although a man may thereby be so restrained from these things as to show himself outwardly righteous, yet inwardly his heart is hostile to the law, and would prefer that there were no law at all.

The other office of preaching is the Gospel, which shows you where that strength is to be obtained that shall enable you to do that which the law demands: this preaching does not force men, nor threaten them, but sweetly invites them.

MARTIN LUTHER

A VEIN OF PURE GOLD

Every word of God is flawless; he is a shield
to those who take refuge in him.

PROVERBS 30:5

This Bible is a Book of authority, it is an authorized Book, for God has written it. Oh, tremble, tremble, lest any of you despise it; mark its authority, for it is the Word of God. Then, since God wrote it, mark its truthfulness.

This is the Word of God; come search, ye critics, and find a flaw; examine it from its Genesis to its Revelation, and find an error. This is a vein of pure gold, unalloyed by quartz, or any earthy substance. This is a star without a speck, a sun without a blot! A light without darkness; a moon without its paleness; a glory without a dimness. O Bible!

It cannot be said of any other book that it is perfect and pure, but of thee we can declare all wisdom is gathered up in thee, without a particle of folly. This is the judge that ends the strife where wit and reason fail. This is the book untainted by any error; it is pure, unalloyed, perfect truth. Why? Because God wrote it.

CHARLES SPURGEON

CLEAVE TO THE WORD

I rejoice in following your statutes as
one rejoices in great riches.

PSALM 119:14

The true difference between godly faith and human faith consists also in this, that human faith cleaves to the person of the preacher, believes, trusts, and honors the Word for the sake of him who spake it. But godly faith, on the other hand, cleaves to the Word, which is God Himself; he believes, trusts, and honors the Word, not because of him who preaches it, but because he feels so surely the truth that no one can ever turn him again from it, even if the same preacher were to try to do it.

This was proved by the Samaritans when they had heard first of Christ from the heathen woman and upon her word they went out of the city to Christ. After they themselves heard Christ, they said to the woman, "Now we believe, not because of thy speaking: for we have heard for ourselves, and know that this is indeed the Savior of the world."

MARTIN LUTHER

THE MYSTERIES OF GOD'S WORD

He makes known his ways to Moses,
his deeds to the people of Israel.

PSALM 103:7

Bless the Lord," said David, "O my soul, and all that is within me bless his holy name!" If there is a curiosity within us, it ought to be employed and developed in a search after truth. "All that is within me," sanctified by the Spirit, should be developed. And verily, the Christian man feels an intense longing to bury his ignorance and receive wisdom. If he, when in his natural estate panted for terrestrial knowledge, how much more ardent is the wish to unravel, if possible, the sacred mysteries of God's Word!

A true Christian is always intently reading and searching the Scripture that he may be able to certify himself as to its main and cardinal truths. I do not think much of that man who does not wish to understand doctrines; I cannot conceive him to be in a right position when he thinks it is no matter whether he believes a lie or truth. God's Word will ever be to a Christian a source of great anxiety: a sacred instinct within will lead him to pry into it; he will seek to understand it.

CHARLES SPURGEON

GOD'S WORDS ARE TRUE

All your words are true; all your
righteous laws are eternal.

PSALM 119:160

For general faith is no other than that which believeth that all the words of God are true, and that God hath a good-will to mankind; particular faith believeth nothing contrary to this; only that which is common to all the faithful applieth particularly to himself, believing that God is not well minded toward others alone, but even unto him also.

So then it bringeth the whole into parts, and that which is general into particularities. For whereas by general faith he believeth that all the words of God are true, in the same sort by particular faith he doth believe that the soul is immortal, that our bodies rise again, that the faithful shall be saved, the unbelievers destroyed, and whatsoever else is of this sort taught to be believed in the Word of God.

MARTIN LUTHER

A VIEW OF PROVIDENCE

Let all the earth fear the LORD; let all
the people of the world revere him.

PSALM 33:8

In the Bible, we have an account of the whole scheme of Providence, from the beginning of the world to the end of it, either in history or prophecy, and are told what will become of things at last; how they will issue in the subduing of God's enemies, and in the salvation and glory of His church, and setting up of the everlasting kingdom of His Son.

How rational, worthy, and excellent a revelation is this! And how excellent a book is the Bible, which contains so much beyond all other books in the world! And what characters are here of its being indeed a divine Book! A Book that the great Jehovah has given to mankind for their instruction, without which we should be left in miserable darkness and confusion. From what has been said, we may see the glorious majesty and power of God in this affair of redemption.

JONATHAN EDWARDS

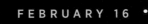
RENEWED BY THE WORD

Let the peoples renew their strength.

ISAIAH 41:1 ESV

All things on earth need to be renewed. No created thing continueth by itself. "Thou renewest the face of the year" was the psalmist's utterance. Even the trees, which wear not themselves with care, nor shorten their lives with labour, must drink of the rain of heaven and suck from the hidden treasures of the soil. The cedars of Lebanon, which God has planted, only live because day by day they are full of sap fresh drawn from the earth.

Neither can man's life be sustained without renewal from God. As it is necessary to repair the waste of the body by the frequent meal, so we must repair the waste of the soul by feeding upon the Book of God, or by listening to the preached Word, or by the soul-fattening table of the ordinances. How depressed are our graces when means are neglected! What poor starvelings some saints are who live without the diligent use of the Word of God and secret prayer! If our piety can live without God, it is not of divine creating, it is but a dream; for if God had begotten it, it would wait upon Him as the flowers wait upon the dew.

CHARLES SPURGEON

AN INNER COURT
TO CREATION

He is altogether lovely.

SONG OF SONGS 5:16

The soul that is familiar with the Lord worships Him in the outer court of nature, wherein it admires His works, and is charmed by every thought of what He must be who made them all. When that soul enters the nearer circle of inspiration and reads the wonderful words of God, it is still more enraptured, and its admiration is heightened. In revelation, we see the same all-glorious Lord as in creation, but the vision is more clear, and the consequent love is more intense. The Word is an inner court to the creation, but there is yet an innermost sanctuary, and blessed are they who enter it and have fellowship with the Lord Himself.

We come to Christ, and in coming to Him we come to God, for Jesus says, "He that hath seen Me hath seen the Father." When we know the Lord Jesus, we stand before the mercy seat, where the glory of Jehovah shineth forth. I like to think of the text as belonging to those who are as priests unto God and stand in the Holy of holies, while they say, "Yea, He is altogether lovely." His works are marvellous, His words are full of majesty, but He Himself is altogether lovely.

CHARLES SPURGEON

THE SOURCE OF ALL INSPIRATION

In the beginning was the Word, and the Word
was with God, and the Word was God.

JOHN 1:1

To this our Saviour's words refer, "My Father worketh hitherto, and I work" (John 5:17). In thus affirming, that from the foundation of the world He constantly worked with the Father, He gives a clearer explanation of what Moses simply touched. The meaning therefore is, that God spoke in such a manner as left the Word His peculiar part in the work, and thus made the operation common to both.

But the clearest explanation is given by John when he states that the Word—which was from the beginning God and with God—was, together with God the Father, the Maker of all things. For he both attributes a substantial and permanent essence to the Word, assigning to it a certain peculiarity and distinctly showing how God spoke the world into being. Therefore, as all revelations from heaven are duly designated by the title of the Word of God, so the highest place must be assigned to that substantial Word, the Source of all inspiration, which, as being liable to no variation, remains forever one and the same with God, and is God.

JOHN CALVIN

MEDITATE ON THE WORD

Blessed is the one . . . whose delight
is in the law of the LORD.

PSALM 1:1-2

Study the Bible, dear brethren, through and through, with all helps that you can possibly obtain. Remember that the appliances now within the reach of ordinary Christians are much more extensive than they were in our fathers' days, and therefore you must be greater biblical scholars if you would keep in front of your hearers. Intermeddle with all knowledge, but, above all things, meditate day and night in the law of the Lord.

Be well instructed in theology, and do not regard the sneers of those who rail at it because they are ignorant of it. Many preachers are not theologians, and hence the mistakes which they make. It cannot do any hurt to the most lively evangelist to be also a sound theologian, and it may often be the means of saving him from gross blunders.

Had [our fathers] been able to compare spiritual things with spiritual, had they understood the analogy of the faith, and had they been acquainted with the holy learning of the great Bible students of past ages, they would not have been quite so fast in vaunting their marvelous knowledge.

CHARLES SPURGEON

THE WORD SATISFIES

*As for God, his way is perfect: the
LORD's word is flawless.*

PSALM 18:30

Angels being the ministers appointed to execute the commands of God must, of course, be admitted to be His creatures, but to stir up questions concerning the time or order in which they were created[1] bespeaks more perverseness than industry. Moses relates that the heavens and the earth were finished, with all their host; what avails it anxiously to inquire at what time other more hidden celestial hosts than the stars and planets also began to be?

Not to dwell on this, let us here remember that on the whole subject of religion one rule of modesty and soberness is to be observed, and it is this, in obscure matters not to speak or think, or even long to know, more than the Word of God has delivered. A second rule is that in reading the Scriptures we should constantly direct our inquiries and meditations to those things which tend to edification, not indulge in curiosity, or in studying things of no use. And since the Lord has been pleased to instruct us, not in frivolous questions, but in solid piety, in the fear of his name, in true faith, and the duties of holiness, let us rest satisfied with such knowledge.

JOHN CALVIN

TAUGHT OF THE LORD

The people who know their God shall
stand firm and take action.

DANIEL 11:32 ESV

Every believer understands that to know God is the highest and best form of knowledge, and this spiritual knowledge is a source of strength to the Christian. It strengthens his faith. Believers are constantly spoken of in the Scriptures as being persons who are enlightened and taught of the Lord; they are said to "have an unction from the Holy One," and it is the Spirit's peculiar office to lead them into all truth, and all this for the increase and the fostering of their faith.

Knowledge strengthens love as well as faith. Knowledge opens the door, and then through that door we see our Saviour. Or, to use another similitude, knowledge paints the portrait of Jesus, and when we see that portrait then we love Him; we cannot love a Christ whom we do not know at least in some degree. If we know but little of the excellences of Jesus, what He has done for us, and what He is doing now, we cannot love Him much; but the more we know Him, the more we shall love Him.

CHARLES SPURGEON

THE PRECEDENCE OF DOCTRINE

*Unlike so many, we do not peddle
the word of God for profit.*

2 CORINTHIANS 2:17

Small faults grow into big faults. To tolerate a trifling error inevitably leads to crass heresy. The doctrine of the Bible is not ours to take or to allow liberties with. We have no right to change even a tittle of it. When it comes to life, we are ready to do, to suffer, to forgive anything our opponents demand as long as faith and doctrine remain pure and uncorrupt.

The apostle James says, "For whosoever shall keep the whole law and yet offend in one point, he is guilty of all." This passage supports us over against our critics, who claim that we disregard all charity to the great injury of the churches. We protest we desire nothing more than peace with all men. The pure doctrine takes precedence before charity, apostles, or an angel from heaven. Let others praise charity and concord to the skies; we magnify the authority of the Word and faith. Charity may be neglected at times without peril, but not the Word and faith. If we do not love God and His Word, what difference does it make if we love anything at all?

MARTIN LUTHER

WAITING OUT THE PROMISES

"The revelation awaits an appointed time; it speaks of an end and will not prove false."

HABAKKUK 2:3

On the whole, how necessary the reinforcements of hope are to establish faith will better appear if we reflect on the numerous forms of temptation by which those who have embraced the Word of God are assailed and shaken. First, the Lord often keeps us in suspense, by delaying the fulfillment of His promises much longer than we could wish. Here the office of hope is to perform what the prophet enjoins, "Though it tarry, wait for it" (Habakkuk 2:3). Here there is still greater necessity for the aid of hope, that we may be able to say with another prophet, "I will wait upon the LORD that hideth his face from the house of Jacob, and I will look for him" (Isaiah 8:17).

On account of this connection and affinity Scripture sometimes confounds the two terms *faith* and *hope*. For when Peter says that we are "kept by the power of God through faith until salvation, ready to be revealed in the last times" (1 Peter 1:5), he attributes to faith what more properly belongs to hope. And not without cause, since we have already shown that hope is nothing else than the food and strength of faith.

JOHN CALVIN

THE WORD OF LIFE

In him was life, and that life was
the light of all mankind.

JOHN 1:4

Just as the word *life* was interpreted differently from the meaning intended by the Evangelist, so was also the word *light*. There has been much foolish speculation as to how the Word of God in its divinity could be a light, which naturally shines and has always given light to the minds of men even among the heathen. Therefore the light of reason has been emphasized and based upon this passage of Scripture. These are all human, Platonic, and philosophical thoughts, which lead us away from Christ into ourselves; but the Evangelist wishes to lead us away from ourselves into Christ.

For he would not deal with the divine, almighty, and eternal Word of God, nor speak of it, otherwise than as flesh and blood that sojourned upon earth. He would not have us diffuse our thoughts among the creatures which He has created, so as to pursue Him, search for Him, and speculate about Him as the Platonic philosophers do; but he wishes to lead us away from those vague and high-flown thoughts and bring us together in Christ.

MARTIN LUTHER

THE AROMA OF CHRIST

*We are to God the pleasing aroma of
Christ among those who are being saved
and those who are perishing.*

2 CORINTHIANS 2:15

We should always read Scripture in this light: we should consider the Word to be as a mirror into which Christ looks down from heaven; and then we, looking into it, see His face reflected as in a glass—darkly, it is true, but still in such a way as to be a blessed preparation for seeing Him as we shall see Him face-to-face.

This volume contains Jesus Christ's letters to us, perfumed by His love. These pages are the garments of our King, and they all smell of myrrh, and aloes, and cassia. Scripture is the royal chariot in which Jesus rides, and it is paved with love for the daughters of Jerusalem. The Scriptures are the swaddling bands of the holy Child, Jesus; unroll them and you find your Savior. The quintessence of the Word of God is Christ.

CHARLES SPURGEON

THE LAW AND THE GOSPEL

*In the past God spoke to our ancestors through
the prophets at many times and in various ways,
but in these last days he has spoken to us by his
Son, whom he appointed heir of all things, and
through whom also he made the universe.*

HEBREWS 1:1-2

The majority of men, blinded by the just judgement of God, have indeed never seriously considered what curse the Law subjects us to, nor why it has been ordained by God. And, as for the Gospel, they have nearly always thought that it was nothing other than a second Law, more perfect than the first. From this has come the erroneous distinction between precept and advice; there has followed, little by little, the total ruin of the benefit of Jesus Christ.

Now, we must besides consider these things. The Law and the Gospel have in common that they are both from the one true God, always consistent with Himself (Heb 1:1–2). We must not therefore think that the Gospel abolishes the essence of the Law. On the contrary, the Law establishes the essence of the Gospel (Rom 10:2–4). For both set before us the same God and the essence of the same righteousness (Rom 3:31), which resides in perfect love to God and our neighbour.

THEODORE BEZA

HOLD FAST TO THE TRUTH

Do not treat prophecies with contempt but test them all; hold on to what is good, reject every kind of evil.

1 THESSALONIANS 5:20-22

Like Paul, we struggle with the Word of God against the fanatical Anabaptists of our day; and our efforts are not entirely in vain. The trouble is there are many who refuse to be instructed. They will not listen to reason; they will not listen to the Scriptures, because they are bewitched by the tricky devil who can make a lie look like the truth. Since the devil has this uncanny ability to make us believe a lie until we would swear a thousand times it were the truth, we must not be proud but walk in fear and humility, and call upon the Lord Jesus to save us from temptation.

Although I am a doctor of divinity, and have preached Christ and fought His battles for a long time, I know from personal experience how difficult it is to hold fast to the truth. I cannot always shake off Satan. I cannot always apprehend Christ as the Scriptures portray Him. Sometimes the devil distorts Christ to my vision. But thanks be to God, who keeps us in His Word, in faith, and in prayer.

MARTIN LUTHER

ASKING FOR ILLUMINATION

Guide me in your truth and teach me, for you are my
God my Savior, and my hope is in you all day long.

PSALM 25:5

We have known other men who were not so strong, who felt that they could not even understand the Word of God without divine illumination, and who went to the great Father of lights for that illumination. Trembling and afraid, they have asked to be helped to speak the mind of God, and not their own mind; and God has spoken through them, and they have been strong.

They were weak, for they were afraid lest their thoughts should stand in the way of God's thoughts; they were fearful lest their mind should darken the Word of God. Yet they have been truly strong, and humble people have listened to them and said that God spake through them. Sinners have listened, and though they have become angry, they have come again, and at last have yielded themselves to Christ. Verily, God spoke through that Man.

CHARLES SPURGEON

GOVERNED BY THE SPIRIT

The mind governed by the flesh is death, but the
mind governed by the Spirit is life and peace.

ROMANS 8:6

If it were not for the example of the Galatian churches I would never have thought it possible that anybody who had received the Word of God with such eagerness as they had, could so quickly let go of it. Good Lord, what terrible mischief one single false statement can create. The article of justification is fragile. Not in itself, of course, but in us.

I know how quickly a person can forfeit the joy of the Gospel. I know in what slippery places even those stand who seem to have a good footing in the matters of faith. In the midst of the conflict, when we should be consoling ourselves with the Gospel, the Law rears up and begins to rage all over our conscience.

I say the Gospel is frail because we are frail. What makes matters worse is that one-half of ourselves, our own reason, stands against us. As Paul puts it, "The flesh lusteth against the Spirit." Therefore we teach that to know Christ and to believe in Him is no achievement of man, but the gift of God.

MARTIN LUTHER

JUST AS THE BIBLE SAYS

*The shepherds returned, glorifying and
praising God for all the things that they had
heard and seen, as it was told unto them.*

LUKE 2:20 KJV

If you have seen Jesus with the God-giving sight of faith, suffer no cobwebs to linger among the harp strings, but loud to the praise of sovereign grace, awake your psaltery and harp. One point for which [the shepherds] praised God was the agreement between what they had heard and what they had seen. Observe the last sentence—"As it was told unto them." Have you not found the Gospel to be in yourselves just what the Bible said it would be? Jesus said He would give you rest—have you not enjoyed the sweetest peace in Him? He said you should have joy, and comfort, and life through believing in Him—have you not received all these? Are not His ways of pleasantness, and His paths of peace? Surely you can say with the queen of Sheba, "The half has not been told me."

I have found Christ more sweet than His servants ever said He was. I looked upon His likeness as they painted it, but it was a mere daub compared with Himself; for the King in His beauty outshines all imaginable loveliness.

CHARLES SPURGEON

GOSPEL DOCTRINE

These are written that you may believe that
Jesus is the Messiah, the Son of God, and that
by believing you may have life in his name.

JOHN 20:31

They have omitted nothing of that which is necessary to salvation. And when we say that the apostles and evangelists have faithfully recorded all the doctrine of the Gospel, we understand they have truly added nothing of their own as far as the substance of the doctrine is concerned,[2] but they have obeyed with precision and simplicity what the Lord had said to them: "Go, preach all that I have commanded you" (Matthew 28:20).

Saint Paul (Acts 20:27; Galatians 1:9) and Saint Peter (1 Peter 1:25) testify how conscientious they have been and how particular in this area.[3] That is why Saint Jerome, writing on this subject, says, "Chatter and babbling must not be believed without the authority of Holy Scripture." And Saint Augustine says even more clearly, "It is true that the Lord Jesus did many things which have not all been written down; for the Evangelist himself testifies that Jesus Christ said and did much that has not been written down. But God has chosen to have written down those things which are sufficient for the salvation of those who believe."[4]

THEODORE BEZA

THE PURE GOSPEL

My eyes have seen your salvation.

LUKE 2:30

If Joseph and Mary had judged according to outward appearances, they would have considered Christ no more than a poor child. But they disregard the outward appearance and cling to the words of Simeon with a firm faith, therefore they marvel at his speech. Thus we must also disregard all the senses when contemplating the works of God, and only cling to His words, so that our eyes and our senses may not offend us.

The fact that they were marveling at the words of Simeon is also mentioned to teach us that the Word of God is never preached in vain, as we read in Isaiah 55:11: "So shall my word be that goeth forth out of my mouth: it shall not return unto me void, but it shall accomplish that which I please, and it shall prosper in the thing whereto I sent it." Thus the Evangelist would say that Simeon delivered a warmhearted, beautiful sermon, preaching the pure Gospel and the Word of God. For the Gospel is nothing but a sermon whose theme is Christ, declaring Him to be the Savior, light, and glory of all the world. Such preaching fills the heart with joy and wonder at this great grace and comfort, if it is received in faith.

MARTIN LUTHER

LIGHT FOR THE DARKNESS

Your word is a lamp for my feet, a light on my path.

PSALM 119:105

Keep the light of truth burning, and thieves will not dare to plunder your house. Oh, for a church of believers in Jesus who know why they believe in Him; persons who believe the Bible and know what it contains; who believe the doctrines of grace and know the bearings of those truths; who know where they are and what they are, and who therefore dwell in the light, and cannot be deceived by the prince of darkness!

Do, dear friends—I speak specially to the younger among us—let there be plenty of teaching in your ministry. I fear that sermons are too often judged by their words rather than by their sense. Let it not be so with you. Feed the people always with knowledge and understanding, and let your preaching be solid, containing food for the hungry, healing for the sick, and light for those who sit in darkness.

CHARLES SPURGEON

HOLINESS THROUGH THE WORD

As obedient children, do not conform to the evil desires
you had when you lived in ignorance. But just as
he who called you is holy, so be holy in all you do.

1 PETER 1:14-15

Ministers of the Gospel, public officials, parents, children, masters, servants, etc., are true saints when they take Christ for their wisdom, righteousness, sanctification, and redemption, and when they fulfill the duties of their several vocations according to the standard of God's Word and repress the lust and desires of the flesh by the Spirit.

Not everybody can resist temptations with equal facilities. Imperfections are bound to show up. But this does not prevent them from being holy. Their unintentional lapses are forgiven if they pull themselves together by faith in Christ. God forbid that we should sit in hasty judgment on those who are weak in faith and life, as long as they love the Word of God and make use of the Supper of the Lord.

I thank God that He has permitted me to see (what as a monk I so earnestly desired to see) not one but many saints, whole multitudes of true saints.

MARTIN LUTHER

GOD OPENS EYES

Give me understanding to learn your commands.

PSALM 119:73

The psalmist had the Law, comprehending in it all the wisdom that could be desired, and yet not contented with this, he prays, "Open thou mine eyes, that I may behold wondrous things out of thy law" (Psalm 119:18). By this expression, he certainly intimates that it is like sunrise to the earth when the Word of God shines forth; but that men do not derive much benefit from it until He Himself, who is for this reason called the Father of lights (James 1:17), either gives eyes or opens them; because whatever is not illuminated by His Spirit is wholly darkness.

The apostles had been duly and amply instructed by the best of teachers. Still, as they wanted the Spirit of truth to complete their education in the very doctrine which they had previously heard, they were ordered to wait for Him (John 14:26). If we confess that what we ask of God is lacking to us, and He by the very thing promised intimates our want, no man can hesitate to acknowledge that he is able to understand the mysteries of God, only insofar as illuminated by His grace.

JOHN CALVIN

THE ILLUMINATED WORD

Open my eyes that I may see
wonderful things in your law.

PSALM 119:18

Perhaps the best way in which the Holy Ghost leads us into all truth is by illumination. He illuminates the Bible. Now, have you an illuminated Bible at home "Yes, I have a large family Bible with pictures in it." There is a picture of John the Baptist baptizing Christ by pouring water on His head and many other nonsensical things; but that is not what I mean. Have you an illuminated Bible? "Yes, I have a Bible with splendid engravings in it." Yes, I know you may have, but have you an illuminated Bible? "I don't understand what you mean by an 'illuminated Bible.'"

Well, it is the Christian man who has an illuminated Bible. He does not buy it illuminated originally, but when he reads it, "a glory gilds the sacred page, majestic like the sun: it gives a light to every age; it gives, but borrows none."[5] There is nothing like reading an illuminated Bible, beloved. You may read to all eternity and never learn anything by it, unless it is illuminated by the Spirit; and then the words shine forth like stars.

CHARLES SPURGEON

THE CROSS IN THE FOREFRONT

Grow in the grace and knowledge of
our Lord and Savior Jesus Christ.

2 PETER 3:18

It is a main part of our religion humbly to accept what God has revealed. Perhaps the highest form of adoration possible, on this side the vale, is the bowing of our entire mental and spiritual being before the revealed mind of God; the kneeling of the understanding in that sacred presence whose glory causes angels to veil their faces. Let those who please to do so, worship science, reason, and their own clear judgments; it is our delight to prostrate ourselves before the Lord our God, and to say, "This God is our God forever and ever: He will be our guide even unto death."

Rally to the old standard. Fight to the death for the old Gospel, for it is your life. Whatever forms of expression you may use as you advance in knowledge, ever keep the cross of Jesus Christ in the forefront, and let all the blessed truths which gather around it be heartily maintained.

CHARLES SPURGEON

THE WORD OF GOD ABIDES

The grass withers and the flowers fall, but
the word of our God endures forever.

ISAIAH 40:8

When I first took over the defense of the Gospel, I remembered what [a colleague] said to me. "I like it well," he said, "that the doctrine which you proclaim gives glory to God alone and none to man. For never can too much glory, goodness, and mercy be ascribed unto God." These words of the worthy doctor comforted and confirmed me. The Gospel is true because it deprives men of all glory, wisdom, and righteousness and turns over all honor to the Creator alone. It is safer to attribute too much glory unto God than unto man.

You may argue that the church and the fathers are holy. Yet the church is compelled to pray, "Forgive us our trespasses." I am not to be believed, nor is the church to be believed, or the fathers, or the apostles, or an angel from heaven, if they teach anything contrary to the Word of God. Let the Word of God abide forever.

MARTIN LUTHER

AT THE TABLE

Taste and see that the LORD is good.

PSALM 34:8

We have had deep draughts; we have thought that we could take in all of Christ, but when we have done our best we have had to leave a vast remainder. We have sat at the table of the Lord's love and said, "Nothing but the infinite can ever satisfy me; I am such a great sinner that I must have infinite merit to wash my sin away," but we have had our sin removed and found that there was merit to spare; we have had our hunger relieved at the feast of sacred love and found that there was a redundance of spiritual meat remaining.

There are certain sweet things in the Word of God which we have not enjoyed yet, and which we are obliged to leave for a while; for we are like the disciples to whom Jesus said, "I have yet many things to say unto you, but ye cannot bear them now." Yes, there are graces to which we have not attained, places of fellowship nearer to Christ which we have not reached, and heights of communion which our feet have not climbed. At every banquet of love there are many baskets of fragments left.

CHARLES SPURGEON

HE HAS SAID

Those who know your name trust in you, for you,
Lord, have never forsaken those who seek you.

PSALM 9:10

There may be a promise in the Word which would exactly fit your case, but you may not know of it, and therefore you miss its comfort. You are like prisoners in a dungeon, and there may be one key in the bunch which would unlock the door, and you might be free; but if you will not look for it, you may remain a prisoner still, though liberty is so near at hand.

Should you not, besides reading the Bible, store your memories richly with the promises of God? Ought you not to be profound in your knowledge of the words of God, so that you may be able to quote them readily when you would solve a difficulty or overthrow a doubt? Since "he hath said" is the source of all wisdom, and the fountain of all comfort, let it dwell in you richly, as "a well of water, springing up unto everlasting life." So shall you grow healthy, strong, and happy in the divine life.

CHARLES SPURGEON

LIBERTY ACCORDING TO THE WORD

"If the Son sets you free, you will be free indeed."

JOHN 8:36

We shall appreciate this liberty all the more when we bear in mind that it was Jesus Christ, the Son of God, who purchased it with His own blood. Hence, Christ's liberty is given us not by the Law, or for our own righteousness, but freely for Christ's sake. In the eighth chapter of the Gospel of Saint John, Jesus declares: "If the Son shall make you free, ye shall be free indeed." He only stands between us and the evils which trouble and afflict us and which He has overcome for us.

Reason cannot properly evaluate this gift. Who can fully appreciate the blessing of the forgiveness of sins and of everlasting life? Our opponents claim that they also possess this liberty. But they do not. When they are put to the test all their self-confidence slips from them. What else can they expect when they trust in works and not in the Word of God?

MARTIN LUTHER

THE COVENANT

He provided redemption for his people; he ordained
his covenant forever—holy and awesome is his name.

PSALM 111:9

The Lord's people delight in the covenant itself. It is an unfailing source of consolation to them so often as the Holy Spirit leads them into its banqueting house and waves its banner of love. They delight to contemplate the antiquity of that covenant, remembering that before the daystar knew its place, or planets ran their round, the interests of the saints were made secure in Christ Jesus.

It is peculiarly pleasing to them to remember the sureness of the covenant while meditating upon "the sure mercies of David." They delight to celebrate it as "signed, and sealed, and ratified, in all things ordered well." It often makes their hearts dilate with joy to think of its immutability, as a covenant which neither time nor eternity, life nor death, shall ever be able to violate—a covenant as old as eternity and as everlasting as the Rock of ages.

They rejoice also to feast upon the fulness of this covenant, for they see in it all things provided for them. God is their Portion, Christ their Companion, the Spirit their Comforter, earth their lodge, and heaven their home.

CHARLES SPURGEON

FAITH ALONE

FAITH REQUIRES KNOWLEDGE

Faith comes from hearing the message, and the message is heard through the word about Christ.

ROMANS 10:17

Faith is the simplest of all things, and perhaps because of its simplicity it is the more difficult to explain. What is faith? It is made up of three things—knowledge, belief, and trust. Knowledge comes first. "How shall they believe in him of whom they have not heard?" I want to be informed of a fact before I can possibly believe it. "Faith cometh by hearing"; we must first hear, in order that we may know what is to be believed. "They that know thy name shall put their trust in thee." A measure of knowledge is essential to faith; hence the importance of getting knowledge.

"Incline your ear, and come unto me; hear, and your soul shall live." Such was the word of the ancient prophet, and it is the word of the Gospel still. Search the Scriptures and learn what the Holy Spirit teacheth concerning Christ and His salvation. Seek to know God: "For he that cometh to God must believe that he is, and that he is a rewarder of them that diligently seek him." May the Holy Spirit give you the spirit of knowledge, and of the fear of the Lord!

CHARLES SPURGEON

FAITH THAT PRODUCES WISDOM

That they may know the mystery of God,
namely, Christ, in whom are hidden all the
treasures of wisdom and knowledge.

COLOSSIANS 2:2-3

There remaineth now for me to declare the virtue and effect of true faith. This hath the holy apostle Paul done very excellently well in the eleventh chapter to the Hebrews. He is compelled notwithstanding to confess that he cannot reckon up all; therefore at this time I mean to rehearse a few virtues of faith.

True faith before all things bringeth with it true knowledge, and maketh us wise indeed. For by faith we know God, and judge aright of the judgments and works of God, of virtues and vices. The wisdom that it bringeth with it is without doubt the true wisdom. Many men hope that they can attain to true wisdom by the study of philosophy; but they are deceived as far as heaven is broad. For philosophy doth falsely judge and faultily teach many things touching God, the works of God, the chief goodness, the end of good and evil, and touching things to be desired and eschewed. But the very same things are rightly and truly taught in the Word of God, and understood and perceived by faith.

MARTIN LUTHER

FAITH CONSISTS IN KNOWLEDGE

*For this reason, make every effort to add to your
faith goodness; and to goodness, knowledge.*

2 PETER 1:5

Is it faith to understand nothing, and merely submit your convictions implicitly to the church? Faith consists not in ignorance, but in knowledge—knowledge not of God merely, but of the divine will. We do not obtain salvation either because we are prepared to embrace every dictate of the church as true, or leave to the church the province of inquiring and determining; but when we recognize God as a propitious Father through the reconciliation made by Christ, and Christ as given to us for righteousness, sanctification, and life. By this knowledge, I say, not by the submission of our understanding, we obtain an entrance into the kingdom of heaven.

For when the apostle says, "With the heart man believeth unto righteousness; and with the mouth confession is made unto salvation" (Romans 10:10), he intimates that it is not enough to believe implicitly without understanding or even inquiring. The thing requisite is an explicit recognition of the divine goodness in which our righteousness consists.

JOHN CALVIN

A DOCTRINE OF GREAT IMPORTANCE

The Gentiles, who did not pursue righteousness,
have obtained it, a righteousness that is by faith.

ROMANS 9:30

The Scripture treats this doctrine as a doctrine of very great importance. That there is a certain doctrine of justification by faith, in opposition to justification by the works of the Law, which the apostle Paul insists upon as of the greatest importance, none will deny; because there is nothing in the Bible more apparent. The apostle, under the infallible conduct of the Spirit of God, thought it worth his most strenuous and zealous disputing about and defending.

He speaks of the contrary doctrine as fatal and ruinous to the souls of men, in the latter end of the ninth chapter of Romans, and beginning of the tenth. He speaks of it as subversive of the Gospel of Christ, and calls it "another gospel," and says concerning it, "Though an angel from heaven preach it, let him be accursed" (Galatians 1:6–9). Certainly we must allow the apostles to be good judges of the importance and tendency of doctrines; at least the Holy Ghost in them.

JONATHAN EDWARDS

THE LIFEBLOOD OF FAITH

Cast your cares on the LORD and he will sustain
you; he will never let the righteous be shaken.

PSALM 55:22

Trust is the lifeblood of faith; there is no saving faith without it. The Puritans were accustomed to explain faith by the word "recumbency." It meant leaning upon a thing. Lean with all your weight upon Christ. It would be a better illustration still if I said, fall at full length, and lie on the Rock of ages. Cast yourself upon Jesus; rest in Him; commit yourself to Him. That done, you have exercised saving faith.

Faith is not a blind thing, for faith begins with knowledge. It is not a speculative thing, for faith believes facts of which it is sure. It is not an unpractical, dreamy thing, for faith trusts, and stakes its destiny upon the truth of revelation. That is one way of describing what faith is. Let me try again. Faith is believing that Christ is what He is said to be, and that He will do what He has promised to do, and then to expect this of Him.

CHARLES SPURGEON

DEPENDENT ON GOD'S POWER

It is by grace you have been saved, through faith—
and this is not from yourselves, it is the gift of God.

EPHESIANS 2:8

We are dependent on God's power through every step of our redemption. We are dependent on the power of God to convert us and give faith in Jesus Christ, and the new nature. 'Tis a work of creation: "If any man be in Christ, he is a new creature" (2 Corinthians 5:17). "We are created in Christ Jesus" (Ephesians 2:10). The fallen creature cannot attain to true holiness, but by being created again, Ephesians 4:24: "And that ye put on the new man, which after God is created in righteousness and true holiness." It is a raising from the dead, Colossians 2:12–13: "Wherein ye also are risen with him, through the faith of the operation of God, who hath raised him from the dead."

Yea, it is a more glorious work of power than mere creation, or raising a dead body to life, in that the effect attained is greater and more excellent. That holy and happy being and spiritual life which is reached in the work of conversion is a far greater and more glorious effect than mere being and life.

JONATHAN EDWARDS

FAITH BRINGS HOLINESS

Abraham "believed God, and it was
credited to him as righteousness."

GALATIANS 3:6

By faith alone can we become righteous, for faith invests us with the sinlessness of Christ. The more fully we believe this, the fuller will be our joy. If you believe that sin, death, and the curse are void, why, they are null, zero. Whenever sin and death make you nervous, write it down as an illusion of the devil. There is no sin now, no curse, no death, no devil, because Christ has done away with them.

In the Apostolic Creed we confess, "I believe in the holy Christian church." But if you want to believe your eyes you will find many shortcomings and offenses in the members of the holy church. You see them succumb to temptation, you see them weak in faith, you see them giving way to anger, envy, and other evil dispositions. "How can the church be holy?" you ask. It is with the Christian church as it is with the individual Christian. If I examine myself, I find enough unholiness to shock me. But when I look at Christ in me, I find that I am altogether holy. And so it is with the church.

MARTIN LUTHER

FAITH THE JEWEL

Jesus said to her, "Woman, you have great
faith! Your request is granted." And her
daughter was healed at that moment.

MATTHEW 15:28

Jesus Christ always puts faith in the seat of honor. When that poor woman came whose daughter was ill, He said, "O woman, great is thy faith!'" He might have said, "Woman, great is thy love," for it was great love that made her force her way through the crowd and speak on her daughter's behalf, or "Great is thy patience," for when He called her "dog," she still stuck to Him, and would not depart; or He might have said, "Great is thy courage," for she said, "Yet the dogs eat of the crumbs." Or He might have said, "Great is thy wisdom," for she was a wise woman to extract sweets out of the bitters, and to say, "Truth, Lord, but the dogs eat of the crumbs."

But He overlooks all that and says, "Great is thy faith." Well, if Christ thinks so much of faith, ought we not to esteem it most highly? Is it possible to think too highly of that jewel which Christ reckons to be the most valuable?

CHARLES SPURGEON

FAITH MAKETH ALIVE

Blessed are those whose transgressions are
forgiven, whose sins are covered.

ROMANS 4:7

It is best to hear the testimonies out of the Scriptures. Faith maketh us happy. For to Saint Peter, confessing the Lord Jesus by true faith, it is said: "Happy art thou, Simon, the son of Jonas. Flesh and blood hath not revealed this to thee, but my Father which is in heaven." Saint Paul, for the proof of faith, bringeth in that sentence of David: "Happy are they whose iniquities are forgiven, and whose sins are covered. Blessed is the man to whom the Lord shall impute no sin." Faith quickeneth or maketh alive. For "the just liveth by faith." This doth Paul very often in his writings allege out of the prophets.

The same Paul also saith: "The life which now I live in flesh, I live by faith in the Son of God, who loved me and gave himself for me." Faith joineth us to the eternal and chief goodness, and so maketh us to enjoy the chief goodness, that God may dwell in us and we in God.

MARTIN LUTHER

FAITH AND KNOWLEDGE

"This is eternal life: that they know you, the only true God, and Jesus Christ, whom you have sent."

JOHN 17:3

Faith consists in the knowledge of God and Christ, not in reverence for the church. Sometimes even the most monstrous errors [are] received by the ignorant as oracles without any discrimination, provided they are prescribed to them under the name of the church. This inconsiderate facility, though the surest precipice to destruction, is, however, excused on the ground that it believes nothing definitely, but only with the appended condition, *if such is the faith of the church.* Thus they pretend to find truth in error, light in darkness, true knowledge in ignorance.

Not to dwell longer in refuting these views, we simply advise the reader to compare them with ours. The clearness of truth will itself furnish a sufficient refutation. For the question they raise is not whether there may be an implicit faith with many remains of ignorance, but they maintain that persons living and even indulging in a stupid ignorance duly believe, provided, in regard to things unknown, they assent to the authority and judgment of the church; as if Scripture did not uniformly teach, that with faith understanding is conjoined.

JOHN CALVIN

FAITH PROVIDES THE MIGHT OF GOD

With your help I can advance against a troop; with my God I can scale a wall.

PSALM 18:29

Faith links me with divinity. Faith clothes me with the robes of deity. Faith engages on my side the omnipotence of Jehovah. Faith gives me the might of God, for it ensures that power on my behalf. It gives me to defy the hosts of hell. It makes me march triumphant over the necks of my enemies. But without faith, how can I receive anything of the Lord? Let not him that wavereth —who is like a wave of the sea—expect that he will receive anything of God!

O then, Christians, watch well thy faith; for with it thou canst win all things, however poor thou art, but without it thou canst obtain nothing. It is said of Midas that he had the power to turn everything into gold by the touch of his hand; and it is true of faith—it can turn everything into gold. But destroy faith, we have lost our all; we are miserably poor, because we can hold no fellowship with the Father and with His Son, Jesus Christ.

CHARLES SPURGEON

FAITH LOOKS TO CHRIST

"The enemy is puffed up; his desires are not upright—
but the righteous person will live by his faithfulness."

HABAKKUK 2:4

The true Gospel has it that we are justified by faith alone, without the deeds of the Law. The false gospel has it that we are justified by faith, but not without the deeds of the Law. The false apostles preached a conditional gospel. So do the papists. They admit that faith is the foundation of salvation. But they add the conditional clause that faith can save only when it is furnished with good works. This is wrong. The true Gospel declares that good works are the embellishment of faith, but that faith itself is the gift and work of God in our hearts.

Faith is able to justify because it apprehends Christ, the Redeemer. Human reason can think only in terms of the Law. It mumbles, "This I have done, this I have not done." But faith looks to Jesus Christ, the Son of God, given into death for the sins of the whole world. To turn one's eyes away from Jesus means to turn them to the Law. True faith lays hold of Christ and leans on Him alone.

MARTIN LUTHER

HEIRS BY FAITH

If we are children, then we are heirs—
heirs of God and co-heirs with Christ.

ROMANS 8:17

We may infer that those who so persistently demand a reward for their works, and say that they will cease working the works of God if no reward awaits the works, have the souls of slaves. For slaves work for reward only. But they that have faith are untiring in the work of God, like the son of the house. He has not merited by works his being the heir of the estate,; but when he was born, he was the heir of his father's possessions through birth, not through merit. And when he is untiring in work, he does not demand a reward, for he knows that all things are his.

So the sons of God who have faith know that by divine birth, that is, the birth of the Spirit, and by free election they are sons of God, not slaves. Since, then, they are sons of the house, they ask not what reward awaits them, for all things are ours. Freely, therefore, gladly, and without weariness they labor, indeed there is no work so great that they do not believe it is accomplished by His power in whom we trust, not by our own.

ULRICH ZWINGLI

AN INCREASE OF FAITH

"You of little faith, why are you so afraid?"

MATTHEW 8:26

How can we obtain an increase of faith? This is a very earnest question to many. They say they want to believe, but cannot. A great deal of nonsense is talked upon this subject. Let us be strictly practical in our dealing with it. Common sense is as much needed in religion as anywhere else. "What am I to do in order to believe?" One who was asked the best way to do a certain simple act replied that the best way to do it was to do it at once. We waste time in discussing methods when the action is simple. The shortest way to believe is to believe.

If the Holy Spirit has made you candid, you will believe as soon as truth is set before you. You will believe it because it is true. The Gospel command is clear: "Believe in the Lord Jesus Christ, and thou shalt be saved." The order is plain; let it be obeyed. But still, if you have difficulty, take it before God in prayer. Tell the great Father exactly what it is that puzzles you, and beg Him by His Holy Spirit to solve the question.

CHARLES SPURGEON

CHILDREN OF ABRAHAM

Those who have faith are children of Abraham.

GALATIANS 3:7

Know ye therefore that they which are of faith, the same are the children of Abraham. This is the main point of Paul's argument against the Jews: the children of Abraham are those who believe and not those who are born of Abraham's flesh and blood. This point Paul drives home with all his might because the Jews attached saving value to the genealogical fact: "We are the seed and children of Abraham."

Let us begin with Abraham and learn how this friend of God was justified and saved. Not because he left his country, his relatives, his father's house; not because he was circumcised; not because he stood ready to sacrifice his own son Isaac, in whom he had the promise of posterity. Abraham was justified because he believed.

Paul's argumentation runs like this: "Since this is the unmistakable testimony of Holy Writ, why do you take your stand upon circumcision and the Law? Was not Abraham, your father, of whom you make so much, justified and saved without circumcision and the Law by faith alone?" Paul therefore concludes: "They which are of faith, the same are the children of Abraham."

MARTIN LUTHER

GRASPING FAITH

"I will uphold you with my righteous right hand."

ISAIAH 41:10

The faith which saves has its analogies in the human frame. It is the eye which looks. By the eye we bring into the mind that which is far away; we can bring the sun and the far-off stars into the mind by a glance of the eye. So by trust we bring the Lord Jesus near to us; and though He be far away in heaven, He enters into our heart. Only look to Jesus; for the hymn is strictly true: "There is life in a look at the Crucified One, there is life at this moment for thee."

Faith is the hand which grasps. When our hand takes hold of anything for itself, it does precisely what faith does when it appropriates Christ and the blessings of His redemption. Faith says, "Jesus is mine." Faith hears of the pardoning blood and cries, "I accept it to pardon me." Faith calls the legacies of the dying Jesus her own; and they are her own, for faith is Christ's heir; He has given Himself and all that He has to faith.

CHARLES SPURGEON

THE HINGE OF FAITH

Since we have been justified through faith, we have
peace with God through our Lord Jesus Christ.

ROMANS 5:1

The principal hinge on which faith turns is this: we must not suppose that any promises of mercy which the Lord offers are only true out of us, and not at all in us; we should rather make them ours by inwardly embracing them. In this way only is engendered that confidence which He elsewhere terms "peace" (Romans 5:1); though perhaps He rather means to make peace follow from it.

This is the security which quiets and calms the conscience in the view of the judgment of God, and without which it is necessarily vexed and almost torn with tumultuous dread, unless when it happens to slumber for a moment, forgetful both of God and of itself. In one word, he only is a true believer who, firmly persuaded that God is reconciled, and is a kind Father to him, hopes everything from His kindness; who, trusting to the promises of the divine favor, with undoubting confidence anticipates salvation; as the apostle shows in these words: "We are made partakers of Christ, if we hold the beginning of our confidence steadfast unto the end" (Hebrews 3:14).

JOHN CALVIN

GREAT TO PERFORM YOUR DUTY

*The LORD who rescued me from the paw of
the lion and the paw of the bear will rescue
me from the hand of this Philistine.*

1 SAMUEL 17:37

Take care of your faith, because otherwise you cannot well perform your duty. Love can make the feet move more swiftly, but faith is the foot which carries the soul. Faith is the oil enabling the wheels of holy devotion and of earnest piety to move well. With faith I can do all things; without faith I shall neither have the inclination nor the power to do anything in the service of God.

If there are great battles and great works to do, there must be great faith. Assurance can carry mountains on its back; little faith stumbles at a molehill. Great faith, like Behemoth, can "snuff" up Jordan at a draught. Little faith is drowned in a drop of rain: it beginneth to think of going back at the slightest trouble. Great faith can build temples; she can pile castles; she can preach the gospel; she can proclaim Christ's name before enemies; she can do all things; and if you would be great indeed, and serve your Master much, as I trust you will, you will seek increased faith!

CHARLES SPURGEON

FAITH IN CHRIST'S PROMISES

The LORD has heard my cry for mercy;
the LORD accepts my prayer.

PSALM 6:9

Faith presupposes the assurance of God's mercy. This assurance takes in the confidence that our sins are forgiven for Christ's sake. Never will the conscience trust in God unless it can be sure of God's mercy and promises in Christ.

Now all the promises of God lead back to the first promise concerning Christ: "And I will put enmity between thee and the woman, and between thy seed and her seed; it shall bruise thy head, and thou shalt bruise his heel." The faith of the fathers in the Old Testament era, and our faith in the New Testament, are one and the same faith in Christ Jesus, although times and conditions may differ. Peter acknowledged this in the words: "We believe that through the grace of the Lord Jesus Christ we shall be saved" (Acts 15:11). And Paul writes: "And did all drink the spiritual drink; for they drank of that spiritual Rock that followed them: and that Rock was Christ" (1 Corinthians 10:4).

MARTIN LUTHER

LIFE DEMANDS FAITH

Trust in the LORD with all your heart, and
lean not on your own understanding.

PROVERBS 3:5

The pursuits of life illustrate faith in many ways. The farmer buries good seed in the earth and expects it not only to live but to be multiplied. He has faith in the covenant arrangement, that "seed-time and harvest shall not cease," and he is rewarded for his faith. The merchant places his money in the care of a banker and trusts altogether to the honesty and soundness of the bank. He entrusts his capital to another's hands and feels far more at ease than if he had the solid gold locked up in an iron safe. The sailor trusts himself to the sea. When he swims he takes his foot from the bottom and rests upon the buoyant ocean. He could not swim if he did not wholly cast himself upon the water.

You cannot turn anywhere in life without seeing faith in operation between man and man, or between man and natural law. Now, just as we trust in daily life, even so are we to trust in God as He is revealed in Christ Jesus.

CHARLES SPURGEON

INSTILLED IN OUR MINDS

Be transformed by the renewing of your mind.

ROMANS 12:2

As soon as the minutest particle of faith is instilled into our minds, we begin to behold the face of God placid, serene, and propitious; far off, indeed, but still so distinct as to assure us that there is no delusion in it. In proportion to the progress we afterwards make, we obtain a nearer and surer view, the very continuance making it more familiar to us.

Thus we see that a mind illumined with the knowledge of God is at first involved in much ignorance—ignorance, however, which is gradually removed. Still this partial ignorance or obscure discernment does not prevent that clear knowledge of the divine favor which holds the first and principal part in faith. For as one shut up in a prison, where from a narrow opening he receives the rays of the sun indirectly and in a manner divided, though deprived of a full view of the sun, has no doubt of the source from which the light comes, and is benefited by it; so believers, while bound with the fetters of an earthly body, though surrounded on all sides with much obscurity, are so far illumined by any slender light which beams upon them and displays the divine mercy as to feel secure.

JOHN CALVIN

CLING TO CHRIST

The righteous will live by faith.

ROMANS 1:17

Thousands of God's people have no more faith than this: they know enough to cling to Jesus with all their heart and soul, and this suffices for present peace and eternal safety. Jesus Christ is to them a Savior strong and mighty, a Rock immovable and immutable; they cling to Him for dear life, and this clinging saves them.

Reader, cannot you cling? Do so at once. Faith is seen when one man relies upon another from a knowledge of the superiority of the other. This is a higher faith: the faith which knows the reason for its dependence, and acts upon it. I do not think the limpet knows much about the rock: but as faith grows it becomes more and more intelligent. A blind man trusts himself with his guide because he knows that his friend can see, and, trusting, he walks where his guide conducts him. If the poor man is born blind he does not know what sight is; but he knows that there is such a thing as sight, and that it is possessed by his friend and therefore he freely puts his hand into the hand of the seeing one, and follows his leadership. "We walk by faith, not by sight."

CHARLES SPURGEON

FAITH IN GOD'S LOVE

The Lord disciplines the ones he loves.

HEBREWS 12:6

Whether adverse circumstances betoken the wrath of God, or conscience finds the subject and matter within itself, unbelief thence draws weapons and engines to put faith to flight, the aim of all its efforts being to make us think that God is adverse and hostile to us, and thus, instead of hoping for any assistance from Him, to make us dread Him as a deadly foe.

To withstand these assaults, faith arms and fortifies itself with the Word of God. When the temptation suggested is that God is an enemy because He afflicts, faith replies that while He afflicts He is merciful, His chastening proceeding more from love than anger. To the thought that God is the Avenger of wickedness, it opposes the pardon ready to be bestowed on all offences whenever the sinner retakes himself to the divine mercy. Thus the pious mind, how much soever it may be agitated and torn, at length rises superior to all difficulties, and allows not its confidence in the divine mercy to be destroyed. Nay, rather, the disputes which exercise and disturb it tend to establish this confidence.

JOHN CALVIN

FAITH BRINGS BLESSINGS

Let us then approach God's throne of grace with
confidence, so that we may receive mercy and
find grace to help us in our time of need.

HEBREWS 4:16

Christian, take good care of thy faith, for recollect faith is the only way whereby thou canst obtain blessings. If we want blessings from God, nothing can fetch them down except faith. Prayer cannot draw down answers from God's throne except it is the earnest prayer of the man who believes. Faith is the ladder on which my soul must walk to ascend to heaven. If I break that ladder, how can I ever approach my God?

Faith is the angelic messenger between the soul and heaven. Let that angel be withdrawn, I can neither send prayer up nor receive the answers down. Faith is the telegraphic wire which links earth and heaven—on which God's blessings move so fast that before we call He answers, and while we are yet speaking He hears us. But if that telegraphic wire of faith be snapped, how can we receive the promise? Am I in trouble? I can obtain help for trouble by faith. Am I beaten about by the enemy? My soul on that dear Refuge leans by faith.

CHARLES SPURGEON

FAITH TAKES HOLD OF CHRIST

*I have been crucified with Christ and I no
longer live, but Christ lives in me.*

GALATIANS 2:20

In order to have faith you must paint a true portrait of Christ.
The scholastics caricature Christ into a judge and tormentor.
But Christ is no lawgiver. He is the Lifegiver. He is the Forgiver
of sins. You must believe that Christ might have atoned for the
sins of the world with one single drop of His blood. Instead, He
shed His blood abundantly in order that He might give abundant satisfaction for our sins.

Here let me say that these three things—faith, Christ, and
imputation of righteousness—are to be joined together. Faith
takes hold of Christ. God accounts this faith for righteousness.
This imputation of righteousness we need very much, because
we are far from perfect. As long as we have this body, sin will
dwell in our flesh. Then, too, we sometimes drive away the Holy
Spirit; we fall into sin, like Peter, David, and other holy men.
Nevertheless we may always take recourse to this fact, "that our
sins are covered" and that "God will not lay them to our charge."

MARTIN LUTHER

FAITH IS OUR SHIELD

Take up the shield of faith, with which you can
extinguish all the flaming arrows of the evil one.

EPHESIANS 6:16

The truth is that unbelief reigns not in the hearts of believers, but only assails them from without; does not wound them mortally with its darts, but annoys them, or, at the utmost, gives them a wound which can be healed. Faith, as Paul declares, is our shield, which receiving these darts, either wards them off entirely, or at least breaks their force and prevents them from reaching the vitals. Hence when faith is shaken, it is just as when, by the violent blow of a javelin, a soldier standing firm is forced to step back and yield a little; and again when faith is wounded, it is as if the shield were pierced, but not perforated by the blow.

The pious mind will always rise, and be able to say with David, "Yea, though I walk through the valley of the shadow of death, I will fear no evil: for thou art with me" (Psalm 23:4). Since the prevailing thought is that God is present and providing for [our] safety, the feeling of security overcomes that of fear.

JOHN CALVIN

ONE TRUE FAITH

*In the gospel the righteousness of God is revealed—a
righteousness that is by faith from first to last.*

ROMANS 1:17

Faith is the saving grace—it is the connecting link between the soul and Christ. Take that away and all is gone. Remove faith, you have sawn through the ship's keel, and she must sink. Take away faith, you have taken away my shield and I must be slain. Remove faith, and Christian life becomes a nonentity: it is extinct at once, for "the just shall live by faith"; and without faith how could they live at all?

Consider then, that since faith is so important in salvation, it becomes each of us more earnestly to inquire whether we have faith or not. O my brethren, there are a thousand shams in the world—a thousand imitations of faith—but there is only one true vital saving faith. There are scores of notional faiths—a faith which consists in holding a sound creed, a faith which bids men believe a lie, by wrapping them up with assurances of their safety when they are still in the gall of bitterness and the bonds of iniquity, a faith which consists in presumptuously trusting to ourselves. There are scores of false faiths; but there is only one true one.

CHARLES SPURGEON

GOD WILL NEVER FAIL US

I remain confident of this: I will see the goodness
of the LORD in the land of the living.

PSALM 27:13

The divine favor to which faith is said to have respect, we understand to include in it the possession of salvation and eternal life. For if, when God is propitious, no good thing can be wanting to us, we have ample security for our salvation when assured of His love. "Turn us again, O God, and cause thy face to shine," says the prophet, "and we shall be saved" (Psalm 80:3). Hence the Scriptures make the sum of our salvation to consist in the removal of all enmity, and our admission into favor; thus intimating that when God is reconciled all danger is past, and everything good will befall us.

Wherefore, faith apprehending the love of God has the promise both of the present and the future life, and ample security for all blessings (Ephesians 2:14). The nature of this must be ascertained from the Word. Faith does not promise us length of days, riches, and honors, but is contented with the assurance that however poor we may be in regard to present comforts, God will never fail us.

JOHN CALVIN

FAITH WORKS BY LOVE

*It is with your heart that you
believe and are justified.*

ROMANS 10:10

When we believe in Christ, and the heart has come into the possession of God, then we are saved from sin and are moved toward repentance, holiness, zeal, prayer, consecration, and every other gracious thing. "What oil is to the wheels, what weights are to a clock, what wings are to a bird, what sails are to a ship, that faith is to all holy duties and services."[1] Have faith, and all other graces will follow and continue to hold their course.

Faith, again, has the power of working by love; it influences the affections toward God and draws the heart after the best things. He that believes in God will beyond all question love God. Faith is an act of the understanding, but it also proceeds from the heart. "With the heart man believeth unto righteousness"; and hence God gives salvation to faith because it resides next door to the affections, and is near akin to love; and love is the parent and the nurse of every holy feeling and act. Love to God is obedience, love to God is holiness.

CHARLES SPURGEON

FAITH IS SINCERE

*What good is it, my brothers and sisters, if
someone claims to have faith but has no deeds?*

JAMES 2:14

In Jesus Christ neither circumcision availeth anything, nor uncircumcision, but faith which worketh by love. Faith must of course be sincere. It must be a faith that performs good works through love. If faith lacks love, it is not true faith. Thus the apostle bars the way of hypocrites to the kingdom of Christ on all sides. He declares on the one hand, "In Christ Jesus circumcision availeth nothing," i.e., works avail nothing, but faith alone, and that without any merit whatever, avails before God.

On the other hand, the apostle declares that without fruits faith serves no purpose. To think, *If faith justifies without works, let us work nothing*, is to despise the grace of God. Idle faith is not justifying faith. In this terse manner Paul presents the whole life of a Christian. Inwardly it consists in faith toward God, outwardly in love toward our fellow men.

MARTIN LUTHER

FAITH DRIVES OUT FEAR

*You are receiving the end result of your
faith, the salvation of your souls.*

1 PETER 1:9

God gives all heavenly gifts to faith, for this reason among others, that faith worketh in us the life and spirit which are to be eternally manifested in the upper and better world. Faith furnishes us with armor for this life, and education for the life to come. It enables a man both to live and to die without fear; it prepares both for action and for suffering; and hence the Lord selects it as a most convenient medium for conveying grace to us, and thereby securing us for glory.

Certainly faith does for us what nothing else can do: it gives us joy and peace, and causes us to enter into rest. Why do men attempt to gain salvation by other means? An old preacher says, "A silly servant who is bidden to open a door, sets his shoulder to it and pushes with all his might; but the door stirs not. Another comes with a key, and easily unlocks the door, and enters right readily. Those who would be saved by works are pushing at heaven's gate without result; but faith is the key which opens the gate at once."[2]

CHARLES SPURGEON

THE DOCTRINE OF FAITH

If you point these things out to the brothers and
sisters, you will be a good minister of Christ
Jesus, nourished on the truths of the faith and
of the good teaching that you have followed.

1 TIMOTHY 4:6

The true knowledge of Christ consists in receiving Him as He is offered by the Father, namely, as invested with His Gospel. For, as He is appointed as the end of our faith, so we cannot directly tend toward Him except under the guidance of the Gospel. Therein are certainly unfolded to us treasures of grace. Did these continue shut, Christ would profit us little. Hence Paul makes faith the inseparable attendant of doctrine in these words: "Ye have not so learned Christ; if so be that ye have heard him, and have been taught by him, as the truth is in Jesus" (Ephesians 4:20–21).

Still I do not confine faith to the Gospel in such a sense as not to admit that enough was delivered to Moses and the prophets to form a foundation of faith; but as the Gospel exhibits a fuller manifestation of Christ, Paul justly terms it *the doctrine of faith* (1 Timothy 4:6).

JOHN CALVIN

CONFIRMATION OF FAITH

I will always remind you of these things,
even though you know them and are firmly
established in the truth you now have.

2 PETER 1:12

Christ is God by nature. At the same time, Paul confirms our creed "that Christ is very God." We need such frequent confirmation of our faith, for Satan will not fail to attack it. He hates our faith. He knows that it is the victory which overcometh him and the world.

That Christ is very God is apparent in that Paul ascribes to Him divine powers equally with the Father, as for instance, the power to dispense grace and peace. This Jesus could not do unless He were God. To bestow peace and grace lies in the province of God, who alone can create these blessings. The angels cannot. The apostles could only distribute these blessings by the preaching of the Gospel. In attributing to Christ the divine power of creating and giving grace, peace, everlasting life, righteousness, and forgiveness of sins, the conclusion is inevitable that Christ is truly God. Hence, the gifts which we receive from the Father and from the Son are one and the same.

MARTIN LUTHER

HEAR THE GOSPEL

"Very truly I tell you, whoever hears my word and believes him who sent me has eternal life."

JOHN 5:24

It is written, "Faith cometh by hearing"; therefore hear often. If I earnestly and attentively hear the Gospel, one of these days I shall find myself believing that which I hear, through the blessed operation of the Spirit of God upon my mind.

I would add next, consider the testimony of others. The Samaritans believed because of what the woman told them concerning Jesus. I believe that there is such a country as Japan; I never saw it, and yet I believe that there is such a place because others have been there. I believe that I shall die; I have never died, but a great many have done so whom I once knew, and therefore I have a conviction that I shall die also. The testimony of many convinces me of that fact.

Listen, then, to those who tell you how they were saved, how they were pardoned, how they were changed in character. If you will look into the matter, you will find that somebody just like yourself has been saved.

CHARLES SPURGEON

BY FAITH WE APPREHEND

*"What no eye has seen, what no ear has heard,
and what no human mind has conceived"—the
things God has prepared for those who love him.*

1 CORINTHIANS 2:9

It is in vain for any to reason as philosophers on the workmanship of the world, except those who, having been first humbled by the preaching of the Gospel, have learned to submit the whole of their intellectual wisdom (as Paul expresses it) to the foolishness of the cross (1 Corinthians 1:21). Nothing shall we find, I say, above or below, which can raise us up to God, until Christ shall have instructed us in His own school.

Yet this cannot be done, unless we, having emerged out of the lowest depths, are borne up above all heavens, in the chariot of His cross, that there by faith we may apprehend those things which the eye has never seen, the ear never heard, and which far surpass our hearts and minds. For the earth, with its supply of fruits for our daily nourishment, is not there set before us; but Christ offers Himself to us unto life eternal.

JOHN CALVIN

JUSTIFIED BY FAITH

*The words "it was credited to him" were not
written for him alone, but also for us, to whom
God will credit righteousness—for us who believe
in him who raised Jesus our Lord from the dead.*

ROMANS 4:23-24

Paul taught justification by faith in Christ Jesus, without the deeds of the Law. He reported this to the disciples at Antioch. Among the disciples were some that had been brought up in the ancient customs of the Jews. These rose against Paul in quick indignation, accusing him of propagating a gospel of lawlessness. Great dissension followed. Paul and Barnabas stood up for the truth. They testified: "Wherever we preached to the Gentiles, the Holy Ghost came upon those who received the Word. This happened everywhere. We preached not circumcision, we did not require observance of the Law. We preached faith in Jesus Christ. At our preaching of faith, God gave to the hearers the Holy Ghost."

From this fact Paul and Barnabas inferred that the Holy Ghost approved the faith of the Gentiles without the Law and circumcision. If the faith of the Gentiles had not pleased the Holy Ghost, He would not have manifested His presence in the uncircumcised hearers of the Word.

MARTIN LUTHER

GUARD YOUR FAITH

Be on your guard; stand firm in the faith.

1 CORINTHIANS 16:13

Take care of your faith, my friends; for it's very often so weak that it demands all your attention. I do not know whether you feel that your faith is too strong, but I never feel mine strong enough. It seems to be exactly strong enough to bear the day's troubles, but it would not stand cutting in the least degree with the plane. I could not afford to take the least atom off; it is just enough, and no more.

As for some of us, our faith is so weak that the least trouble threatens to devour it. The goat passes and nips its tender shoot, the winter chills and freezes it; it is almost ready to die. And my faith very often hangs upon the feeblest thread; it appears ready to expire.

Take care of your faith, Christian, take care of your faith. Whatever you leave out of doors of a night, do not leave that little child of faith; whatsoever plant is exposed to the frost, be sure to put faith within. Take care of faith, for it is so weak generally, it needs well to have a good preservation.

CHARLES SPURGEON

BY FAITH EMBRACE
THE PROMISE

The law was our guardian until Christ came
that we might be justified by faith.

GALATIANS 3:24

The perpetual succession of the church has flowed from this fountain, that the holy fathers, one after another, having by faith embraced the offered promise, were collected together into the family of God in order that they might have a common life in Christ. This we ought carefully to notice, that we may know what is the society of the true church, and what is the communion of faith among the children of God.

Whereas Moses was ordained the teacher of the Israelites, there is no doubt that he had an especial reference to them, in order that they might acknowledge themselves to be a people elected and chosen by God; and that they might seek the certainty of this adoption from the covenant which the Lord had ratified with their fathers, and might know that there was no other God, and no other right faith. But it was also [God's] will to testify to all ages, that whosoever desired to worship God aright, and to be deemed members of the church, must pursue no other course than that which is here prescribed.

JOHN CALVIN

THOSE WHO LIVE BY FAITH

*Have faith in the L*ORD *your God*
and you will be upheld.

2 CHRONICLES 20:20

The doctrines I speak of are those of Christians living by faith, not by sight: their giving glory to God by trusting Him in the dark; living upon Christ, and not upon experiences; not making their good frames the foundation of their faith. These are excellent and important doctrines indeed, rightly understood, but corrupt and destructive, as many understand them.

The Scripture speaks of our living or walking by faith, and not by sight, in no other way than these, namely when we are governed by a respect to eternal things, which are the objects of faith and are not seen, and not by a respect to temporal things, which are seen; when we believe things revealed, that we never saw with bodily eyes, and also exercise faith in the promise of future things, without yet seeing or enjoying the things promised, or knowing the way how they can be fulfilled. This will be easily evident to anyone that looks over the Scriptures, which speak of faith in opposition to sight.

JONATHAN EDWARDS

PURIFIED BY FAITH

He did not discriminate between us and
them, for he purified their hearts by faith.

ACTS 5:9

The Spirit testifies, by the mouth of Peter, that hearts are "purified by faith" (Acts 15:9); and seeing that the purity of the holy patriarchs was of the very same kind, the apostle does not in vain infer that the offering of Abel was, by faith, more excellent than that of Cain. Therefore, in the first place we must hold that all works done before faith, whatever splendor of righteousness may appear in them, were nothing but mere sins, being defiled from their roots, and were offensive to the Lord, whom nothing can please without inward purity of heart.

I wish they who imagine that men, by their own motion of free will, are rendered meet to receive the grace of God, would reflect on this. Certainly, no controversy would then remain on the question, whether God justifies men gratuitously, and that by faith. For this must be received as a settled point, that in the judgment of God, no respect is had to works until man is received into favor.

JOHN CALVIN

FAITH THAT MOVES ONWARD

They go from strength to strength, till
each appears before God in Zion.

PSALM 84:7

Consider the heart's desire of the apostles: "Increase our faith." They did not say, "Lord, keep our faith alive: Lord, sustain it as it is at present," but "Increase our faith." For they knew very well that it is only by increase that the Christian keeps alive at all.

Napoleon once said, "I must fight battles, and I must win them: conquest has made me what I am, and conquest must maintain me." And it is so with the Christian. It is not yesterday's battle that will save me today; I must be going onward. A wheel will remain erect as long as it moves, but when it begins to stand still it falls. Christian men are saved by progress: constantly going onward keeps the Christian alive.

If it were possible for me to stop, I know not where my life would be. The Christian must be going onward; for the arrow will mount while still it is in progress, but it stalls the moment the power stops that keeps it aloft. So the apostles said unto the Lord, "Increase our faith."

CHARLES SPURGEON

THE REVELATION OF JESUS CHRIST

"I am the way and the truth and the life. No one comes to the Father except through me."

JOHN 14:6

Faith is the soul's entirely adhering to and acquiescing in the revelation of Jesus Christ as our Saviour, from a sense of the excellent dignity and sufficiency of the Revealer of the doctrine and of the Saviour. God is the Revealer, and Christ is also the Revealer. Christ's excellency and sufficiency include the excellency of His person, and the excellency of the salvation He has revealed, and His adequateness to the performance, etc., and the excellency of His manner of salvation.

From the excellency and sufficiency of the Revealer and Performer we believe what is said is true, fully believe it; and from the glorious excellency of the Saviour and His salvation, all our inclination closes with the revelation. To depend upon the word of another person imports two things: first, to be sensible how greatly it concerns us, and how much our interest and happiness really depend upon the truth of it; and, secondly, to depend upon the word of another is so to believe it as to dare to act upon it as if it were really true.

JONATHAN EDWARDS

FAITH THAT RECONCILES

Know that a person is not justified by the works
of the law, but by faith in Jesus Christ.

GALATIANS 2:16

He who has God for his inheritance does not exult in fading joy, but, as one already elevated toward heaven, enjoys the solid happiness of eternal life. It is, indeed, to be maintained as an axiom, that all the promises of God made to the faithful flow from the free mercy of God, and are evidences of that paternal love, and of that gratuitous adoption, on which their salvation is founded.

Therefore, we do not say that Abram was justified because he laid hold on a single word, respecting the offspring to be brought forth, but because he embraced God as his Father. And truly faith does not justify us for any other reason than that it reconciles us unto God, and that it does so not by its own merit, but because we receive the grace offered to us in the promises and have no doubt of eternal life, being fully persuaded that we are loved by God as sons.

JOHN CALVIN

FAITH HONORS GOD

"You are my witnesses," declares the LORD, "and my servant whom I have chosen, so that you may know me and believe me and understand that I am he."

ISAIAH 43:10

Faith truly honors God. And because faith honors God, God counts faith for righteousness. Christian righteousness is the confidence of the heart in God through Christ Jesus. Such confidence is accounted righteousness for Christ's sake. Two things make for Christian righteousness: faith in Christ, which is a gift of God; and God's acceptance of this imperfect faith of ours for perfect righteousness.

Because of my faith in Christ, God overlooks my distrust, the unwillingness of my spirit, my many other sins. Because the shadow of Christ's wing covers me I have no fear that God will cover all my sins and take my imperfections for perfect righteousness. God "winks" at my sins and covers them up. God says: "Because you believe in My Son, I will forgive your sins until death shall deliver you from the body of sin." Learn to understand the constitution of your Christian righteousness. Faith is weak, but it means enough to God that He will not lay sin to our charge.

MARTIN LUTHER

SEALED WITH THE HOLY SPIRIT OF PROMISE

I know whom I have believed, and am
convinced that he is able to guard what I
have entrusted to him until that day.

2 TIMOTHY 1:12

There are different sorts of faith that are not true and saving, as is evident by what the apostle James says: "Show me thy faith without thy works, and I will show thee my faith by my works," where it is supposed that there may be a faith without works, which is not the right faith. When he says, "I will show thee my faith by my works," nothing else can be meant, than that *I will show thee that my faith is right.* It is a trusting in Christ.

"Kiss the Son, lest he be angry, and ye perish from the way, when his wrath is kindled but a little: blessed are all they that put their trust in him." "That we should be to the praise of his glory, who first trusted in Christ: in whom ye also trusted, after that ye heard the word of truth, the gospel of your salvation; in whom also, after that ye believed, ye were sealed with that Holy Spirit of promise."

JONATHAN EDWARDS

THE HAPPIEST OF BELIEVERS

These three remain: faith, hope and love.
But the greatest of these is love.

1 CORINTHIANS 13:13

The lovers of Jesus are charmed with His character, and delighted with His mission; they are carried away by the lovingkindness that He has manifested, and therefore they cannot help trusting Him, because they so much admire, revere, and love Him.

The way of loving trust in the Savior may thus be illustrated. A lady is the wife of the most eminent physician of the day. She is seized with a dangerous illness, and is smitten down by its power; yet she is wonderfully calm and quiet, for her husband has made this disease his special study, and has healed thousands who were similarly afflicted. She is not in the least troubled, for she feels perfectly safe in the hands of one so dear to her, and in whom skill and love are blended in their highest forms. Her faith is reasonable and natural; her husband, from every point of view, deserves it of her. This is the kind of faith which the happiest of believers exercise toward Christ.

CHARLES SPURGEON

FAITH IS THE INSTRUMENT

In the gospel the righteousness of God is revealed—a
righteousness that is by faith from first to last.

ROMANS 1:17

Here is the explanation of our justification by faith alone: faith is the instrument which receives Jesus Christ and, consequently, which receives His righteousness, that is to say, all perfection. When therefore, after Saint Paul we say that we are justified by faith alone, or freely, or by faith without works (for all these ways of speaking give the same sense),[3] we do not say that faith is a virtue which makes us righteous, in ourselves, before God. For this would be to put faith in the place of Jesus Christ who is, alone, our perfect and entire righteousness.

But we speak thus with the apostle, and we say that by faith alone we are justified, insomuch as it embraces Him who justifies us, Jesus Christ, to whom it unites and joins us. We are then made partakers of Him and the benefits which He possesses. These, being imputed and gifted to us, are more than sufficient to make us acquitted and accounted righteous before God.

THEODORE BEZA

CHRIST: THE OBJECT OF FAITH

Believe in the Lord Jesus, and you will be saved.

ACTS 16:31

In contrast to the doting dreams of the scholastics, we teach this: First a person must learn to know himself from the Law. With the prophet he will then confess: "All have sinned, and come short of the glory of God." And "there is none that doeth good, no, not one." And "against thee, thee only, have I sinned." Having been humbled by the Law, and having been brought to a right estimate of himself, a man will repent. He finds out that he is so depraved that no strength, no works, no merits of his own will ever deliver him from his guilt. He will then understand the meaning of Paul's words: "I am sold under sin" and "they are all under sin."

At this state a person begins to lament: "Who is going to help me?" In due time comes the word of the Gospel and says: "Son, thy sins are forgiven thee. Believe in Jesus Christ who was crucified for your sins. Remember, your sins have been imposed upon Christ." In this way are we delivered from sin. In this way are we justified and made heirs of everlasting life.

MARTIN LUTHER

FAITH IN GOD'S WILL

Every word of God is flawless; he is a shield
to those who take refuge in him.

PROVERBS 30:5

Paul designates faith as the obedience which is given to the Gospel (Romans 1:5); and writing to the Philippians, he commends them for the obedience of faith (Philippians 2:17). For faith includes not merely the knowledge that God is, but also, nay chiefly, a perception of His will toward us. It concerns us to know not only what He is in Himself, but also in what character He is pleased to manifest Himself to us.

We now see, therefore, that faith is the knowledge of the divine will in regard to us, as ascertained from His Word. And the foundation of it is a previous persuasion of the truth of God. So long as your mind entertains any misgivings as to the certainty of the Word, its authority will be weak and dubious, or rather it will have no authority at all. Nor is it sufficient to believe that God is true, and cannot lie or deceive, unless you feel firmly persuaded that every word which proceeds from Him is sacred, inviolable truth.

JOHN CALVIN

BLESSED ARE THE BELIEVERS

"Because you have seen me, you have
believed; blessed are those who have
not seen and yet have believed."

JOHN 20:29

This verse is as good an image of faith as well can be; we know that Jesus has about Him merit, and power, and blessing, which we do not possess, and therefore we gladly trust ourselves to Him to be to us what we cannot be to ourselves. We trust Him as the blind man trusts his guide. He never betrays our confidence, but He "is made of God unto us wisdom, and righteousness, and sanctification, and redemption."

Every boy that goes to school has to exert faith while learning. His schoolmaster teaches him geography and instructs him as to the form of the earth, and the existence of certain great cities and empires. The boy does not himself know that these things are true, except that he believes his teacher, and the books put into his hands.

That is what you will have to do with Christ, if you are to be saved; you must simply know because He tells you, believe because He assures you it is even so, and trust yourself with Him because He promises you that salvation will be the result.

CHARLES SPURGEON

PRESERVING OUR LIBERTY

It is for freedom that Christ has set us free.
Stand firm, then, and do not let yourselves
be burdened again by a yoke of slavery.

GALATIANS 5:1

On the question of justification we must remain adamant, or else we shall lose the truth of the Gospel. It is a matter of life and death. It involves the death of the Son of God, who died for the sins of the world. If we surrender faith in Christ as the only thing that can justify us, the death and resurrection of Jesus are without meaning; that Christ is the Savior of the world would be a myth. God would be a liar, because He would not have fulfilled His promises.

Our stubbornness is right, because we want to preserve the liberty which we have in Christ. Only by preserving our liberty shall we be able to retain the truth of the Gospel inviolate. Some will object that the Law is divine and holy. Let it be divine and holy. The Law has no right to tell me that I must be justified by it.

MARTIN LUTHER

AN INSTRUMENT
OF FAITH

*"God did not send his Son into the world to condemn
the world, but to save the world through him."*

JOHN 3:17

It is necessary therefore that with all this, the good Father, who chose us for His glory, should come to multiply His mercy toward His enemies. In declaring to us that He has given His own only Son so that whosoever takes hold of Him by faith should not perish (John 3:16), He creates also in us this instrument of faith which He requires from us.

Now, the faith of which we speak does not consist only in believing that God is God, and that the contents of His Word are true; for the devils indeed have this faith, and it only makes them tremble (James 2:19). But we call *faith* a certain knowledge which, by His grace and goodness alone, the Holy Spirit engraves more and more in the hearts of the elect of God (1 Corinthians 2:6–8). By this knowledge, each of them, being assured in his heart of his election, appropriates to himself and applies to himself the promise of his salvation in Jesus Christ.

THEODORE BEZA

FAITH THAT FACES ENEMIES

Though an army besiege me, my heart will
not fear; though war break out against
me, even then I will be confident.

PSALM 27:3

My friends, take care of your faith perpetually, because of your enemies; for if you do not want faith when you are with friends, you will require it when you have to deal with your foes. That good old warrior, Paul, once led the Ephesians into the armoury, and after he had shown them the shoes they were to wear, the girdle, the breast plate, the helmet, and the sword, he solemnly said, "Above all take the shield of faith."

Even if you forget the helmet, be quite sure of the shield, for if your helmet should be off you may ward off a blow with the shield, and save it from your head. You had better put on the "shoes of peace and the breast-plate of righteousness," but if you omit one of them, take care that you have "the shield of faith, where with you shall be able to quench all the fiery darts of the wicked one." Faith makes a man very mighty when he deals with enemies.

CHARLES SPURGEON

THE POWER OF FAITH IN CHRIST

But now that you have been set free from sin and
have become slaves of God, the benefit you reap
leads to holiness, and the result is eternal life.

ROMANS 6:22

Now, the effects which Jesus Christ produces in us, when we have taken hold of Him by faith, are two. In the first place, there is the testimony which the Holy Spirit gives to our spirit that we are children of God, and enables us to cry with assurance, "Abba, Father". (Rom 8:16; Gal 4:6). In the second place, we must understand that when we apply to ourselves Jesus Christ by faith, this is not by some silly and vain fancy and imagining, but really and in fact, though spiritually (Rom 6:14; 1 John 1:6; 2:5; 3:7). In the same way as the soul produces its effects when it is naturally united to the body, so, when, by faith, Jesus Christ dwells in us in a spiritual manner, His power produces there and reveals there His graces. These are described in Scripture by the words 'regeneration' and 'sanctification', and they make us new creatures with regard to the qualities that we can have (John 3:3; Eph 4:21–24).

THEODORE BEZA

FAITH IN CHRIST

Salvation is found in no one else, for there
is no other name under heaven given to
mankind by which we must be saved.

ACTS 4:12

It is true, indeed, that faith has respect to God only; but to this we should add that it acknowledges Jesus Christ whom He has sent. God would remain far off, concealed from us, were we not irradiated by the brightness of Christ. All that the Father had, He deposited with His only begotten Son, in order that He might manifest Himself in Him, and thus by the communication of blessings express the true image of His glory. Since, as has been said, we must be led by the Spirit, and thus stimulated to seek Christ, so must we also remember that the invisible Father is to be sought nowhere but in this image.

For which reason Augustine treating of the object of faith, elegantly says, "The thing to be known is, whither we are to go, and by what way," and immediately after infers that "the surest way to avoid all errors is to know him who is both God and man. It is to God we tend, and it is by man we go, and both of these are found only in Christ."[4]

JOHN CALVIN

FAITH FROM LOVE

To all who did receive him, to those who believed in his name, he gave the right to become children of God.

JOHN 1:12

Almost all that you and I know has come to us by faith. A scientific discovery has been made, and we are sure of it. On what grounds do we believe it? On the authority of certain well-known men of learning, whose reputations are established. We believe their witness.

You must do the like with regard to Jesus: because He teaches you certain truths you are to be His disciple, and believe His words; because He has performed certain acts you are to be His client, and trust yourself with Him. He is infinitely superior to you, and presents Himself to your confidence as your Master and Lord. If you will receive Him and His words, you shall be saved.

Another and a higher form of faith is that faith which grows out of love. Why does a boy trust his father? Because he loves him. Blessed and happy are they who have a sweet faith in Jesus, intertwined with deep affection for Him, for this is a restful confidence.

CHARLES SPURGEON

ALL THAT IS NECESSARY

There is now no condemnation for
those who are in Christ Jesus.

ROMANS 8:1

There [are] two points which should be noted well. On the one side, where there is no Word of God but only the word of man, whoever he be, there is no faith there, but only a dream or an opinion which cannot fail to deceive us.[5] On the other side, faith embraces and appropriates Jesus Christ and all that is in Him, since He has been given to us on the condition of believing in Him (John 17:20–21; Romans 8:9).

There follows one of two things: either all that is necessary for our salvation is not in Jesus Christ, or if all is indeed there, he who has Jesus Christ by faith has everything. Now, to say that all which is necessary for our salvation is not in Jesus Christ is a very horrible blasphemy, for this would only make Him a Saviour in part (Matthew 1:21). There remains therefore the other part: in having Jesus Christ, by faith, we have in Him all that is required for our salvation (Romans 5:1.)

THEODORE BEZA

LOOK TO CHRIST

Trust in the LORD and do good; dwell
in the land and enjoy safe pasture.

PSALM 37:3

After we have taught faith in Christ, we teach good works. "Since you have found Christ by faith," we say, "begin now to work and do well. Love God and your neighbor. Call upon God, give thanks unto Him, praise Him, confess Him. These are good works. Let them flow from a cheerful heart, because you have remission of sin in Christ."

When crosses and afflictions come our way, we bear them patiently. "For Christ's yoke is easy, and His burden is light." When sin has been pardoned, and the conscience has been eased of its dreadful load, a Christian can endure all things in Christ. To give a short definition of a Christian: a Christian is not somebody chalks sin, because of his faith in Christ. This doctrine brings comfort to consciences in serious trouble. When a person is a Christian he is above law and sin. When the Law accuses him, and sin wants to drive the wits out of him, a Christian looks to Christ. A Christian is free. He has no master except Christ. A Christian is greater than the whole world.

MARTIN LUTHER

HEIRS OF THE PROMISE

If you are Christ's, then you are Abraham's seed.

GALATIANS 3:29 NKJV

We, brethren, are children of the promise, born not after the flesh, nor according to the energy of nature, but by the power of God. We trace our new birth not to blood, nor to the will of the flesh, nor to the will of man, but to God alone. We owe our conversion neither to the reasoning of the logician nor to the eloquence of the orator, neither to our natural betterness nor to our personal efforts; we are, as Isaac was, the children of God's power according to the promise.

Now, to us the covenant belongs, for it has been decided—and the apostle has declared the decision in the name of God—that "to Abraham and his seed were the promises made. He saith not, And to seeds, as of many; but as of one, and to thy seed, which is Christ. . . . And if ye be Christ's, then are ye Abraham's seed, and heirs according to the promise" (Galatians 3:16, 29). We are altogether saved by faith.

CHARLES SPURGEON

FAITH EXALTS GOD

Humble yourself before the Lord,
and he will lift you up.

JAMES 4:10

Faith is a sensibleness of what is real in the work of redemption; and as we do really wholly depend on God, so the soul that believes doth entirely depend on God for all salvation, in its own sense and act. Faith abases men and exalts God, it gives all the glory of redemption to God alone. It is necessary in order to saving faith that man should be emptied of himself, that he should be sensible that he is "wretched, and miserable, and poor, and blind, and naked." Humility is a great ingredient of true faith: he that truly receives redemption, receives it as a little child, Mark 10:15: "Whosoever shall not receive the kingdom of heaven as a little child, he shall not enter therein."

It is the delight of a believing soul to abase itself and exalt God alone: that is the language of it, Psalm 115:1: "Not unto us, O Lord, not unto us, but to thy name give glory." Let us be exhorted to exalt God alone, and ascribe to Him all the glory of redemption.

JONATHAN EDWARDS

NOT BY WORKS

We have this hope as an anchor for
the soul, firm and secure.

HEBREWS 6:19

The true way of becoming a Christian is to be justified by faith in Jesus Christ, and not by the works of the Law. We know that we must also teach good works, but they must be taught in their proper turn, when the discussion is concerning works and not the article of justification. Here the question arises: By what means are we justified? We answer with Paul, "By faith only in Christ are we pronounced righteous, and not by works."

Not that we reject good works. Far from it. But we will not allow ourselves to be removed from the anchorage of our salvation. The Law is a good thing. But when the discussion is about justification, then is no time to drag in the Law. When we discuss justification we ought to speak of Christ and the benefits He has brought us. Christ is no sheriff. He is "the Lamb of God, which taketh away the sin of the world" (John 1:29)

MARTIN LUTHER

FAITH BEHOLDS RIGHTEOUSNESS

Through the Spirit we eagerly await by faith
the righteousness for which we hope.

GALATIANS 5:5

The brightest day that ever dawned upon us was the day in which we first "looked unto Him, and were lightened." It was all dark till faith beheld the Sun of Righteousness. The dawn of faith was to us the morning of life; by faith only we began to live. We have since then walked by faith. Whenever we have been tempted to step aside from the path of faith, we have been like the foolish Galatians, and we have smarted for our folly. I trust we have not "suffered so many things in vain" (Galatians 3:4).

We began in the Spirit, and if we have sought to be made perfect in the flesh, we have soon discovered ourselves to be sailing upon the wrong tack, and nearing sunken rocks. "The just shall live by faith" is a truth which has worked itself out in our experience, for often and often have we felt that, in any other course, death stares us in the face; and therefore "we through the Spirit wait for the hope of righteousness by faith" (Galatians 5:5).

CHARLES SPURGEON

FAITH CREATES CONFIDENCE

In him and through faith in him we may
approach God with freedom and confidence.

EPHESIANS 3:12

To be assured of one's salvation through faith in Jesus Christ is not at all arrogance or presumption. It is established that to be assured of one's salvation through faith is not only neither presumption nor arrogance, but, on the contrary, is the sole means of stripping oneself of all pride, to give all glory to God.[6] Faith alone teaches us to go out of ourselves, and compels us to Jesus Christ. It teaches us and assures us that we shall find salvation before God through His righteousness alone.

Truly, all that is in Jesus Christ, that is to say, all the righteousness and perfection (in Him there was no sin, and moreover He has fulfilled all the righteousness of the Law), is placed to our account and gifted to us as if it were our own, provided that we embrace Him by faith.

THEODORE BEZA

OVERCOMING THE DEVIL

Where, O death, is your victory?
Where, O death, is your sting?

1 CORINTHIANS 15:55

By faith in Christ a person may gain such sure and sound comfort, that he need not fear the devil, sin, death, or any evil. "Sir Devil," he may say, "I am not afraid of you. I have a Friend whose name is Jesus Christ, in whom I believe. He has abolished the Law, condemned sin, vanquished death, and destroyed hell for me. He is bigger than you, Satan. He has licked you, and holds you down. You cannot hurt me." This is the faith that overcomes the devil.

Paul manhandles the Law. He treats the Law as if it were a thief and a robber. He treats the Law as contemptible to the conscience, in order that those who believe in Christ may take courage to defy the Law, and say: "Mr. Law, I am a sinner. What are you going to do about it?" Or take death. Christ is risen from death. Why should we now fear the grave? Against my death I set another death, or rather life, my life in Christ. Oh, the sweet name of Jesus!

MARTIN LUTHER

FAITH IS PRECIOUS

To those who through the righteousness of our
God and Savior Jesus Christ have received a faith
as precious as ours: Grace and peace be yours.

2 PETER 1:1-2

Take heed of your faith, because Christ thinks much of it. There are three things in the New Testament which are called "precious": one of them, you know, is the precious blood of Christ; another is the exceeding great and precious promises; and faith has the honor of being the third thing—"To them that have obtained like precious faith." So that faith is one of God's three precious things.

It is one of the things which He values above all others. I was astonished yesterday when I met with an idea in an old divine, concerning the honor which God puts on faith: says he, "Christ takes the crown off His own head to put it on to faith's head." Mark you how often He says, "Thy faith hath saved thee." Now it is not faith that saves, it is Christ that saves. "Thy faith hath healed thee," says Christ. Now faith did not heal, it was Christ that healed, but Christ did uncrown Himself to crown faith.

CHARLES SPURGEON

ONE IN CHRIST

I am again in the pains of childbirth
until Christ is formed in you.

GALATIANS 4:19

With Christ domiciling in me, the old Adam has to stay outside and remain subject to the Law. Think what grace, righteousness, life, peace, and salvation there is in me, thanks to that inseparable conjunction between Christ and me through faith! Paul has a peculiar style, a celestial way of speaking. "I live," he says, "I live not; I am dead, I am not dead; I am a sinner, I am not a sinner; I have the Law, I have no Law." When we look at ourselves we find plenty of sin. But when we look at Christ, we have no sin. Whenever we separate the person of Christ from our own person, we live under the Law and not in Christ; we are condemned by the Law, dead before God.

Faith connects you so intimately with Christ, that He and you become as it were one person. As such you may boldly say: "I am now one with Christ. Therefore Christ's righteousness, victory, and life are mine."

MARTIN LUTHER

THE SOLE VESSEL

He has given us his very great and precious
promises, so that through them you may
participate in the divine nature.

2 PETER 1:4

The Holy Spirit makes us partakers of Jesus Christ by faith alone. The Holy Spirit is therefore the One through whom the Father places and maintains His elect in possession of Jesus Christ, His Son; and, consequently, of all the graces which are necessary to their salvation. But it is necessary, in the first place, that the Holy Spirit makes us suitable and ready to receive Jesus Christ. This is what He does in creating in us, by His pure goodness and divine mercy, that which we call "faith,"[7] the sole instrument by which we take hold of Jesus Christ when He is offered to us, the sole vessel to receive Him (John 3:1–13, 33–36). The means which the Holy Spirit uses to create and preserve faith in us in order to create in us this instrument of faith, and also to feed and strengthen it more and more, [are] the preaching of the Word of God, and His sacraments.[8]

THEODORE BEZA

MORE FAITH, PLEASE

The apostles said the Lord, "Increase our faith!"

LUKE 17:5

The apostles said to the Lord, "Increase our faith!" They went to the right person. They did not say to themselves, "I will increase my faith," they did not cry to the minister, "Preach a comforting sermon, and increase my faith," they did not say, "I will read such-and-such a book, and that will increase my faith." No, they said to the Lord, "Increase our faith."

Faith's Author can alone increase it. I could inflate your faith till it turned into presumption, but I could not make it grow. It is God's work to feed faith, as well as to give it life at first; and if you desire to have a growing faith, go and take your burden this morning to God's throne, crying, "Lord, increase our faith!" If you feel that your troubles have been increased, go to the Lord, and say, "Increase our faith!" If your money is accumulating, go to the Lord, and say, "Increase our faith"; for you will want more faith as you get more prosperity. If your property is diminishing, go to Him and say, "Increase our faith," so that what you lose in one scale you may gain in the other.

CHARLES SPURGEON

FAITH PERVADES
EVERY ACTION

Faith is confidence in what we hope for and
assurance about what we do not see.

HEBREWS 11:1

In the Word of God, all things that are attributed to works are attributable to faith. Faith is the divinity of works. Faith permeates all the deeds of the believer, as Christ's divinity permeated His humanity. Abraham was accounted righteous because faith pervaded his whole personality and his every action. When you read how the fathers, prophets, and kings accomplished great deeds, remember to explain them as the epistle to the Hebrews accounts for them: "Who through faith subdued kingdoms, wrought righteousness, obtained promises, stopped the mouths of lions" (Hebrews 11:33). In this way will we correctly interpret all those passages that seem to support the righteousness of works. The Law is truly observed only through faith.

Supposing that this explanation will not satisfy the scholastics, supposing that they should completely wrap me up in their arguments (they cannot do it), I would rather be wrong and give all credit to Christ alone. Here is Christ. Paul, Christ's apostle, declares that "Christ hath redeemed us from the curse of the law, being made a curse for us" (Galatians 3:13.) I hear with my own ears that I cannot be saved except by the blood and death of Christ.

MARTIN LUTHER

A PROFESSION OF FAITH

Salvation is found in no one else.

ACTS 4:12

When the apostle speaks of a profession of our faith in Christ, as one duty which all Christians ought to perform as they seek salvation, it is the profession of a saving faith. His words plainly imply it: "If thou shalt confess with thy mouth the Lord Jesus, and shalt believe in thine heart that God hath raised him from the dead, thou shalt be saved." The faith which was to be professed with the mouth was the same which the apostle speaks of as in the heart, but that is saving faith. The latter is yet plainer in the following words: "For with the heart man believeth unto righteousness, and with the mouth confession is made unto salvation."

Believing unto righteousness is saving faith; but it is evidently the same faith which is spoken of, as professed with the mouth, in the next words in the same sentence. And that the Gentiles, in professing the Christian religion, or swearing to Christ, should profess saving faith, is implied Isaiah 45:23–24: "Every tongue shall swear; surely shall one say, In the Lord have I righteousness and strength"; i.e., should profess entirely to depend on Christ's righteousness and strength.

JONATHAN EDWARDS

EMBRACING THE PROMISES

Let us hold unswervingly to the hope we
profess, for he who promised is faithful.

HEBREWS 10:23

Let us attempt great things, for those who believe in the name of the Lord succeed beyond all expectation. By faith the worker lives. The right noble Earl of Shaftesbury said, the other afternoon, of Ragged school teachers and their work, "It was evident to all thinking persons that we had a great danger in the ignorance of the children of the lower classes, and so the senators began to think of it, and the philosophers began to think of it, and good men of all sorts began to think of it; but while they were all engaged in thinking, a few plain, humble people opened Ragged schools, and did it. This is the kind of faith of which we need more and more; we need so to trust in God as to put our hand to the plough in His name. It is idle to spend time in making and altering plans and doing nothing else; the best plan for doing God's work is to do it."

Brothers, if you do not believe in anybody else, believe in God without stint. Believe up to the hilt. Bury yourselves, both as to your weakness and your strength, in simple trust in God.

CHARLES SPURGEON

FAITH IS WORSHIP

*Without faith it is impossible to please God, because
anyone who comes to him must believe he exists
and that he rewards those who earnestly seek him.*

HEBREWS 11:6

Faith in God constitutes the highest worship, the prime duty, the first obedience, and the foremost sacrifice. Without faith God forfeits His glory, wisdom, truth, and mercy in us. The first duty of man is to believe in God and to honor Him with his faith. Faith is truly the height of wisdom, the right kind of righteousness, the only real religion. Faith says to God: "I believe what You say."

When we pay attention to reason, God seems to propose impossible matters in the Christian creed. To reason it seems absurd that Christ should offer His body and blood in the Lord's Supper; that baptism should be the washing of regeneration; that the dead shall rise; that Christ the Son of God was conceived in the womb of the Virgin Mary, etc. Reason shouts that all this is preposterous. Are you surprised that reason thinks little of faith? Reason thinks it ludicrous that faith should be the foremost service any person can render unto God. Let your faith supplant reason.

MARTIN LUTHER

FAITH THAT SECURES

This is his command: to believe in the
name of his Son, Jesus Christ.

1 JOHN 3:23

We ought, my friends, to be extremely careful of our faith—both of its rightness and of its strength, first of all, when we consider the position which faith occupied in salvation. Faith is the salvation-grace. We are not saved by love, but we are saved by grace, and we are saved by faith. We are not saved by courage, we are not saved by patience; but we are saved by faith. That is to say, God gives His salvation to faith and not to any other virtue.

It is nowhere written, *He that loveth shall be saved.* It is nowhere recorded that a patient sinner shall be saved. But it is said, "He that believeth and is baptized shall be saved." Faith is the vital part of salvation. If a man lacks faith he lacks everything. "Without faith it is impossible to please God." If a man has true faith—however little he has of any other virtue—that man is secure.

CHARLES SPURGEON

THE MERIT OF WORKS CEASES

This righteousness is given through faith in Jesus Christ to all who believe.

ROMANS 3:22

Whosoever obtains righteousness by works, his merits come into the account before God. But we apprehend righteousness by faith, when God freely reconciles us to Himself. Whence it follows that the merit of works ceases when righteousness is sought by faith; for it is necessary that this righteousness should be freely given by God, and offered in His Word, in order that anyone may possess it by faith.

To render this more intelligible, when Moses says that faith was imputed to Abram for righteousness, he does not mean that faith was that first cause of righteousness, but only the formal cause; as if he had said that Abram was therefore justified, because, relying on the paternal lovingkindness of God, he trusted to His mere goodness, and not to himself, nor to his own merits. For it is especially to be observed that faith borrows a righteousness elsewhere, of which we, in ourselves, are destitute; otherwise it would be in vain for Paul to set faith in opposition to works, when speaking of the mode of obtaining righteousness.

JOHN CALVIN

THE MOTHER OF VIRTUES

For this very reason, make every effort to
add to your faith goodness; and to goodness,
knowledge; and to knowledge, self-control;
and to self-control, perseverance; and to
perseverance, godliness; and to godliness, mutual
affection; and to mutual affection, love.

2 PETER 1:5-7

Faith is the root-grace: all other virtues and graces spring from it. Tell me of love: how can I love Him in whom I do not believe? If I do not believe that there is a God, and that He is the rewarder of all them that diligently seek him, how can I possibly love Him? Tell me of patience: How can I exercise patience unless I have faith? For faith looks to the recompense of the reward: she says that "all things are working together for our good," she believes that from our distresses the greater glory shall spring, and therefore she can endure. Tell me of courage: but who can have courage if he has not faith?

Take what virtue you will, and you will see that it depends on faith. Faith is the silver thread upon which the pearls of the graces are to be strung. Break that, and you have broken the string—the pearls lie scattered on the ground, nor can you wear them for your own adornment. Faith is the mother of virtues.

CHARLES SPURGEON

• GRACE ALONE •

THE FOUNTAINHEAD OF SALVATION

He does not treat us as our sins deserve or repay us according to our iniquities. For as high as the heavens are above the earth, so great is his love for those who fear him.

PSALM 103:10-11

By grace are ye saved, through faith" (Ephesians 2:8). I think it well to turn a little to one side that I may ask my reader to observe adoringly the fountainhead of our salvation, which is the grace of God. "By grace are ye saved." Because God is gracious, therefore sinful men are forgiven, converted, purified, and saved. It is not because of anything in them, or that ever can be in them, that they are saved; but because of the boundless love, goodness, pity, compassion, mercy, and grace of God.

Tarry a moment, then, at the wellhead. Behold the pure river of the water of life, as it proceeds out of the throne of God and of the Lamb! What an abyss is the grace of God! Who can measure its breadth? Who can fathom its depth? Like all the rest of the divine attributes, it is infinite.

CHARLES SPURGEON

A PERFECT SAVIOR

Be strong in the grace that is in Christ Jesus.

2 TIMOTHY 2:1

The innocence, purity, and righteousness of Christ, which He offered up for our guilt and condemnation, deliver us from sin, guilt, and suffering; and we are reckoned worthy of the favor of God for the reason that Christ, who was absolutely free from all sinful inclination, was able to satisfy fully the justice of God. Although He is so high and holy, namely, very God, He nevertheless is our Savior.

From this it follows that His righteousness and innocence, which are wanting in us, are also imputed to us; for God made Him unto us wisdom, righteousness, sanctification, and redemption. So we now have access to God through Christ, because He is our Savior and a pledge of the grace of God unto us. He is our Surety, our Bondsman, our Mediator, our Advocate, and our Intercessor; yea, He is a perfect Savior to us. Those who have thus received the Gospel and assuredly trust therein are born of God; for the shortsightedness of the human mind can neither perceive nor understand the heavenly and mysterious council of God's grace.

ULRICH ZWINGLI

UNMIXED GRACE

[God] made us alive with Christ even
when we were dead in transgressions.

EPHESIANS 2:5

Paul asserts that the salvation of the Ephesians was entirely the work, the gracious work of God. But then they had obtained this grace by faith. On one side, we must look at God, and, on the other, at man. God declares that He owes us nothing, so that salvation is not a reward or recompense, but unmixed grace.

The next question is, in what way do men receive that salvation which is offered to them by the hand of God? The answer is by faith; and hence he concludes that nothing connected with it is our own. If, on the part of God, it is grace alone, and if we bring nothing but faith, which strips us of all commendation, it follows that salvation does not come from us. Ought we not then to be silent about free will, and good intentions, and fancied preparations, merits, and satisfactions? There is none of these which does not claim a share of praise in the salvation of men, so that the praise of grace would not, as Paul shews, remain undiminished.

JOHN CALVIN

A STATE OF GRACE

Through faith [we] are shielded by God's
power until the coming of the salvation that
is ready to be revealed in the last time.

1 PETER 1:5

'Tis by God's power also that we are preserved in a state of grace. As grace is at first from God, so 'tis continually from Him, and is maintained by Him, as much as light in the atmosphere is all day long from the sun. Men are dependent on the power of God for every exercise of grace, and for carrying on the work of grace in the heart, for the subduing of sin and corruption, and increasing holy principles, and enabling to bring forth fruit in good works, and at last bringing grace to its perfection, in making the soul completely amiable in Christ's glorious likeness, and filling it with a satisfying joy and blessedness; and for the raising of the body to life, and to such a perfect state, that it shall be suitable for a habitation and organ for a soul so perfected and blessed. These are the most glorious effects of the power of God that are seen in the series of God's acts with respect to the creatures.

JONATHAN EDWARDS

CREATED IN CHRIST

*We are His workmanship, created in Christ
Jesus for good works, which God prepared
beforehand that we should walk in them.*

EPHESIANS 2:10 NKJV

or we are His work. By setting aside the contrary supposition, [Paul] proves his statement that by grace we are saved, that we have no remaining works by which we can merit salvation; for all the good works which we possess are the fruit of regeneration. Hence it follows that works themselves are a part of grace.

When he says that "we are the work of God," this does not refer to ordinary creation, by which we are made men. We are declared to be new creatures because, not by our own power, but by the Spirit of Christ, we have been formed to righteousness. This applies to none but believers. As the descendants of Adam, they were wicked and depraved; but by the grace of Christ, they are spiritually renewed and become new men. Everything in us, therefore, that is good is the supernatural gift of God. The context explains his meaning. We are His work, because we have been created, not in Adam, but in Christ Jesus, not to every kind of life, but to good works.

JOHN CALVIN

GROW IN GRACE

Grow in the grace and knowledge of
our Lord and Savior Jesus Christ.

2 PETER 3:18

Men ought to be truthful not only in words but also in all their actions, never pretending to be what they are not, nor falsely representing anything in their dealings. As the heart the spring of action is, so should the countenance, the eyes, and all one's manner be. He who feigns the gait of another thereby discloses the fact that his step does not correspond to his character; in other words, that his heart is unchaste and frivolous. What more shall I say?

Let every youth diligently see to it that he drinks from the clear and pure fountain of life, which is the Lord Jesus Christ. He who does this will be shown by Christ how to live, how to speak, and how to act. He will no more regard himself above exercising piety and doing right; he will never despair. He will grow in grace daily; nevertheless he will observe that he often fails and falters. In this way he will make rapid progress, but he will still count himself among the most unworthy. He will do good to all men and will revile no one; for thus did Christ set an example.

ULRICH ZWINGLI

TRUSTING GOD'S GRACE

"I am the Lord's servant," Mary answered.
"May your word to me be fulfilled."

LUKE 1:38

Why have we not taught that one should certainly trust in the grace of God, and count our works as of no value: or that they are not ours, be they ever so good, but God's? For if the works were good according to the judgment of men, we would value our works so high that no one would be able to reward us. Therefore should we learn our humility from Mary: to submit ourselves wholly to God, so that if God speaks a word, we submit ourselves to it and believe it; although according to our understanding it appears impossible, we can say with her: "Lord, my mind is weak; but what Thou sayest, must take place. I am Thy servant; be it unto me according to Thy word!"

Now will every foolish question cease, for everyone would know before he does anything good (that is, what we call "good") how much it will help him, but we will rest ourselves with trustful hearts wholly and unconditionally on the grace of God, who knows what we need before we ask Him, and knows what is proper to give us.

MARTIN LUTHER

GRACE: A CHANGE AGENT

Pursue righteousness, faith, love and peace.

2 TIMOTHY 2:22

Wherever the grace of God has appeared to a man it has trained him to deny ungodliness and worldly lusts, and to live soberly, righteously, and godly in this present evil world: and, dear reader, it will do the same for you. "I cannot make this change," says one. Who said you could? The Scripture which we have quoted speaks not of what man will do, but of what God will do. It is God's promise, and it is for Him to fulfill His own engagements. Trust in Him to fulfill His Word to you, and it will be done.

"But how is it to be done?" What business is that of yours? Must the Lord explain His methods before you will believe Him? The Lord's working in this matter is a great mystery: the Holy Ghost performs it. He who made the promise has the responsibility of keeping the promise, and He is equal to the occasion. God, who promises this marvelous change, will assuredly carry it out in all who receive Jesus, for to all such He gives power to become the Sons of God. O that you would believe it!

CHARLES SPURGEON

GIFTS OF GRACE

How abundant are the good things that you
have stored up for those who fear you.

PSALM 31:19

You remember well, I am sure, the beautiful story of the patriarch Joseph, that when he was viceroy of Egypt his brothers who were in Mesopotamia came several times to him to be helped by him in their extreme necessity, when they were reduced by the famine in their country. You know that they returned each time to their father laden with corn. But when they brought little Benjamin they did not return as at other times laden merely with corn and such things given solely by measure, but with rich gifts and with chariots of all that could be desired.

From this let us see what the eternal Father does in our day; for although the ancient Law bestowed many great benefits upon its people, it was always by measure. But on the other hand, in the new law, when He entered into His glory, He opened His generous hand most liberally to scatter gifts and graces on His faithful, as He said by the prophet Joel, that He would pour out His Spirit upon all flesh, that is, upon all men and not merely upon the apostles.

MARTIN LUTHER

CLEANSED BY GRACE

*If we confess our sins, he is faithful and
just and will forgive us our sins and
purify us from all unrighteousness.*

1 JOHN 1:9

When we say that grace was obtained for us by the merit of Christ, our meaning is that we were cleansed by His blood, that His death was an expiation for sin: "His blood cleanses us from all sin" (1 John 1:7); "This is my blood, which is shed for the remission of sins" (Luke 22:20). If the effect of His shed blood is that our sins are not imputed to us, it follows that by that price the justice of God was satisfied.

To the same effect are the Baptist's words, "Behold the Lamb of God, which taketh away the sin of the world" (John 1:29). For he contrasts Christ with all the sacrifices of the Law, showing that in Him alone was fulfilled what these figures typified. But we know the common expression in Moses—*Iniquity shall be expiated, sin shall be wiped away and forgiven.* In short, we are admirably taught by the ancient figures what power and efficacy there is in Christ's death.

JOHN CALVIN

INFINITE GRACE

The Spirit of the LORD will rest on him—
the Spirit of wisdom and of understanding,
the Spirit of counsel and of might, the Spirit
of the knowledge and fear of the LORD.

ISAIAH 11:2

You know also what Isaiah said of our Lord, that He received infinite grace and the gifts of the Spirit rested upon His head. The Spirit of the Lord, said he, would rest upon Him, the spirit of wisdom and of understanding, the spirit of counsel and strength, the spirit of knowledge and of piety, and He would be filled with the fear of the Lord.

But wherefore did the prophet say that all these gifts would rest upon our Lord when He could have had no need of them, seeing that He Himself was the Source of all grace? It was not otherwise than for us, to cause us to understand that all graces and heavenly blessings must be given to us by Him who is our Head, who distributes them to us who are His members, that is, children of the holy church of which He is the Head. And as a proof of this truth hear what He said in the Song of Songs to His well-beloved: "Open to Me, My spouse, My sister." He called her "spouse" because of the greatness of His love, and His "sister" as an evidence of the purity and chasteness of that love.

MARTIN LUTHER

GRACE AND VICTORY

Having disarmed the powers and authorities,
he made a public spectacle of them,
triumphing over them by the cross.

COLOSSIANS 2:15

Hence it appears that this redemption is not a mere manumission, such as that in which a master, without any price, sets free his slaves; nor is it simply an act of power by which captives are rescued from the hand of an enemy; nor a bare exchange, such as that of prisoners of war. It is a real satisfaction, such as a surety makes by paying in full for the debtor. Our deliverance, indeed, is procured without any price paid on our part, and purely through the free grace and mercy of God (Romans 3:24; Ephesians 2:8).

The divine power too is displayed gloriously in emancipating us from the tyrannical dominion of Satan, over whom Christ obtains a victory and triumph (Colossians 2:15). There is also an exchange in respect of Christ, who was substituted in our place and suffered the punishment due to us. Yet in relation to the justice of God there is a real and perfect satisfaction made.

FRANCIS TURRETIN

DEPENDENT ON GRACE

All are justified freely by his grace through
the redemption that came by Christ Jesus.

ROMANS 3:24

Man hath now a greater dependence on the grace of God than he had before the fall. He depends on the free goodness of God for much more than he did then: then he depended on God's goodness for conferring the reward of perfect obedience, for God was not obliged to promise and bestow that reward. Now we are dependent on the grace of God for much more.

We stand in need of grace, not only to bestow glory upon us, but to deliver us from hell and eternal wrath. Under the first covenant we depended on God's goodness to give us the reward of righteousness; and so we do now. And not only so, but we stand in need of God's free and sovereign grace to give us that righteousness; and yet not only so, but we stand in need of His grace to pardon our sin and release us from the guilt and infinite demerit of it.

JONATHAN EDWARDS

HE DELIGHTS IN MERCY

Who is a God like you, who pardons
sin and forgives the transgression of
the remnant of his inheritance?

MICAH 7:18

Only God can justify the ungodly, but He can do it to perfection. He casts our sins behind His back, He blots them out; He says that though they be sought for, they shall not be found. With no other reason for it but His own infinite goodness, He has prepared a glorious way by which He can make scarlet sins as white as snow, and remove our transgressions from us as far as the east is from the west. One of old called out in amazement, "Who is a God like unto thee, that pardoneth iniquity, and passeth by the transgression of the remnant of his heritage? He retaineth not his anger forever, because he delighteth in mercy" (Micah 7:18).

If you profess to deal with the righteous Lord on law terms, everlasting wrath threatens you, for that is what you deserve. Blessed be His name, He has not dealt with us after our sins; He treats with us on terms of free grace and infinite compassion, and He says, "I will receive you graciously, and love you freely."

CHARLES SPURGEON

ALL THAT IS GOOD

*It is by grace you have been saved, through faith—
and this is not from yourselves, it is the gift of
God—not by works, so that no one can boast.*

EPHESIANS 2:8-9

We must look to Paul's design. He intends to shew that we have brought nothing to God by which He might be laid under obligations to us; and he shews that even the good works which we perform have come from God. Hence it follows that we are nothing except through the pure exercise of His kindness.

Some, on the other hand, infer that the half of our justification arises from works. But what has this to do with Paul's intention, or with the subject which he handles? It is one thing to inquire in what righteousness consists, and another thing to follow up the doctrine that it is not from ourselves by this argument, that we have no right to claim good works as our own, but have been formed by the Spirit of God through the grace of Christ to all that is good. When Paul lays down the cause of justification, he dwells chiefly on this point, that our consciences will never enjoy peace till they rely on the propitiation of sins.

JOHN CALVIN

THE POWER LIES IN GRACE

"If you have faith as small as a mustard seed,
you can say to this mulberry tree, 'Be uprooted
and planted in the sea' and it will obey you."

LUKE 17:6

Grace is the powerful engine, and faith is the chain by which the carriage of the soul is attached to the great motive power. The peace within the soul is not derived from the contemplation of our own faith; it comes to us from Him who is our Peace, the hem of whose garment faith touches, and virtue comes out of Him into the soul.

See then, dear friend, that the weakness of your faith will not destroy you. A trembling hand may receive a golden gift. The Lord's salvation can come to us though we have only faith as a grain of mustard seed. The power lies in the grace of God, and not in our faith. Great messages can be sent along slender wires, and the peace-giving witness of the Holy Spirit can reach the heart by means of a thread-like faith which seems almost unable to sustain its own weight. Think more of Him to whom you look than of the look itself.

CHARLES SPURGEON

GRACE TO BE HOLY

It is written: "Be holy, because I am holy."

1 PETER 1:16

We were in our first estate dependent on God for holiness: we had our original righteousness from Him; but then holiness was not bestowed in such a way of sovereign good pleasure as it is now. Man was created holy, and it became God to create holy all the reasonable creatures He created: it would have been a disparagement to the holiness of God's nature if He had made an intelligent creature unholy.

But now when a man is made holy, it is from mere and arbitrary grace; God may forever deny holiness to the fallen creature if He pleases, without any disparagement to any of His perfections. And we are not only indeed more dependent on the grace of God, but our dependence is much more conspicuous, because our own insufficiency and helplessness in ourselves is much more apparent in our fallen and undone state than it was before we were either sinful or miserable. We are more apparently dependent on God for holiness, because we are first sinful, and utterly polluted, and afterward holy: so the production of the effect is sensible, and its derivation from God more obvious.

JONATHAN EDWARDS

EXPECTANT GRACE

*Being confident of this, that he who began
a good work in you will carry it on to
completion until the day of Christ Jesus.*

PHILIPPIANS 1:6

One of these days you who are now a "babe" in Christ shall be a "father" in the church. Hope for this great thing; but hope for it as a gift of grace, and not as the wages of work, or as the product of your own energy. The inspired apostle Paul speaks of these people as to be confirmed unto the end. He expected the grace of God to preserve them personally to the end of their lives, or till the Lord Jesus should come. Indeed, he expected that the whole church of God in every place and in all time would be kept to the end of the dispensation, till the Lord Jesus as the Bridegroom should come to celebrate the wedding-feast with his perfected Bride. All who are in Christ will be confirmed in Him till that illustrious day.

Has He not said, "Because I live ye shall live also"? He also said, "I give unto my sheep eternal life; and they shall never perish, neither shall any man pluck them out of my hand." He that hath begun a good work in you will confirm it unto the day of Christ.

CHARLES SPURGEON

GRACE AND MERCY
WE PROCLAIM

Am I now trying to win the approval of
human beings, or of God? Or am I trying to
please people? If I were still trying to please
people, I would not be a servant of Christ.

GALATIANS 1:10

We say that we obtain grace by the free mercy of God alone for Christ's sake. This is no preaching to please men. This sort of preaching procures for us the hatred and disfavor of the world, persecutions, excommunications, murders, and curses. "Can't you see that I seek no man's favor by my doctrine?" asks Paul. "If I were anxious for the favor of men I would flatter them. But what do I do? I condemn their works. I teach things only that I have been commanded to teach from above. For that I bring down upon my head the wrath of Jews and Gentiles. My doctrine must be right. It must be divine. Any other doctrine cannot be better than mine. Any other doctrine must be false and wicked."

With Paul we boldly pronounce a curse upon every doctrine that does not agree with ours. We do not preach for the praise of men, or the favor of princes. We preach for the favor of God alone whose grace and mercy we proclaim.

MARTIN LUTHER

GRACE OUTDOES SIN

The law was brought in so that the trespass
might increase. But where sin increased,
grace increased all the more.

ROMANS 5:20

Grace outdoes sin, for it lifts us higher than the place from which we fell. And again, "Where sin abounded, grace did much more abound," because the sentence of the Law may be reversed, but that of grace never can. I stand here and feel condemned, yet perhaps I have a hope that I may be acquitted. There is a dying hope of acquittal still left. But when we are justified, there is no fear of condemnation. I cannot be condemned if I am once justified; fully absolved I am by grace. I defy Satan to lay hands on me, if I am a justified man.

The state of justification is an unvariable one, and is indissolubly united to glory. "Who shall lay anything to the charge of God is elect? It is God that justifieth. Who is he that condemneth? It is Christ that died, yea, rather, that is risen again who is even at the right hand of God who also maketh intercession for us. Who shall separate us from the love of Christ?

CHARLES SPURGEON

GRACE AND PEACE

Grace and peace to you from God the
Father and the Lord Jesus Christ.

2 THESSALONIANS 1:2

Grace remits sin, and peace quiets the conscience. Sin and conscience torment us, but Christ has overcome these fiends now and forever. Only Christians possess this victorious knowledge given from above. These two terms, "grace" and "peace," constitute Christianity. Grace involves the remission of sins, peace, and a happy conscience. Sin is not canceled by lawful living, for no person is able to live up to the Law. The Law reveals guilt, fills the conscience with terror, and drives men to despair. Much less is sin taken away by man-invented endeavors. The fact is, the more a person seeks credit for himself by his own efforts, the deeper he goes into debt. Nothing can take away sin except the grace of God. In actual living, however, it is not so easy to persuade oneself that by grace alone, in opposition to every other means, we obtain the forgiveness of our sins and peace with God.

MARTIN LUTHER

POWER AND GRACE

In order that in the coming ages he might show
the incomparable great riches of his grace,
expressed in his kindness to us in Christ Jesus.

EPHESIANS 2:7

So much the greater concern any one has with, and dependence upon, the power and grace of God, so much the greater occasion has he to take notice of that power and grace. So much the greater and more immediate dependence there is on the divine holiness, so much the greater occasion to take notice of and acknowledge that. So much the greater and more absolute dependence we have on the divine perfections, as belonging to the several persons of the Trinity, so much the greater occasion have we to observe and own the divine glory of each of them.

That which we are most concerned with is surely most in the way of our observation and notice; and this kind of concern with anything, namely dependence, does especially tend to commend and oblige the attention and observation. Those things that we are not much dependent upon, 'tis easy to neglect; but we can scarce do any other than mind that which we have a great dependence on.

JONATHAN EDWARDS

ABUNDANT PARDON

Here is a trustworthy saying that deserves full
acceptance: Christ Jesus came into the world
to save sinners—of whom I am the worst.

1 TIMOTHY 1:15

May I urge upon any who have no good thing about them—who fear that they have not even a good feeling, or anything whatever that can recommend them to God— that they will firmly believe that our gracious God is able and willing to take them without anything to recommend them, and to forgive them spontaneously, not because they are good, but because He is good.

Does He not make His sun to shine on the evil as well as on the good? Does He not give fruitful seasons, and send the rain and the sunshine in their time upon the most ungodly nations? Ay, even Sodom had its sun, and Gomorrah had its dew. Oh friend, the great grace of God surpasses my conception and your conception, and I would have you think worthily of it! As high as the heavens are above the earth; so high are God's thoughts above our thoughts. He can abundantly pardon. Jesus Christ came into the world to save sinners: forgiveness is for the guilty.

CHARLES SPURGEON

GRATUITOUS MERCY

Noah was a righteous man, blameless
among the people of his time, and he
walked faithfully with God.

GENESIS 6:9

Noah found grace in the eyes of the Lord." This is a Hebrew phrase, which signifies that God was propitious to him, and favored him. For so the Hebrews are accustomed to speak: "If I have found grace in Thy sight" instead of "If I am acceptable to Thee" or "If Thou wilt grant me thy benevolence or favor." Which phrase requires to be noticed, because certain unlearned men infer with futile subtlety that if men find grace in God's sight, it is because they seek it by their own industry and merits. I acknowledge, indeed, that here Noah is declared to have been acceptable to God, because, by living uprightly and holily, he kept himself pure from the common pollutions of the world; whence, however, did he attain this integrity, but from the preventing grace of God? The commencement, therefore, of this favor was gratuitous mercy. Afterwards, the Lord, having once embraced him, retained him under His own hand, lest he should perish with the rest of the world.

JOHN CALVIN

THE SYSTEM OF GRACE

"The Son of Man came to seek and to save the lost."

LUKE 19:10

I say that the Lord of love had just such as you are in His eye when He arranged the system of grace. Suppose a man of generous spirit were to resolve to forgive all those who were indebted to him; it is clear that this can only apply to those really in his debt. Each one has but to have his bill receipted, and the liability is wiped out. But the most generous person cannot forgive the debts of those who do not owe him anything. It is out of the power of omnipotence to forgive where there is no sin.

Pardon, therefore, cannot be for you who have no sin. Pardon must be for the guilty. Forgiveness must be for the sinful. It were absurd to talk of forgiving those who do not need forgiveness—pardoning those who have never offended. Do you think you must be lost because you are a sinner? This is the reason why you can be saved. Because you own yourself to be a sinner, I would encourage you to believe that grace is ordained for such as you are.

CHARLES SPURGEON

GRACE: THE FRUIT OF MERCY

To each one of us grace has been given
as Christ apportioned it.

EPHESIANS 4:7

Grace is properly set in opposition to offense; the gift which proceeds from grace, to death. Hence grace means the free goodness of God or gratuitous love, of which He has given us a proof in Christ that He might relieve our misery: and gift is the fruit of this mercy, and hath come to us, even the reconciliation by which we have obtained life and salvation, righteousness, newness of life, and every other blessing.

We hence see how absurdly the schoolmen have defined *grace*, who have taught that it is nothing else but a quality infused into the hearts of men. For grace, properly speaking, is in God; and what is in us is the effect of grace. And [Paul] says that it is by one Man; for the Father has made Him the Fountain out of whose fullness all must draw. And thus he teaches us that not even the least drop of life can be found out of Christ—that there is no other remedy for our poverty and want than what He conveys to us from His own abundance.

JOHN CALVIN

COME AS YOU ARE

To the one who does not work but trusts
God who justifies the ungodly, their
faith is credited as righteousness.

ROMANS 4:5

Wait not for reformation, but come at once for salvation. God justifieth the ungodly, and that takes you up where you now are: it meets you in your worst estate. Come to your heavenly Father in all your sin and sinfulness. Come to Jesus just as you are, leprous, filthy, naked, neither fit to live nor fit to die. Come, you that are the very sweepings of creation; come, though you hardly dare to hope for anything but death. Come, though despair is brooding over you, pressing upon your bosom like a horrible nightmare. Come and ask the Lord to justify another ungodly one.

Why should He not? Come, for this great mercy of God is meant for such as you are. I put it in the language of the text, and I cannot put it more strongly: the Lord God Himself takes to Himself this gracious title, "Him that justifieth the ungodly." He makes just, and causes to be treated as just, those who by nature are ungodly. Is not that a wonderful word for you?

CHARLES SPURGEON

GOD'S GRACE SET FORTH

If, by the trespass of the one man, death reigned
through that one man, how much more will
those who receive God's abundant provision
of grace and of the gift of righteousness reign
in life through the one man, Jesus Christ!

ROMANS 5:17

The grace of God might be worthily set forth, that men might be led from self-confidence to trust in Christ, that having obtained His grace they might enjoy full assurance; and hence at length arises gratitude. The sum of the whole is this: that Christ surpasses Adam; the sin of one is overcome by the righteousness of the other; the curse of one is effaced by the grace of the other; from one, death has proceeded, which is absorbed by the life which the other bestows.

But the parts of this comparison do not correspond; instead of adding "the gift of life shall more fully reign and flourish through the exuberance of grace," [Paul] says that "the faithful shall reign," which amounts to the same thing; for the reign of the faithful is in life, and the reign of life is in the faithful.

JOHN CALVIN

THE COVENANT OF GRACE

He gives us more grace.

JAMES 4:6

Remember that the Lord Jesus came to take away sin in three ways: He came to remove the penalty of sin, the power of sin, and, at last, the presence of sin. At once you may reach to the second part—the power of sin may immediately be broken; and so you will be on the road to the third, namely, the removal of the presence of sin. "We know that he was manifested to take away our sins." The angel said of our Lord, "Thou shalt call his name Jesus, for he shall save his people from their sins." Our Lord Jesus came to destroy in us the works of the devil. That which was said at our Lord's birth was also declared in His death; for when the soldier pierced His side forthwith came there out blood and water, to set forth the double cure by which we are delivered from the guilt and the defilement of sin.

If, however, you are troubled about the power of sin, and about the tendencies of your nature, as you well may be, here is a promise for you. Have faith in it, for it stands in that covenant of grace which is ordered in all things and sure.

CHARLES SPURGEON

GRACE COMES TO HELP

As sin reigned in death, even so grace might
reign through righteousness to eternal
life through Jesus Christ our Lord.

ROMANS 5:21 NKJV

Grace has superabounded. After sin has held men sunk in ruin, grace then comes to their help; for He teaches us that the abundance of grace becomes for this reason more illustrious: while sin is overflowing, [grace] pours itself forth so exuberantly that it not only overcomes the flood of sin, but wholly absorbs it. And we may hence learn that our condemnation is not set before us in the Law that we may abide in it, but that having fully known our misery, we may be led to Christ, who is sent to be a Physician to the sick, a Deliverer to the captives, a Comforter to the afflicted, a Defender to the oppressed (Isaiah 61:1).

As sin is said to be the sting of death, and as death has no power over men, except on account of sin, so sin executes its power by death: it is hence said to exercise thereby its dominion. In the last clause the order of the words is deranged, but yet not without reason. The simple contrast might have been thus formed, "That righteousness may reign through Christ."

JOHN CALVIN

A MIRACLE OF GRACE

You have been born again, not of perishable
seed, but of imperishable, through the
living and enduring word of God.

1 PETER 1:23

The Lord knows right well that you cannot change your own heart, and cannot cleanse your own nature; but He also knows that He can do both. He can cause the Ethiopian to change his skin, and the leopard his spots. Hear this, and be astonished: He can create you a second time; He can cause you to be born again. This is a miracle of grace, but the Holy Ghost will perform it.

It would be a very wonderful thing if one could stand at the foot of the Niagara Falls, and could speak a word which should make the river Niagara begin to run upstream, and leap up that great precipice over which it now rolls in stupendous force. Nothing but the power of God could achieve that marvel; but that would be more than a fit parallel to what would take place if the course of your nature were altogether reversed. All things are possible with God. He can make your whole being tend upward toward God.

CHARLES SPURGEON

GOD'S PLEASURE: SAVING SINNERS

"A bruised reed he will not break, and a smoldering wick he will not snuff out."

ISAIAH 42:3

The Law is a mirror to show a person what he is like, a sinner who is guilty of death, and worthy of everlasting punishment. What is this bruising and beating by the hand of the Law to accomplish? This, that we may find the way to grace. God is the God of the humble, the miserable, the afflicted. It is His nature to exalt the humble, to comfort the sorrowing, to heal the brokenhearted, to justify the sinners, and to save the condemned. The fatuous idea that a person can be holy by himself denies God the pleasure of saving sinners.

God must therefore first take the sledgehammer of the Law in His fists and smash the beast of self-righteousness and its brood of self-confidence, self-wisdom, self-righteousness, and self-help. When the conscience has been thoroughly frightened by the Law it welcomes the Gospel of grace with its message of a Savior who came into the world, not to break the bruised reed, nor to quench the smoking flax, but to preach glad tidings to the poor, to heal the brokenhearted, and to grant forgiveness of sins to all the captives.

MARTIN LUTHER

THE SPIRIT ENLIGHTENS

Repent, then, and turn to God, so that
your sins may be wiped out, that times of
refreshing may come from the Lord.

ACTS 3:19

Repentance of sin is as truly the work of grace as the making of an atonement by which sin is blotted out. Salvation, from first to last, is of grace alone. It is not the Holy Spirit who repents. He has never done anything for which He should repent. We must ourselves repent of our own sin, or we are not saved from its power. It is not the Lord Jesus Christ who repents. What should He repent of? We ourselves repent with the full consent of every faculty of our mind.

The will, the affections, the emotions all work together most heartily in the blessed act of repentance for sin; and yet at the back of all that there is a secret holy influence which melts the heart, gives contrition, and produces a complete change. The Spirit of God enlightens us to see what sin is, and also turns us toward holiness, makes us heartily to appreciate, love, and desire it, and thus gives us the impetus by which we are led onward from stage to stage of sanctification.

CHARLES SPURGEON

DIVINE GRACE

Because of his great love for us, God, who
is rich in mercy, made us alive with Christ
even when we were dead in transgressions—
it is by grace you have been saved.

EPHESIANS 2:4-5

Behold, this divine promise of grace and forgiveness of sin is rightly called "the Gospel." And I say here again that by the Gospel you must by no means understand anything else than the divine promise of God's grace and His forgiveness of sin. For thus it was that Paul's epistles were never understood, nor can they be understood by the papists, because they do not know what the Law and the Gospel really mean. They hold Christ to be a lawmaker, and the Gospel a mere doctrine of a new law. That is nothing else than locking up the Gospel and entirely concealing it.

Now, the word *Gospel* is of Greek origin and signifies in German *Frohliche Botschaft*, that is, *glad tidings*, because it proclaims the blessed doctrine of life eternal by divine promise, and offers grace and forgiveness of sin. Therefore, works do not belong to the Gospel, as it is not a law; only faith belongs to it, as it is altogether a promise and an offer of divine grace.

MARTIN LUTHER

CONTINUAL GRACE

He did not take away the pillar of cloud by day or
the pillar of fire by night from before the people.

EXODUS 13:22 NKJV

The sun shall not smite thee by day, nor the moon by night" (Psalm 121:6) refers not to a single day, but to all ages. The statement of Moses, then, that "He took not away the pillar of the cloud by day, nor the pillar of fire by night" is a blessing which God extends to us, as well as to them, except only the visible symbol, which was temporary on account of the infirmity of the people.

As to his saying that God always appeared to them, that they might march by night as well as by day, he does not mean that they went on continually without any rest, since he had just before mentioned that their first station was in Succoth, from whence they encamped in Etham, but merely informs us that the flow of God's grace was continual: the token of His favor and protection shone forth no less amidst the darkness of the night than at midday itself.

JOHN CALVIN

MORE GRACE

God is able to bless you abundantly, so that
in all things at all times, having all that you
need, you will abound in every good work.

2 CORINTHIANS 9:8

Between this hour and the consummation of all things, every promise of God and every provision of the covenant of grace will be brought into requisition. The urgent need of the believing soul is confirmation, continuance, final perseverance, preservation to the end. This is the great necessity of the most advanced believers, for Paul was writing to saints at Corinth, who were men of a high order, of whom he could say, "I thank my God always on your behalf, for the grace of God which is given you by Jesus Christ." Such men are the very persons who most assuredly feel that they have daily need of new grace if they are to hold on, and hold out, and come off conquerors at the last.

If you were not saints you would have no grace, and you would feel no need of more grace; but because you are men of God, therefore you feel the daily demands of the spiritual life.

CHARLES SPURGEON

THE GRACE OF CHRIST

Do not be afraid, Daughter Zion; see, your
king is coming, seated on a donkey's colt.

JOHN 12:15

The Gospel encourages and demands faith, for it prefigures Christ coming with grace, whom none may receive or accept save he who believes Him to be the Man, and has the mind, as this Gospel portrays in Christ. Nothing but the mercy, tenderness, and kindness of Christ are here shown, and he who so receives and believes on Him is saved.

He sits not upon a proud steed, an animal of war, nor does He come in great pomp and power, but sitting upon an ass, an animal of peace fit only for burdens and labor and a help to man. He indicates by this that He comes not to frighten man, nor to drive or crush him, but to help him and to carry his burden for him. And although it was the custom of the country to ride on asses and to use horses for war, as the Scriptures often tell us, yet here the object is to show that the entrance of this King shall be meek and lowly.

MARTIN LUTHER

A PLEDGE OF GOD'S FAVOR

We have peace with God through our Lord Jesus
Christ, through whom we have gained access
by faith into this grace in which we now stand.
And we boast in the hope of the glory of God.

ROMANS 5:1-2

Our reconciliation with God depends only on Christ; for He only is the beloved Son, and we are all by nature the children of wrath. But this favor is communicated to us by the Gospel; for the Gospel is the ministry of reconciliation, by the means of which we are in a manner brought into the kingdom of God.

Rightly then does Paul set before our eyes in Christ a sure pledge of God's favor, that he might more easily draw us away from every confidence in works. And as he teaches us by the word "access," that salvation begins with Christ, he excludes those preparations by which foolish men imagine that they can anticipate God's mercy; as though he said, "Christ comes not to you, nor helps you, on account of your merits." He afterwards immediately subjoins that it is through the continuance of the same favor that our salvation becomes certain and sure; by which he intimates that perseverance is not founded on our power and diligence, but on Christ.

JOHN CALVIN

STANDING IN GRACE

*He is able to save completely those who
come to God through him, because he
always lives to intercede for them.*

HEBREWS 7:25

We ought to feel sure that we stand in the grace of God, not in view of our own worthiness, but through the good services of Christ. As certain as we are that Christ pleases God, so sure ought we to be that we also please God, because Christ is in us. And although we daily offend God by our sins, yet as often as we sin, God's mercy bends over us. Therefore sin cannot get us to doubt the grace of God. Our certainty is of Christ, that mighty Hero who overcame the Law, sin, death, and all evils. So long as He sits at the right hand of God to intercede for us, we have nothing to fear from the anger of God.

This inner assurance of the grace of God is accompanied by outward indications such as gladly to hear, preach, praise, and to confess Christ, to do one's duty in the station in which God has placed us, to aid the needy, and to comfort the sorrowing. These are the affidavits of the Holy Spirit testifying to our favorable standing with God.

MARTIN LUTHER

PARDON GRANTED

In him we have redemption through his
blood, the forgiveness of sins, in accordance
with the riches of God's grace.

EPHESIANS 1:7

There is a wide difference between a payment made by a debtor in his own person, and a payment made by a surety. As to the reality of payment there is no difference in the eye of the law, but in relation to grace there is a striking difference. When a debtor pays out of his own purse his debts, it cannot be said that the creditor has forgiven him the debt or shown him favour, but if the debt has been paid by another and that other has been found out by the creditor, then grace may be said to have been shown. Satisfaction and remission are inconsistent with each other, when referred to the same thing, but not so when they are referred to different things. Satisfaction has God for its object, remission man for its object. Satisfaction is made by Christ to God for man, and yet man is freely pardoned. Justice and mercy kiss each other. Justice is exercised against sin as imputed to Christ, and mercy, free and sovereign mercy, is shown to sinners. The pardon granted to us is entirely of grace, while full satisfaction is demanded of the surety.

FRANCIS TURRETIN

ASSURED OF GRACE

By him we cry, "Abba, Father."

ROMANS 8.15

We are born in sin. To doubt the goodwill of God is an inborn suspicion of God with all of us. Besides, the devil, our adversary, goeth about seeking to devour us by roaring: "God is angry at you and is going to destroy you forever." In all these difficulties we have only one support, the Gospel of Christ.

Especially in times of trials a Christian feels the power of sin, the infirmity of his flesh, the goading darts of the devil, the agues of death, the scowl and judgment of God. All these things cry out against us. The Law scolds us, sin screams at us, death thunders at us, the devil roars at us. In the midst of the clamor the Spirit of Christ cries in our hearts: "Abba, Father." And this little cry of the Spirit transcends the hullabaloo of the Law, sin, death, and the devil, and finds a hearing with God. The Spirit cries in us because of our weakness. Because of our infirmity the Holy Ghost is sent forth into our hearts to pray for us according to the will of God and to assure us of the grace of God.

MARTIN LUTHER

GRACE TO PERSEVERE

May our Lord Jesus Christ himself and God our
Father, who loved us and by his grace gave us eternal
encouragement and good hope, encourage your hearts.

2 THESSALONIANS 2:16–17

Whosoever has obtained the gift of true faith has also by the same grace and liberality of God obtained the gift of perseverance, so that in all manner of temptations and afflictions he doubts not to call upon God, with sure confidence to obtain his request (as far as it is expedient for him), knowing that he is of the number of God's children, who cannot fail him.

Moreover he never swerves so from the right way, but at length by the benefit of God's grace, he returns again: for although faith sometime seems in the elect (as it were for a time) hid and buried, so that a man would think it were utterly quenched (which God allows, that men might know their own weakness), yet it does never so far leave them, that the love of God and their neighbor is altogether plucked out of their hearts. For no man is justified in Christ, who also is not sanctified in him, and framed to good works, which God prepared that we should walk therein.

THEODORE BEZA

DEEDS OF GRACE

*Sin shall no longer be your master, because you
are not under the law, but under grace.*

ROMANS 6:14

The whole Bible tells us, from beginning to end, that salvation is not by the works of the Law, but by the deeds of grace. Martin Luther declared that he constantly preached justification by faith alone "because," said he, "the people would forget it; so that I was obliged almost to knock my Bible against their heads, to send it into their hearts." So it is true we constantly forget that salvation is by grace alone.

We always want to be putting in some little scrap of our own virtue; we want to be doing something. I remember a saying of old Matthew Wilkes: "Saved by your works! You might as well try to go to America in a paper boat!" Saved by your works! It is impossible! Oh no; the poor legalist is like a blind horse going round and round the mill, or like the prisoner going up the treadmill, and finding himself no higher after all he has done; he has no solid confidence, no firm ground to rest upon. He has not done enough—"Never enough." Conscience always says, "This is not perfection; it ought to have been better."

CHARLES SPURGEON

NEVER DESPAIR

The LORD is close to the brokenhearted and
saves those who are crushed in spirit.

PSALM 34:18

Now if anyone so sins as even to be driven quite back, or to fall prostrate on the ground, yet he is not to be rejected, as if he belongs not at all to Christ's kingdom. Christ must and will be ever like Himself, and in His kingdom must remain mere grace and mercy so that He will ever continue to help those who feel their misery and wretchedness, and who desire to be rescued from their sufferings. Thus it will always be a kingdom of help and comfort.

And He will be a comforting, gentle Shepherd who invites and allures everyone to come to Him. Moreover, all these things are administered by the Gospel only. By this the weak are made strong, the sick healed. For the Word is of that nature, that it serves for all things which the conscience lacks, and gives to all so much comfort, that however great a sinner one may be, one need not despair. Christ alone therefore is the true and real Shepherd, who heals every wound, and lifts up everyone that is fallen.

MARTIN LUTHER

THE FULLNESS OF HIS GRACE

Out of his fullness we have all received grace in place of grace already given.

JOHN 1:16

We have the greater occasion to take notice of God's all-sufficiency when all our sufficiency is thus every way of Him. We have the more occasion to contemplate Him as an infinite good, and as the fountain of all good. Such a dependence on God demonstrates God's all-sufficiency. So much as the dependence of the creature is on God, so much the greater does the creature's emptiness in himself appear to be; and so much the greater the creature's emptiness, so much the greater must the fulness of the Being be who supplies him.

Our having all of God shows the fullness of His power and grace; our having all through Him shows the fullness of His merit and worthiness; and our having all in Him demonstrates His fullness of beauty, love, and happiness. And the redeemed, by reason of the greatness of their dependence on God, haven't only so much the greater occasion but obligation to contemplate and acknowledge the glory and fullness of God.

JONATHAN EDWARDS

HE IS OUR DEFENDER

If God is for us, who can be against us?

ROMANS 8:31

This is the chief and the only support which can sustain us in every temptation. For except we have God propitious to us, though all things should smile on us, yet no sure confidence can be attained: but, on the other hand, His favor alone is a sufficient solace in every sorrow, a protection sufficiently strong against all the storms of adversities.

And on this subject there are many testimonies of Scripture, which show that when the saints rely on the power of God alone, they dare to despise whatever is opposed to them in the world: "When I walk in the midst of the shadow of death, I shall not fear evils, for thou art with me" (Psalm 23:4). "In the Lord I trust: what shall flesh do to me?" (Psalm 56:11). "I shall not fear the thousands of the people who beset me" (Psalm 3:6). For there is no power either under or above the heavens, which can resist the arm of God. Having Him then as our Defender, we need fear no harm whatever.

JOHN CALVIN

THE GIFT OF GRACE

It is by grace you have been saved.

EPHESIANS 2:5

We can run a golden link from hence up to Jesus Christ Himself, through a holy succession of mighty fathers who all held these glorious truths; and we can say to them, Where will you find holier and better men in the world? We are not ashamed to say of ourselves, that however much we may be maligned and slandered, ye will not find a people who will live closer to God than those who believe that they are saved not by their works, but by free grace alone.

But oh! ye believers in free grace, be careful. Our enemies hate the doctrine; and if one falls, "Ah there," say they, "see the tendency of your principles." *Nay*, we might reply, *see what is the tendency of your doctrine.* The exception in our case proves the rule is true, that after all, our Gospel does lead us to holiness. Of all men, those have the most disinterested piety, the sublimest reverence, the most ardent devotion, who believe that they are saved by grace, without works, through faith, and that not of themselves, it is the gift of God.

CHARLES SPURGEON

FULL OF GRACE

The Mighty One has done great things
for me—holy is his name.

LUKE 1:49

When the angel came in unto Mary, he greeted her with these words: "Hail, thou art full of grace! The Lord is with thee, blessed art thou among women." Here it is to be noticed that this term "full of grace" is translated from the Greek word *kecharitomene*, which means "beloved," or "filled with grace," "highly favored," whereby we understand that the term "full of grace" should not be taken to mean that she was from herself full of grace, but that all the grace with which she was so rich and full was from God.

For grace is only the favor of God. So if I should say that God has given much grace to men, I should say nothing else than God has been very favorable to men and done loving things for them. Therefore is the pure Mary full of grace from God, as she herself sings: "He hath done to me great things." She says not: "I am great from mine own grace," but "the Almighty hath done to me great things."

MARTIN LUTHER

SUPPORTED BY GOD'S HANDS

The Spirit also helpeth our infirmities: for we know not what we should pray for as we ought: but the Spirit itself maketh intercession for us with groanings which cannot be uttered.

ROMANS 8:26 KJV

The faithful may not make this objection, that they are so weak as not to be able to bear so many and so heavy burdens, [Paul] brings before them the aid of the Spirit, which is abundantly sufficient to overcome all difficulties. We are sustained by a celestial power. The Spirit takes on Himself a part of the burden, by which our weakness is oppressed; so that He not only helps and succors us but lifts us up, as though He went under the burden with us.

The word *infirmities,* being in the plural number, is expressive of extremity. For as experience shows, that except we are supported by God's hands, we are soon overwhelmed by innumerable evils. Paul reminds us that though we are in every respect weak, and various infirmities threaten our fall, there is yet sufficient protection in God's Spirit to preserve us from falling, and to keep us from being overwhelmed by any mass of evils.

JOHN CALVIN

GRACE MAKES US USEFUL

Each of you has your own gift from God.

1 CORINTHIANS 7:7

God, by using us as instruments, confers upon us the highest honor which men can receive. It should make our hearts burn at the thought of it. It makes us feel thrice honored that God should use us to convert souls; and it is only the grace of God which teaches us, on the other hand, that it is grace and grace alone which makes us useful, which can keep us humble under the thought that we are bringing souls to the Savior. It is a work which he who has once entered, if God has blessed him, cannot renounce. He will be impatient; he will long to win more souls to Jesus; he will think that labor is but ease so that by any means he may save some and bring men to Jesus.

Glory and honor, praise and power, be unto God, that He thus honors His people. But when He exalts us most, we will still conclude, "Not unto us, not unto us, but unto thy name be all the glory forever and ever."

CHARLES SPURGEON

JULY 17

PARTAKERS OF
GOD BY GRACE

*I say to the LORD, "You are my Lord; apart
from you I have no good thing."*

PSALM 16:2

The redeemed have all their inherent good in God. Inherent good is twofold; 'tis either excellency or pleasure. These the redeemed not only derive from God, as caused by Him, they have spiritual excellency and joy by a kind of participation of God. They are made excellent by a communication of God's excellency: God puts His own beauty, i.e., His beautiful likeness, upon their souls: they are made partakers of the divine nature, or moral image of God (2 Peter 1:4). They are holy by being made partakers of God's holiness (Hebrews 12:10).

The saints are beautiful and blessed by a communication of God's holiness and joy, as the moon and planets are bright by the sun's light. The saint hath spiritual joy and pleasure by a kind of effusion of God on the soul. In these things the redeemed have communion with God; that is, they partake with Him and of Him.

JONATHAN EDWARDS

ABOUNDING GRACE

Grace and peace be yours in abundance.

1 PETER 1:2

Grace doth "much more abound" because a time shall come when the world shall be all full of grace. There has never been a period in this world's history when it was wholly given up to sin. When Adam and Eve rebelled against God, there was still a display of grace in the world; for in the garden, at the close of the day, God said, "I will put enmity between thee and the woman, and between thy seed and her seed; it shall bruise thy head, and thou shalt bruise his heel"; and since that first transgression, there has never been a moment when grace has entirely lost its footing in the earth.

God has always had His servants on earth; at times they have been hidden by fifties in the caves, but they have never been utterly cut off. Grace might be low; the stream might be very shallow, but it has never been wholly dry. There has always been a salt of grace in the world to counteract the power of sin.

CHARLES SPURGEON

GRACE LEADS TO PRAYER

The Spirit himself testifies with our spirit that we are God's children.

ROMANS 8:16

When the Spirit testifies to us that we are the children of God, He at the same time pours into our hearts such confidence that we venture to call God our Father. And doubtless since the confidence of the heart alone opens our mouth, except the Spirit testifies to our heart respecting the paternal love of God, our tongues would be dumb, so that they could utter no prayers. For we must ever hold fast this principle, that we do not rightly pray to God unless we are surely persuaded in our hearts that He is our Father, when we so call Him with our lips.

To this there is a corresponding part, that our faith has no true evidence except we call upon God. It is not then without reason that Paul, bringing us to this test, shows that it then only appears how truly anyone believes when they who have embraced the promise of grace exercise themselves in prayers.

JOHN CALVIN

A SUPREME GIFT

The grace of God has appeared that offers salvation
to all people. It teaches us to say "No" to ungodliness
and worldly passions, and to live self-controlled,
upright and godly lives in this present age.

TITUS 2:11–12

When supreme goodness intended to bestow the supreme gift, it gave the most precious thing it could bring out of its treasure chest, namely itself, that the heart of man, ever eager for something greater, should not even have a way left to wonder how this angelic or human victim could be so great as to be sufficient for all, or how one could put unshaken trust in a creature. The Son of God has, therefore, been given to us as a confirmation of His mercy, as a pledge of pardon, as the price of righteousness, and as a rule of life, to make us sure of the grace of God and to teach us the law of living.

Who could worthily extol the greatness of this divine goodness and generosity? We had deserved to be disowned, and He honors us with being chosen. We had destroyed the way of life, and He has restored it. Thus, then, we have been redeemed and renewed by divine goodness so completely as to be acceptable through His mercy, and to be justified and blameless through His atoning sacrifice.

ULRICH ZWINGLI

THE ALPHA AND OMEGA

"These are the very Scriptures
that testify about me."

JOHN 5:39

Jesus Christ is the Alpha and Omega of the Bible. He is the constant theme of its sacred pages; from first to last they testify of Him. At the creation we at once discern Him as one of the sacred Trinity; we catch a glimpse of Him in the promise of the woman's seed; we see Him typified in the ark of Noah; we walk with Abraham as he sees Messiah's day; we dwell in the tents of Isaac and Jacob, feeding upon the gracious promise; we hear the venerable Israel talking of Shiloh; and in the numerous types of the Law, we find the Redeemer abundantly foreshadowed. Prophets and kings, priests and preachers, all look one way—they all stand as the cherubs did over the ark, desiring to look within, and to read the mystery of God's great propitiation.

Still more manifestly in the New Testament we find our Lord the one pervading subject. Here you stand upon a solid floor of gold; for the whole substance of the New Testament is Jesus crucified, and even its closing sentence is bejewelled with the Redeemer's name.

CHARLES SPURGEON

DIVINE INFLUENCE

I will instruct you and teach you in
the way you should go; I will counsel
you with my loving eye on you.

PSALM 32:8

While I admit that those who hold that man has no ability in himself to do righteousness, hold what is most necessary to be known for salvation, I think it ought not to be overlooked that we owe it to the special grace of God whenever, on the one hand, we choose what is for our advantage, and whenever our will inclines in that direction; and on the other, whenever with heart and soul we shun what would otherwise do us harm. And the interference of divine Providence goes to the extent not only of making events turn out as was foreseen to be expedient, but of giving the wills of men the same direction.

If we look at the administration of human affairs with the eye of sense, we will have no doubt that, so far, they are placed at man's disposal; but if we lend an ear to the many passages of Scripture which proclaim that even in these matters the minds of men are ruled by God, they will compel us to place human choice in subordination to His special influence.

JOHN CALVIN

A WORK OF GRACE

God saw that the light was good.

GENESIS 1:4

God saw the light"—He gazed upon it with pleasure, saw that it "was good." If the Lord has given you light, dear reader, He looks on that light with peculiar interest; for not only is it dear to Him as His own handiwork, but because it is like Himself, for "he is light." Pleasant it is to the believer to know that God's eye is thus tenderly observant of that work of grace which He has begun. He never loses sight of the treasure which He has placed in our earthen vessels.

Sometimes we cannot see the light, but God always sees the light, and that is much better than our seeing it. Better for the judge to see my innocence than for me to think I see it. It is very comfortable for me to know that I am one of God's people—but whether I know it or not, if the Lord knows it, I am still safe. You may be sighing and groaning because of inbred sin, and mourning over your darkness, yet the Lord sees "light" in your heart, for He has put it there, and all the cloudiness and gloom of your soul cannot conceal your light from His gracious eye.

CHARLES SPURGEON

THE LIGHT OF GRACE

*In him was life, and that life was
the light of all mankind.*

JOHN 1:4

When now Christ, the light of grace, comes and also teaches that we are to be pious and serve God, He does not extinguish this natural light, but opposes the way and manner of becoming pious and serving God as taught by reason. He says: to become pious is not to do works; no works are good without faith. Then begins the fight. Reason rises up against grace and cries out against its light, accuses it of forbidding good works, protests against not having its own way and standard of becoming pious, being thus set aside; but [it] continually rages about being pious and serving God, and so makes the light of grace foolishness, nay error and heresy, and persists in persecuting and banishing it.

See, this is the virtue of the light of nature, that it raves against the true light, is constantly boasting of piety, piety, and is always crying "Good works!" "Good works!" But it cannot and will not stand to be taught what piety is and what good works are; it insists that which it thinks and proposes must be right and good.

MARTIN LUTHER

ACKNOWLEDGING GOD'S GRACE

Then you say in your heart, "My power and the
might of my hand have gained me this wealth."
And you shall remember the LORD your God, for
it is He who gives you power to get wealth.

DEUTERONOMY 8:17–18 NKJV

This is the principal ground of pride: to assume and assign to ourselves what belongs to God. For nothing so greatly confines us within the boundaries of humility and modesty as the acknowledgment of God's grace; for it is madness and temerity to raise our crests against Him on whom we depend, and to whom we owe ourselves and all we possess.

Rightly, then, does Moses reprove the pride of the human heart which arises from forgetfulness of God, if they think that they have gained by their own exertions (*marte suo*) what God has given them of His own pleasure, in order to lay them under obligation to Himself. "To say in the heart" is a Hebraism for thinking in one's self, or reflecting in one's self. [God] does not, therefore, only require the outward expression of the lips, whereby men profess that they are grateful to God's bounty (for in this there is often nothing more than hypocrisy and vanity); but He would have them seriously persuaded that whatever they possess is derived from His sheer beneficence.

JOHN CALVIN

APPLIED GRACE

*"He himself bore our sins" in his body on the
cross, so that we might die to sins and live for
righteousness; "by his wounds you have been healed."*

1 PETER 2:24

Let us learn to reply in a different manner to the argument of
Satan. You say, Satan, that God is perfectly righteous and the
Avenger of all iniquity. I confess it; but I add another property of
His righteousness which you have left aside: since He is righteous,
He is satisfied with having been paid once. You say next that I
have infinite iniquities which deserve eternal death. I confess it;
but I add what you have maliciously omitted: the iniquities which
are in me have been very amply avenged and punished in Jesus
Christ who has borne the judgement of God in my place (Rom
3:25; 1 Pet 2:24).

That is why I come to a conclusion quite different from
yours. Since God is righteous (Rom 3:26) and does not demand payment twice, since Jesus Christ, God and man (2 Cor.
5:19), has satisfied by infinite obedience (Rom 5:19; Phil 2:8)
the infinite majesty of God (Rom 8:33), it follows that my iniquities can no longer bring me to ruin (Col. 2:14); they are
already blotted out and washed out of my account by the blood
of Jesus Christ who was made a curse for me (Gal 3:13), and
who righteous, died for the unrighteous (1 Pet 2:24).

THEODORE BEZA

THE MOST EXCELLENT GIFT

The LORD longs to be gracious to you; therefore
he will rise up to show you compassion.

ISAIAH 30:18

Spiritual wisdom and grace is the highest and most excellent gift that ever God bestows on any creature: in this the highest excellency and perfection of a rational creature consists. 'Tis also immensely the most important of all divine gifts: 'tis that wherein man's happiness consists, and on which his everlasting welfare depends. How rational is it to suppose that God, however He has left meaner goods and lower gifts to second causes, and in some sort in their power, yet should reserve this most excellent, divine, and important of all divine communications in His own hands, to be bestowed immediately by Himself as a thing too great for second causes to be concerned in!

'Tis rational to suppose that this blessing should be immediately from God; for there is no gift or benefit that is in itself so nearly related to the divine nature; there is nothing the creature receives that is so much of God, of His nature, so much a participation of the deity: 'tis a kind of emanation of God's beauty, and is related to God as the light is to the sun.

JONATHAN EDWARDS

THE SOURCE OF GRACE

The LORD bless you and keep you; the LORD make
his face shine on you and be gracious to you; the
LORD turn his face toward you and give you peace.

NUMBERS 6:24-26

The Lord bless thee. Blessing is an act of His genuine liberality, because the abundance of all good things is derived to us from His favor as their only source. It is next added, that He should "keep" the people, by which clause lie intimates that He is the sole Defender of the church, and protects it under His guardianship. But since the main advantage of God's grace consists in our sense of it, the words "and make his face shine on you" are added; for nothing is more desirable for the consummation of our happiness than that.

We should behold the serene countenance of God, as it is said in Psalm 4:6, "There be many that say, Who will shew us any good? Lord, lift thou up the light of thy countenance upon us." Thus then I interpret this clause that the people may perceive and taste the sweetness of God's goodness, which may cheer them like the brightness of the sun when it illumines the world in serene weather.

JOHN CALVIN

HIS LOVE IS INFINITE

There is no one like the God of Jeshurun,
who rides the heavens to help you, and
in His excellency on the clouds.

DEUTERONOMY 33:26 NKJV

He is the King of glory, the Lord strong and mighty, the Lord mighty in battle: a strong rock, and a high tower. There is none like the God of Jeshurun, who rideth on the heavens in their help, and in His excellency on the sky. The eternal God is [our] Refuge, and underneath are everlasting arms. He is a God that hath all things in His hands, and does whatsoever He pleases: He killeth and maketh alive; He bringeth down to the grave and bringeth up; He maketh poor and maketh rich: the pillars of the earth are the Lord's. Their God is an infinitely holy God; there is none holy as the Lord.

And He is infinitely good and merciful. Many that others worship and serve as gods are cruel beings, spirits that seek the ruin of souls; but this is a God that delighteth in mercy; His grace is infinite and endures forever. He is love itself, an infinite fountain and ocean of it.

JONATHAN EDWARDS

HONORING GOD'S GRACE

*"I cannot do it," Joseph replied to Pharaoh, "but
God will give Pharaoh the answer he desires."*

GENESIS 41:16

Let us learn from the example of holy Joseph to honor the grace of God even among unbelievers; and if they shut the door against the entire and full doctrine of piety, we must at least endeavor to instill some drops of it into their minds. Let us also reflect on this, that nothing is less tolerable than for men to arrogate to themselves anything as their own; for this is the first step of wisdom, to ascribe nothing to ourselves, but modestly to confess that whatever in us is worthy of praise flows only from the fountain of God's grace.

It is especially worthy of notice that as the Spirit of understanding is given to anyone from heaven, he will become a proper and faithful interpreter of God. "God shall give Pharaoh an answer of peace." Joseph added this from the kindly feeling of his heart; for he did not yet comprehend what the nature of the oracle would be.

JOHN CALVIN

SATISFIED WITH GOD'S GRACE

Since we have these promises, dear friends,
let us purify ourselves . . . perfecting
holiness out of reverence for God.

2 CORINTHIANS 7:1

Whosoever now believes the Gospel will receive grace and the Holy Spirit. This will cause the heart to rejoice and find delight in God, and will enable the believer to keep the Law cheerfully, without expecting reward, without fear of punishment, without seeking compensation, as the heart is perfectly satisfied with God's grace, by which the Law has been fulfilled. But all these promises from the beginning are founded on Christ, so that God promises no one this grace except through Christ, who is the Messenger of the divine promise to the whole world. For this reason He came and through the Gospel brought these promises into all the world, which before this time had been proclaimed by the prophets.

It is, therefore, in vain if anyone expects the fulfillment of the divine promises without Christ. All is centered and decreed in Christ. Whosoever will not hear Him shall have no promises of God. For just as God acknowledges no law besides the Law of Moses and the writings of the prophets, so He makes no promises, except through Christ alone.

MARTIN LUTHER

AN INVALUABLE FREEDOM

*In him we have redemption through his
blood, the forgiveness of sins, in accordance
with the riches of God's grace.*

EPHESIANS 1:7

By His death He has restored us to favor with the Father, and therefore we ought always to direct our minds to the blood of Christ as the means by which we obtain divine grace. After mentioning that through the blood of Christ we obtain redemption, [Paul] immediately styles it "the forgiveness of sins" to intimate that we are redeemed because our sins are not imputed to us. Hence it follows that we obtain by free grace that righteousness by which we are accepted of God, and freed from the chains of the devil and of death.

The close connection which is here preserved, between our redemption itself and the manner in which it is obtained, deserves our notice; for so long as we remain exposed to the judgment of God, we are bound by miserable chains, and therefore our exemption from guilt becomes an invaluable freedom. According to the riches of His grace, He now returns to the efficient cause, the largeness of the divine kindness which has given Christ to us as our Redeemer.

JOHN CALVIN

GLAD TIDINGS OF GRACE

"I chose you and appointed you so that
you might go and bear fruit."

JOHN 15:16

Unbounded goodness and love enter into the very essence of the Godhead. It is because "his mercy endureth forever" that men are not destroyed; because "his compassions fail not" that sinners are brought to Him and forgiven. Remember this, or you may fall into error by fixing your minds so much upon the faith which is the channel of salvation as to forget the grace which is the fountain and source even of faith itself.

Faith is the work of God's grace in us. No man can say that Jesus is the Christ but by the Holy Ghost. "No man cometh unto me," saith Jesus, "except the Father which hath sent me draw him." So that faith, which is coming to Christ, is the result of divine drawing. Grace is the first and last moving cause of salvation; and faith, essential as it is, is only an important part of the machinery which grace employs. We are saved "through faith," but salvation is "by grace." Sound forth those words as with the archangel's trumpet: "By grace are ye saved." What glad tidings for the undeserving!

CHARLES SPURGEON

NOT OF WORKS

Not by works, so that no one can boast.

EPHESIANS 2:9

Not of works. Instead of what [Paul] had said, that their salvation is of grace, he now affirms, that "it is the gift of God." Instead of what he had said, "Not of yourselves," he now says, "Not of works." Hence we see that the apostle leaves nothing to men in procuring salvation. In these three phrases—*not of yourselves, it is the gift of God, not of works*—he embraces the substance of his long argument in the epistles to the Romans and to the Galatians that righteousness comes to us from the mercy of God alone, is offered to us in Christ by the gospel, and is received by faith alone, without the merit of works.

This passage affords an easy refutation of the idle cavil by which papists attempt to evade the argument that we are justified without works. Paul, they tell us, is speaking about ceremonies. But the present question is not confined to one class of works. Nothing can be more clear than this. The whole righteousness of man, which consists in works—nay, the whole man, and everything that he can call his own—is set aside.

JOHN CALVIN

A FEAST FOR OUR SOULS

The gift is not like the trespass. For if the many died
by the trespass of the one man, how much more did
God's grace and the gift that came by the grace of
the one man, Jesus Christ, overflow to the many!

ROMANS 5:15

It was of mere grace that God gave us His only begotten Son. The grace is great in proportion to the dignity and excellency of what is given: the gift was infinitely precious, because it was a person infinitely worthy, a person of infinite glory; and also because it was a person infinitely near and dear to God. The grace is great in proportion to the benefit we have given us in Him: the benefit is doubly infinite, in that in Him we have deliverance from an infinite, because an eternal, misery; and do also receive eternal joy and glory. The grace in bestowing this gift is great in proportion to our unworthiness to whom it is given; instead of deserving such a gift, we merited infinitely ill of God's hands. The grace is great according to the manner of giving, or in proportion to the humiliation and expense of the method and means by which way is made for our having of the gift.

JONATHAN EDWARDS

NOTHING BUT DIVINE GRACE

There are different kinds of gifts, but
the same Spirit distributes them.

1 CORINTHIANS 12:4

What remains now for free will if all the good works which proceed from us are acknowledged to have been the gifts of the Spirit of God? Let godly readers weigh carefully the apostle's words. He does not say that we are assisted by God. He does not say that the will is prepared, and is then left to run by its own strength. He does not say that the power of choosing aright is bestowed upon us, and that we are afterwards left to make our own choice. Such is the idle talk in which those persons who do their utmost to undervalue the grace of God are accustomed to indulge.

But the apostle affirms that everything good in us is His creation, by which he means that the whole man is formed by His hand to be good. It is not the mere power of choosing aright, some indescribable kind of preparation, or even assistance, but the right will itself which is His workmanship; otherwise Paul's argument would have no force. Man is nothing but by divine grace.

JOHN CALVIN

A FOUNTAIN
AND STREAM

*"If you knew the gift of God and who it is that
asks you for a drink, you would have asked him
and he would have given you living water."*

JOHN 4:10

Faith occupies the position of a channel or conduit pipe. Grace is the fountain and the stream; faith is the aqueduct along which the flood of mercy flows down to refresh the thirsty sons of men. It is a great pity when the aqueduct is broken. It is a sad sight to see around Rome the many noble aqueducts which no longer convey water into the city, because the arches are broken and the marvelous structures are in ruins. The aqueduct must be kept entire to convey the current; and, even so, faith must be true and sound, leading right up to God and coming right down to ourselves, that it may become a serviceable channel of mercy to our souls.

Still, I again remind you that faith is only the channel or aqueduct, and not the fountainhead, and we must not look so much to it as to exalt it above the divine Source of all blessing which lies in the grace of God.

CHARLES SPURGEON

TREASURES OF DIVINE GRACE

God exalted him to the highest place and gave
him the name that is above every name.

PHILIPPIANS 2:9

When our minds rise to a confident anticipation of right-eousness, salvation, and glory, let us learn to turn them to Christ. We still lie under the power of death, but He, raised from the dead by heavenly power, has the dominion of life. We labor under the bondage of sin and, surrounded by end-less vexations, are engaged in a hard warfare (1 Timothy 1:18). But He, sitting at the right hand of the Father, exercises the highest government in heaven and earth, and triumphs glori-ously over the enemies whom He has subdued and vanquished. We lie here mean and despised; but to Him has been "given a name" (Philippians 2:9) which angels and men regard with rev-erence, and devils and wicked men with dread. We are pressed down here by the scantiness of all our comforts, but He has been appointed by the Father to be the sole Dispenser of all blessings.

For these reasons, we shall find our advantage in directing our views to Christ, that in Him, as in a mirror, we may see the glorious treasures of divine grace.

JOHN CALVIN

• CHRIST ALONE •

CLOTHED IN CHRIST'S PROMISES

Since we have these promises, dear friends,
let us purify ourselves from everything that
contaminates body and spirit, perfecting
holiness out of reverence for God.

2 CORINTHIANS 7:1

Although Christ offers us in the Gospel a present fullness of spiritual blessings, fruition remains in the keeping of hope until we are divested of corruptible flesh, and transformed into the glory of Him who has gone before us. Meanwhile, in leaning on the promises we obey the command of the Holy Spirit.

We have it on the testimony of Paul that "godliness is profitable unto all things, having promise of the life that now is, and of that which is to come" (1 Timothy 4:8); for which reason he glories in being "an apostle of Jesus Christ, according to the promise of life which is in Christ Jesus" (2 Timothy 1:1). And he elsewhere reminds us that we have the same promises which were given to the saints in ancient time (2 Corinthians 7:1). In fine, he makes the sum of our felicity consist in being sealed with the Holy Spirit of promise. Indeed we have no enjoyment of Christ unless by embracing Him as clothed with His own promises.

JOHN CALVIN

LORD OF ALL

You know the message God sent to the people
of Israel, announcing the good news of peace
through Jesus Christ, who is Lord of all.

ACTS 10:36

That the government of the world in all its parts is for the good of such as are to be the eternal subjects of God's goodness is implied in what the Scripture teaches us of Christ being set at God's right hand, made King of angels and men; set at the head of the universe, having all power given Him in heaven and earth, to that end that He may promote their happiness; being made Head over all things to the church, and having the government of the whole creation for their good.

Christ mentions it [in] Mark 2:28 as the reason why the Son of Man is made Lord of the Sabbath, because "the Sabbath was made for man." And if so, we may in like manner argue, that all things were made for man, because the Son of Man is made Lord of all things. That God uses the whole creation, in his government of it, for the good of his people, is most elegantly represented in Deuteronomy 33:26. "There is none like unto the God of Jeshurun, who rideth upon the heaven."

JONATHAN EDWARDS

NOTHING BUT CHRIST

I resolved to know nothing while I was with
you except Jesus Christ and him crucified.

1 CORINTHIANS 2:2

From his first sermon to his last, Paul preached Christ, and nothing but Christ. He lifted up the cross and extolled the Son of God who bled thereon. Follow his example in all your personal efforts to spread the glad tidings of salvation, and let "Christ and him crucified" be your ever-recurring theme.

The Christian should be like those lovely spring flowers which, when the sun is shining, open their golden cups, as if saying, "Fill us with Thy beams!" but when the sun is hidden behind a cloud, they close their cups and droop their heads. So should the Christian feel the sweet influence of Jesus; Jesus must be his Sun, and he must be the flower which yields itself to the Sun of Righteousness.

Oh! To speak of Christ alone, this is the subject which is both "seed for the sower, and bread for the eater." This is the live coal for the lip of the speaker, and the master key to the heart of the hearer.

CHARLES SPURGEON

CHRIST THE DIVINE

"Father, I want those you have given me
to be with me where I am, and to see my
glory, the glory you have given me."

JOHN 17:24

We must hold that as often as Christ, in the character of Mediator, addresses the Father, He, under the term *God*, includes His own divinity also. Thus, when He says to the apostles, "It is expedient for you that I go away," "My Father is greater than I," He does not attribute to Himself a secondary divinity merely, as if in regard to eternal essence He were inferior to the Father; but having obtained celestial glory, He gathers together the faithful to share it with Him.

He places the Father in the higher degree, inasmuch as the full perfection of brightness conspicuous in heaven differs from that measure of glory which He Himself displayed when clothed in flesh. For the same reason Paul says that Christ will restore "the kingdom to God, even the Father," "that God may be all in all" (1 Corinthians 15:24, 28). Nothing can be more absurd than to deny the perpetuity of Christ's divinity.

JOHN CALVIN

GAZE UPON HIM

Let us run with perseverance the race
marked out for us, fixing our eyes on Jesus,
the pioneer and perfecter of faith.

HEBREWS 12:1-2

We are full of sin, but the Saviour bids us lift our eyes to Him, and as we gaze upon His streaming wounds, each drop of blood, as it falls, cries, "It is finished; I have made an end of sin; I have brought in everlasting righteousness." Oh! Sweet language of the precious blood of Jesus! If you have come to that blood once, you will come to it constantly. Your life will be "Looking unto Jesus." Your whole conduct will be epitomized in this: "To whom coming." Not to whom I have come, but to whom I am always coming.

If thou hast ever come to the blood of sprinkling, thou wilt feel thy need of coming to it every day. He who does not desire to wash in it every day has never washed in it at all. The believer ever feels it to be his joy and privilege that there is still a fountain opened.

CHARLES SPURGEON

A STAMP OF DIVINITY

Since the creation of the world God's
invisible qualities—his eternal power and
divine nature—have been clearly seen.

ROMANS 1:20

If Christ should now appear to anyone as He did on the mount at His transfiguration; or if He should appear to the world in His heavenly glory, as He will do at the Day of Judgment; without doubt, His glory and majesty would be such as would satisfy everyone that He was a divine person. And why may there not be that stamp of divinity, or divine glory, on the Word of God, on the scheme and doctrine of the Gospel, that may be in like matter distinguishing and as rationally convincing, provided it be but seen? Supposing that God never had spoken to the world, but we had noticed that He was about to reveal Himself from heaven and speak to us immediately Himself; after what manner should we expect that He would speak?

Would it not be rational to suppose that His speech would be exceeding different from men's speech, that there should be such an excellency and sublimity in His word that the word of the wisest of men should appear mean and base in comparison of it? Doubtless it would be thought rational to expect this, and unreasonable to think otherwise.

JONATHAN EDWARDS

THE GRANDEST FACT

Who will bring any charge against those whom
God has chosen? It is God who justifies.

ROMANS 8:33

The grandest fact under heaven is this: that Christ by His precious blood does actually put away sin, and that God, for Christ's sake, dealing with men on terms of divine mercy, forgives the guilty and justifies them, not according to anything that He sees in them, or foresees will be in them, but according to the riches of His mercy which lie in His own heart. This we have preached, do preach, and will preach as long as we live. "It is God that justifieth"—that justifieth the ungodly; He is not ashamed of doing it, nor are we of preaching it.

The justification which comes from God Himself must be beyond question. If the Judge acquits me, who can condemn me? If the highest court in the universe has pronounced me just, who shall lay anything to my charge? Justification from God is a sufficient answer to an awakened conscience. The Holy Spirit by its means breathes peace over our entire nature, and we are no longer afraid. With this justification we can answer all the roarings and railings of Satan and ungodly men.

CHARLES SPURGEON

A TITLE TO ETERNAL LIFE

If, while we were God's enemies, we were
reconciled to him through the death of his
Son, how much more, having been reconciled,
shall we be saved through his life!

ROMANS 5:10

There is in the obedience of Christ a twofold efficacy. The one is expiatory, that by which we are freed from those punishments to which we were liable on account of sin. The other is a meritorious efficacy, by which, through the remission of our sins, a title to eternal life and salvation has been acquired for us. For as sin has brought upon us two evils—the loss of life and exposure to death—so redemption must procure two benefits—liberation from death and a title to life; or deliverance from hell and an introduction into heaven.

There are various passages of Scripture which clearly express these two benefits: "To make reconciliation for iniquity, and to bring in an everlasting righteousness" (Daniel 9:24). "Christ hath redeemed us from the law, being made a curse for us—that the blessing of Abraham might come on the Gentiles" (Galatians 3:13–14). "God sent forth his Son—to redeem them that were under the law, that we might receive the adoption of sons" (Galatians 4:4).

FRANCIS TURRETIN

THE TRIUMPH OF
THE CROSS

How much more, then, will the blood of Christ, who
through the eternal Spirit offered himself unblemished
to God, cleanse our consciences from acts that lead
to death, so that we may serve the living God!

HEBREWS 9:14

Faith apprehends acquittal in the condemnation of Christ, and blessing in His curse. Hence it is not without cause that Paul magnificently celebrates the triumph which Christ obtained upon the cross, as if the cross, the symbol of ignominy, had been converted into a triumphal chariot. For he says that He blotted out the handwriting of ordinances that was against us, which was contrary to us, and took it out of the way, nailing it to His cross: that "having spoiled principalities and powers he made a show of them openly, triumphing over them in it" (Colossians 2:14–15).

Nor is this to be wondered at; for, as another apostle declares, Christ, "through the eternal Spirit, offered himself without spot to God" (Hebrews 9:14), and hence that transformation of the cross which were otherwise against its nature. But that these things may take deep root and have their seat in our inmost hearts, we must never lose sight of sacrifice and ablution.

JOHN CALVIN

THE LAMB OF GOD

John saw Jesus coming toward him and
said, "Look, the Lamb of God, who
takes away the sin of the world!"

JOHN 1:29

It is Jesus Christ, the Lamb of God. He, He, and no one else either in heaven or on earth takes our sins upon Himself. You yourself could not pay for the very smallest of sins. He alone must take upon Himself not alone your sins, but the sins of the world, and not some sins, but all the sins of the world, be they great or small, many or few. This then is preaching and hearing the pure Gospel, and recognizing the finger of John, who points out to you Christ, the Lamb of God.

Now, if you are able to believe that this voice of John speaks the truth, and if you are able to follow his finger and recognize the Lamb of God carrying your sin, then you have gained the victory, then you are a Christian, a master of sin, death, hell, and all things. Then your conscience will rejoice and become heartily fond of this gentle Lamb of God.

MARTIN LUTHER

THE GRAND TRUTH

God made him who had no sin to be sin for us, so that
in him we might become the righteousness of God.

2 CORINTHIANS 5:21

Endeavor to know more and more of Christ Jesus. Endeavor especially to know the doctrine of the sacrifice of Christ, for the point upon which saving faith mainly fixes itself is this: "God was in Christ, reconciling the world unto himself, not imputing their trespasses unto them." Know that Jesus was "made a curse for us, as it is written, Cursed is every one that hangeth on a tree." Drink deep of the doctrine of the substitution work of Christ, for therein lies the sweetest possible comfort to the guilty sons of men.

Faith begins with knowledge. The mind goes on to believe that these things are true. The soul believes that God is, and that He hears the cries of sincere hearts; that the Gospel is from God; that justification by faith is the grand truth which God hath revealed in these last days by His Spirit more clearly than before. Then the heart believes that Jesus is verily and in truth our God and Savior, the Redeemer of men, the Prophet, Priest, and King of His people.

CHARLES SPURGEON

CHRIST: BRIGHTNESS OF GLORY

"I am the light of the world. Whoever
follows me will never walk in darkness,
but will have the light of life."

JOHN 8:12

Although this only begotten Son, who is now to us the brightness of His Father's glory and the express image of His person, was formerly made known to the Jews, as we have elsewhere shown from Paul that He was the Deliverer under the old dispensation, it is nevertheless true, as Paul himself elsewhere declares, that "God, who commanded the light to shine out of darkness, has shined in our hearts, to give the light of the knowledge of the glory of God in the face of Jesus Christ" (2 Corinthians 4:6); [this is] because, when He appeared in this His image, He in a manner made Himself visible, His previous appearance having been shadowy and obscure.

JOHN CALVIN

PREPARE THE WAY

"I will send my messenger ahead of you, who will prepare your way"—"A voice of one calling in the wilderness, 'Prepare the way for the Lord.'"

MARK 1:2–3

What has been said may show us how great a person Jesus Christ is, and how great His errand into the world, seeing there was so much done to prepare the way for His coming. God had been preparing the way for Him through all ages of the world, from the very beginning. If we had notice of a certain stranger being about to come into a country, and should observe that a great preparation was made for him, great things were done, many alterations made in the state of the whole country, many hands employed, persons of great note engaged in making the preparation, and all the affairs and concerns of the country ordered so as to be subservient to the design of entertaining that person, it would be natural for us to think, *Surely this is some extraordinary person, and it is some very great business that he is coming upon.* How great a person then must He be, for whose coming the great God of heaven and earth, and Governor of all things, spent four thousand years in preparing the way!

JONATHAN EDWARDS

FULLY GOD AND FULLY MAN

The Word became flesh and made his dwelling
among us. We have seen his glory.

JOHN 1:14

The true substance of Christ is most clearly declared in those passages which comprehend both natures at once. Numbers of these exist in the Gospel of John. What we there read as to His having received power from the Father to forgive sins; as to His quickening whom He will; as to His bestowing righteousness, holiness, and salvation; as to His being appointed judge both of the quick and the dead; as to His being honored even as the Father, are not peculiar either to His Godhead or His humanity, but applicable to both.

In the same way He is called the Light of the world, the Good Shepherd, the only Door, the true Vine. With such prerogatives the Son of God was invested on His manifestation in the flesh, and though He possessed the same with the Father before the world was created, still it was not in the same manner or respect; neither could they be attributed to one who was a man and nothing more.

JOHN CALVIN

SUBJECT TO CHRIST

He is the head of the body, the church.

COLOSSIANS 1:18

The whole universe is put in subjection to Jesus Christ; all heaven and earth, angels and men, are subject to Him, as executing this office, and are put under Him to that end, that all things may be ordered by Him, in subservience to the great designs of His redemption. All power, as He says, is given to Him in heaven and in earth, that He may give eternal life to as many as the Father has given Him; and He is exalted far above all principality and power, and might and dominion, and made Head over all things to the church.

The angels are put in subjection to Him, that He may employ them all as ministering spirits for the good of them that shall be the heirs of salvation. And all things are so governed by their Redeemer that all things are theirs, whether things present or things to come; and all God's works of providence in the moral government of the world, which we have an account of in Scripture history, or that are foretold in Scripture prophecy, are evidently subordinate to the great purposes and end of this great work.

JONATHAN EDWARDS

EXCEEDING LOVE

"Greater love has no one than this: to lay
down one's life for one's friends."

JOHN 15:13

The Scripture everywhere represents it, as though the great things Christ did and suffered were in the most direct and proper sense from exceeding love to us. Thus the apostle Paul represents the matter: Galatians 2:20: "Who loved me, and gave himself for me." Ephesians 5:25: "Husbands, love your wives, even as Christ loved the church, and gave himself for it." And Christ Himself, John 17:19: "For their sakes I sanctify myself."

And the Scripture represents Christ as resting in the salvation and glory of His people, when obtained as in what He ultimately sought, as having therein reached the goal, obtained the prize He aimed at, enjoying the travail of His soul in which He is satisfied, as the recompense of His labours and extreme agonies; Isaiah 53:10–11: "When thou shalt make his soul an offering for sin, he shall see his seed, he shall prolong his days, and the pleasure of the Lord shall prosper in his hand. He shall see of the travail of his soul, and shall be satisfied; by his knowledge shall my righteous servant justify many, for he shall bear their iniquities."

JONATHAN EDWARDS

THE GREATEST WONDER

He saved us, not because of righteous things
we had done, but because of his mercy.

TITUS 3:5

Jesus Christ came into the world to save sinners. It is a very surprising thing, a thing to be marveled at most of all by those who enjoy it. I know that it is to me even to this day the greatest wonder that I ever heard of, that God should ever justify me. I feel myself to be a lump of unworthiness, a mass of corruption, and a heap of sin, apart from His almighty love.

I know by a full assurance that I am justified by faith which is in Christ Jesus, and treated as if I had been perfectly just, and made an heir of God and a joint heir with Christ; and yet by nature I must take my place among the most sinful. I, who am altogether undeserving, am treated as if I had been deserving. I am loved with as much love as if I had always been godly, whereas aforetime I was ungodly. Who can help being astonished at this?

CHARLES SPURGEON

HIS OWN PURPOSE AND GRACE

He has saved us and called us to a holy life—
not because anything we have done but
because of his own purpose and grace.

2 TIMOTHY 1:9

In the second epistle to Timothy, first chapter, and ninth verse are these words: "Who hath saved us, and called us with an holy calling." Now, here is a touchstone by which we may try our calling. It is "a holy calling, not according to our works, but according to his own purpose and grace." This calling forbids all trust in our own doings and conducts us to Christ alone for salvation, but it afterwards purges us from dead works to serve the living and true God.

As He that hath called you is holy, so must you be holy. If you are living in sin, you are not called, but if you are truly Christ's, you can say, "Nothing pains me so much as sin; I desire to be rid of it; Lord, help me to be holy." Is this the panting of thy heart? Is this the tenor of thy life toward God, and His divine will?

CHARLES SPURGEON

CHRIST'S DIVINE GLORY

He received honor and glory from God the
Father when the voice came to him from
the Majestic Glory, saying, "This is my Son,
whom I love; with him I am well pleased."

2 PETER 1:17

The apostle Peter mentions it as what gave him and his companions good and well-grounded assurance of the truth of the Gospel, that they had seen the divine glory of Christ—2 Peter 1:16: "For we . . . were eye-witnesses of his majesty." The apostle has respect to that visible glory of Christ which they saw in His transfiguration: that glory was so divine, having such an ineffable appearance and semblance of divine holiness, majesty, and grace, that it evidently denoted Him to be a divine person.

But if a sight of Christ's outward glory might give a rational assurance of His divinity, why may not an apprehension of His spiritual glory do so too? Doubtless Christ's spiritual glory is in itself as distinguishing, and as plainly shows His divinity, as His outward glory—nay, a great deal more: for His spiritual glory of His transfiguration showed Him to be divine, only as it was a remarkable image or representation of that spiritual glory.

JONATHAN EDWARDS

THE POWER OF GOD IN CHRIST

Christ is the culmination of the law so that there may be righteousness for everyone who believes.

ROMANS 10:4

Note this fact carefully, that when you find in the Scriptures the [term] *God's justice*, it is not to be understood of the self-existing, imminent justice of God, as many of the fathers held, lest you be frightened; but, according to the usage of Holy Writ, it means the revealed grace and mercy of God through Jesus Christ in us by means of which we are considered godly and righteous before Him. Hence it is called *God's justice* or *righteousness* effected not by us, but by God through grace, just as God's work, God's wisdom, God's strength, God's Word, and God's mouth signifies what He works and speaks in us.

For therein is revealed a righteousness of God, as it is written in Habakkuk 2:4: "The righteous shall live by his faith." Here you see that he speaks of the righteousness of faith and calls the same the righteousness of God, preached in the Gospel, since the Gospel teaches nothing else but that he who believes has grace and is righteous before God and is saved.

MARTIN LUTHER

OUR SOLE HOPE

We have this hope as an anchor for the
soul, firm and secure. It enters the inner
sanctuary behind the curtain.

HEBREWS 6:19

It is Christ that died. "Who shall lay any thing to the charge of God's elect? It is God that justifieth." Now, poor soul! Will you come into this lifeboat, just as you are? Here is safety from the wreck! Accept the sure deliverance. "I have nothing with me," say you. You are not asked to bring anything with you. Men who escape for their lives will leave even their clothes behind. Leap for it, just as you are.

I will tell you this thing about myself to encourage you: my sole hope for heaven lies in the full atonement made upon Calvary's cross for the ungodly. On that I firmly rely. I have not the shadow of a hope anywhere else. You are in the same condition as I am, for we neither of us have anything of our own worth as a ground of trust. Let us join hands and stand together at the foot of the cross, and trust our souls once for all to Him who shed His blood for the guilty.

CHARLES SPURGEON

NOTHING APART FROM CHRIST

"I am the vine; you are the branches. If you remain in me and I in you, you will bear much fruit; apart from me you can do nothing."

JOHN 15:5

Take heed, therefore, take heed, I say, lest you presume to get rid of the smallest of your sins through your own merit before God, and lest you rob Christ, the Lamb of God, of His credit. John indeed demands that we grow better and repent; but he does not mean us to grow better of ourselves and to strip off our sins by our own strength, this he declares powerfully by adding, "Behold the Lamb of God that taketh away the sin of the world." He means that each one is to know himself and his need of becoming a better man; yet he is not to look for this in himself, but in Jesus Christ alone.

Now may God our Father according to His infinite mercy bestow upon us this knowledge of Christ, and may He send into the world the voice of John, with great numbers of evangelists! Amen.

MARTIN LUTHER

THE GLORY OF THE TRINITY

*"Now the Son of Man is glorified
and God is glorified in him."*

JOHN 13:31

In all this God designed to accomplish the glory of the blessed Trinity in an eminent degree. God had a design of glorifying Himself from eternity; yea, to glorify each person in the Godhead. The end must be considered as first in order of nature, and then the means; and therefore we must conceive that God having professed this end, had then as it were the means to choose; and the principal mean that He adopted was this great work of redemption. It was His design in this work to glorify his only begotten Son, Jesus Christ; and by the Son to glorify the Father: John 13:31–32: "Now is the Son of man glorified, and God is glorified in him. If God be glorified in him, God also shall glorify him in himself, and shall straightway glorify him." It was His design that the Son should thus be glorified, and should glorify the Father by what should be accomplished by the Spirit to the glory of the Spirit, that the whole Trinity, conjunctly, and each person singly, might be exceedingly glorified.

JONATHAN EDWARDS

THE REAL CHRIST

A person is justified by faith apart
from the works of the law.

ROMANS 3:28

All that teach you to do works, instead of teaching you to believe—those who hold forth Christ to you as a law-maker and a judge, and refuse to let Christ be a Helper and a Comforter, torment you, by putting works before and in the way of God in order to atone for your sins and to merit grace: such are the teachings of the pope, priests, monks and their high schools, who with their masses and religious ceremonies cause you to open your eyes and mouth in astonishment, leading you to another Christ and withholding from you the real Christ.

For if you desire to believe rightly and to possess Christ truly, then you must reject all works that you intend to place before and in the way of God. They are only stumbling blocks, leading you away from Christ and from God. Before God no works are acceptable but Christ's own works.

MARTIN LUTHER

THE CHURCH OF
THE REDEEMER

"I lay a stone in Zion, a tested stone, a precious
cornerstone for a sure foundation."

ISAIAH 28:16

The Old Testament church was not wholly without light, but had not the light of the sun directly, only as reflected. Now these prophets were the luminaries that reflected the light of the Sun; and accordingly they spoke abundantly of Jesus Christ, as appears by what we have of their prophecies in writing.

And they made it very much their business, when they studied in their schools or colleges and elsewhere, to search out the work of redemption; agreeable to what the apostle Peter says of them, 1 Peter 1:10–11: "Of which salvation the prophets have inquired, and searched diligently, who prophesied of the grace that should come unto you; searching what, or what manner of time the Spirit of Christ that was in them did signify, when it testified beforehand the sufferings of Christ, and the glory that should follow." We are told that the church of the Redeemer is built on the foundation of the prophets and apostles, the Redeemer himself being the chief Cornerstone (Ephesians 2:20).

JONATHAN EDWARDS

A SAVING FAITH

*"Very truly I tell you, the one who
believes has eternal life."*

JOHN 6:47

Jesus is what He is said to be, Jesus will do what He says He will do; therefore we must each one trust Him, saying, "He will be to me what He says He is, and He will do to me what He has promised to do; I leave myself in the hands of Him who is appointed to save, that He may save me. I rest upon His promise that He will do even as He has said."

This is a saving faith, and he that hath it hath everlasting life. Whatever his dangers and difficulties, whatever his darkness and depression, whatever his infirmities and sins, he that believeth thus on Christ Jesus is not condemned, and shall never come into condemnation. May that explanation direct my reader into immediate peace. "Be not afraid; only believe." Trust, and be at rest. My fear is lest the reader should rest content with understanding what is to be done, and yet never do it. The great matter is to believe on the Lord Jesus at once.

CHARLES SPURGEON

GOD'S MERCY IN CHRIST

"Whoever believes in the Son has eternal life."

JOHN 3:36

This is Christian faith that trusts in God's grace alone, gained for us and bestowed upon us through the blood of Christ, and that counts no work useful or good to win God's favor. For this were too hard for nature, which is conceived and born in sin, and also lives, works, and dies in it if Christ would not come to its help, gaining God's mercy for us by His works alone and not by our own. Through Him too we fulfill the first commandment and have a God on whose mercy we can depend with all confidence, so that without our merit He forgives all our sins and saves us in Christ, as has often already been said.

Therefore it is impossible that this faith should permit beside itself a trust in works, as though anyone could obtain forgiveness of sins and grace and become holy and be saved by them, for this belongs to Christ alone, who does all this through His work. Thus we have only to believe and confidently to entrust ourselves to Him.

MARTIN LUTHER

MIGHTY TO SAVE

*"I tell you, every kind of sin and
slander can be forgiven."*

MATTHEW 12:31

In due time Christ died for the ungodly." If you stand to that truth, your blasphemous thoughts which you have not the strength to drive away will go away of themselves. These thoughts are injections of the devil for which he is responsible, and not you. If you strive against them, they are no more yours than are the cursing and falsehoods of rioters in the street. It is by means of these thoughts that the devil would drive you to despair, or at least keep you from trusting Jesus.

The poor diseased woman could not come to Jesus for the press, and you are in much the same condition, because of the rush and throng of these dreadful thoughts. Still, she put forth her finger and touched the fringe of the Lord's garment, and she was healed. Do you the same. Jesus died for those who are guilty of "all manner of sin and blasphemy," and therefore I am sure He will not refuse those who are unwillingly the captives of evil thoughts. Cast yourself upon Him, thoughts and all, and see if He be not mighty to save.

CHARLES SPURGEON

CONSOLATION IN HIS MERCY

I do not do the good I want to do, but the evil I do not
want to do—this I keep on doing. . . . Thanks be to
God, who delivers me through Jesus Christ our Lord!

ROMANS 7:19, 25

Learn then from this Gospel what takes place when God begins to make us godly, and what the first step is in becoming godly. There is no other beginning than that your King comes to you and begins to work in you. It is done in this way: the Gospel must be the first; this must be preached and heard. In it you hear and learn how all your works count for nothing before God and that everything is sinful that you work and do. Your King must first be in you and rule you.

Behold, here is the beginning of your salvation: you relinquish your works and despair of yourself, because you hear and see that all you do is sin and amounts to nothing, as the Gospel tells you, and you receive your King in faith, cling to Him, implore His grace, and find consolation in His mercy alone.

MARTIN LUTHER

A COMMEMORATION

He took bread, gave thanks and broke it, and
gave it to them, saying, "This is my body given
for you; do this in remembrance of me."

LUKE 22:19

Christ by His death atoned for our sins. The Eucharist is a commemoration of this thing, as He Himself said— "This do in remembrance of me." By this commemoration all the benefits are presented which God has vouchsafed unto us through His Son. Furthermore, by the symbols themselves, namely the bread and wine, Christ Himself is, as it were, presented to our eyes, so that not only the ears but the eyes and the mouth see and perceive the Christ whom the soul has present within and rejoices in.

In regard to the institution of the sacraments, they have the power and grace which belongs to God alone. Since, then, the Deity has never conferred on created things the power which we attribute to them, it is clearly frivolous for us to teach that either the saints or the sacraments remove sins and bestow grace upon us. For who remitted sins save God alone?

ULRICH ZWINGLI

CHRIST THE KING FINDS YOU

See, your king comes to you.

ZECHARIAH 9:9

You do not seek Him, but He seeks you. You do not find Him, He finds you. For the preachers come from Him, not from you; their sermons come from Him, not from you; your faith comes from Him, not from you; everything that faith works in you comes from Him, not from you; and where He does not come, you remain outside; and where there is no Gospel there is no God, but only sin and damnation, free will may do, suffer, work, and live as it may and can.

Therefore you should not ask where to begin to be godly; there is no beginning, except where the King enters and is proclaimed. He cometh "unto thee." Thee, thee, what does this mean? Is it not enough that He is your King? If He is yours, how can He say He comes to you? All this is stated by the prophet to present Christ in an endearing way and invite to faith.

MARTIN LUTHER

JESUS THE SON

If anyone acknowledges that Jesus is the Son of
God, God lives in them and they in God.

1 JOHN 4:15

To the objection that if Christ be properly God, He is improperly called the Son of God, it has been already answered that when one person is compared with another, the name *God* is not used indefinitely, but is restricted to the Father, regarded as the beginning of the Godhead, not by essentiating, as fanatics absurdly express it, but in respect of order.

In this sense are to be understood the words which Christ addressed to the Father: "This is life eternal, that they might know thee the only true God, and Jesus Christ whom thou hast sent" (John 17:3). For speaking in the person of the Mediator, He holds a middle place between God and man; yet so that His majesty is not diminished thereby. For though He humbled (emptied) Himself, He did not lose the glory which He had with the Father, though it was concealed from the world.

JOHN CALVIN

CHRIST THE REDEEMER

"It was for this very reason I came to this hour. Father, glorify your name!"

JOHN 12:27-28

It is manifest from Scripture that God's glory is the last end of that great work of providence, the work of redemption by Jesus Christ. This is manifest from what is just now observed of its being the end ultimately sought Jesus Christ the Redeemer. And if we further consider the texts mentioned in the proof of that and take notice of the context, it will be very evident that it was what Christ sought as His last end, in that great work which He came into the world upon, namely to procure redemption for His people.

It is manifest that Christ professes in John 7:18 that He did not seek His own glory in what He did, but the glory of Him that sent Him. He means, the work of His ministry, the work He performed, and which He came into the world to perform, which is the work of redemption. Christ comforted Himself in the view of the extreme difficulty of His work, in the prospect of the highest, ultimate, and most excellent end of that work, which He set His heart most upon, and delighted most in.

JONATHAN EDWARDS

CHRIST WILL ALWAYS BE GOD

"I and the Father are one."

JOHN 10:30

If He will never cease to be the Son of God, but will ever remain the same that He was from the beginning, it follows that under the name of Father the one divine essence common to both is comprehended. And assuredly Christ descended to us for the very purpose of raising us to the Father, and thereby, at the same time, raising us to Himself, inasmuch as He is one with the Father. It is therefore erroneous and impious to confine the name of God to the Father so as to deny it to the Son.

Accordingly, John, declaring that He is the true God, has no idea of placing Him beneath the Father in a subordinate rank of divinity. I wonder what these fabricators of new gods mean when they confess that Christ is truly God, and yet exclude Him from the Godhead of the Father, as if there could be any true God but the one God, or as if transfused divinity were not a mere modern fiction.

JOHN CALVIN

CHRIST THE SON OF GOD

A voice came from the cloud saying, 'This is my Son, whom I have chosen; listen to him."

LUKE 9:35

The Scriptures speak of Jesus Christ as being God, God is human flesh; as being perfect in His character; as bearing our sins in His own body on the tree. The Scripture speaks of Him as having finished transgression, made an end of sin, and brought in everlasting righteousness. The sacred records further tell us that He "rose again from the dead," that He "ever liveth to make intercession for us," that He has taken possession of heaven on the behalf of His people, and that He will shortly come again "to judge the world in righteousness, and his people with equity."

We are most firmly to believe that it is even so; for this is the testimony of God the Father when He said, "This is my beloved Son; hear ye him." This also is testified by God the Holy Spirit; for the Spirit has borne witness to Christ, both in the inspired Word and by diverse miracles, and by His working in the hearts of men. We are to believe this testimony to be true.

CHARLES SPURGEON

SUMMED UP IN CHRIST

*Jesus Christ is the same yesterday
and today and forever.*

HEBREWS 13:8

We infer that the Old Testament was both established by the free mercy of God and confirmed by the intercession of Christ. For the preaching of the Gospel declares nothing more than that sinners, without any merit of their own, are justified by the paternal indulgence of God. It is wholly summed up in Christ. Who, then, will presume to represent the Jews as destitute of Christ, when we know that they were parties to the Gospel covenant, which has its only foundation in Christ? Who will presume to make them aliens to the benefit of gratuitous salvation, when we know that they were instructed in the doctrine of justification by faith?

And not to dwell on a point which is clear, we have the remarkable saying of our Lord: "Your father Abraham rejoiced to see my day, and he saw it and was glad" (John 8:56). What Christ here declares of Abraham, an apostle shows to be applicable to all believers when he says that Jesus Christ is the "same yesterday, to-day, and forever" (Hebrews 13:8). For he is not there speaking merely of the eternal divinity of Christ, but of His power, of which believers had always full proof.

JOHN CALVIN

REDEMPTION AND RENEWAL

Power belongs to you, God, and with
you, Lord, is unfailing love.

PSALM 62:11–12

Gentleness without righteousness would be no longer gentleness, but carelessness or fear. On the other hand, if you do not temper righteousness with goodness or equity, it becomes the utmost injustice and violence. Since, therefore, we recognize that God is by nature good, we confess at the same time that He is mild, gentle, and bountiful, as well as holy, righteous, and inviolable.

This was the cause of His clothing His only begotten Son with flesh, that He might not only show to, but bestow upon, the whole world these two things: redemption and renewal. For since His goodness, that is, justice and mercy, is inviolable, that is, firm and immutable, His justice required atonement, His mercy pardon, and pardon a new life.

Therefore the Son of the Most High King put on the cloak of the flesh and came forth to be made a victim (for in His divine nature He could not die), to placate unchangeable justice and reconcile it with those who even in their own innocence did not dare to come into the presence of God, because of their consciousness of guilt.

ULRICH ZWINGLI

THE FIRSTBORN OF EVERY CREATURE

The Son is the image of the invisible
God, the firstborn over all creation.

COLOSSIANS 1:15

What Christ said of Himself, "Before Abraham was I am" (John 8:58), was very foreign to His humanity. I am not unaware of the cavil by which erroneous spirits distort this passage—namely that He was before all ages inasmuch as He was foreknown as the Redeemer, as well in the counsel of the Father as in the minds of believers. But seeing He plainly distinguishes the period of His manifestation from His eternal existence, and professedly founds on His ancient government to prove His precedence to Abraham, He undoubtedly claims for Himself the peculiar attributes of divinity.

Paul's assertion that He is "the first-born of every creature," that "he is before all things, and by him all things consist" (Colossians 1:15, 17); His own declaration that He had glory with the Father before the world was, and that He worketh together with the Father, are equally inapplicable to man. These and similar properties must be specially assigned to His divinity.

JOHN CALVIN

CHRIST DIED FOR THE UNGODLY

*At just the right time, when we were still
powerless, Christ died for the ungodly.*

ROMANS 5:6

Happily, it is written, as the commendation of God's love to us: when we were yet without strength, in due time Christ died for the ungodly. Here we see conscious helplessness succored—succored by the interposition of the Lord Jesus. Our helplessness is extreme. It is not written, "When we were comparatively weak Christ died for us"; or "When we had only a little strength"; but the description is absolute and unrestricted: "When we were yet without strength." We had no strength whatever which could aid in our salvation; our Lord's words were emphatically true: "Without me ye can do nothing."

I may go further than the text and remind you of the great love wherewith the Lord loved us, "even when we were dead in trespasses and sins." To be dead is even more than to be without strength. The one thing that the poor strengthless sinner has to fix his mind upon, and firmly retain, as his one ground of hope, is the divine assurance that "in due time Christ died for the ungodly." Believe this, and all inability will disappear.

CHARLES SPURGEON

THE ONLY BEGOTTEN SON

God said to him, "You are my Son."

HEBREWS 5:5

Those of us who are regenerated to a new life God honors with the name of *sons*; the name of *true and only begotten Son* he bestows on Christ alone. But how is He an only Son in so great a multitude of brethren, except that He possesses by nature what we acquire by gift? This honor we extend to His whole character of Mediator, so that He is truly and properly the Son of God; but still in respect of His Godhead, as Paul teaches when he says that he was "made of the seed of David according to the flesh; and declared to be the Son of God with power" (Romans 1:3–4).

When distinctly calling Him the Son of David, why should he also say that He was "declared to be the Son of God" if he meant not to intimate that this depended on something else than His incarnation? He now draws a distinction between the two natures. They must certainly admit, that as on account of His mother He is called the Son of David, so, on account of His Father, He is the Son of God, and that in some respect differing from His human nature.

JOHN CALVIN

A PERFECT PAYMENT

*If anyone is in Christ, the new creation has
come. The old has gone, the new is here!*

2 CORINTHIANS 5:17

If our redemption and salvation are attributed to the death and blood of Christ, this is not done to the exclusion of the obedience of His life; for such a restriction is nowhere mentioned in Scripture. On the contrary, the work of man's salvation is, in many places, attributed to the obedience and righteousness of Christ.

When the death or blood of Christ is mentioned alone, and our redemption ascribed to it, this is done by a synecdoche, a figure which puts a part for the whole. The reason is that His death was the lowest degree of His humiliation and the completion of His obedience, that which supposes all the other parts, and without which they would have been of no avail. No righteousness merits anything unless it is persevered in to the last breath; a payment is never perfectly made, until the last farthing is paid and the bond cancelled.

FRANCIS TURRETIN

ALL POWER TO THE SON

*God placed all things under his feet and appointed
him to be head over everything for the church.*

EPHESIANS 1:22

For the Father has given all power to the Son, that by His hand He may govern, cherish, sustain us, keep us under His guardianship, and give assistance to us. And indeed, His sitting at the right hand of the Father has the same meaning as if He was called the Viceregent of the Father, entrusted with the whole power of government. For God is pleased, mediately (so to speak) in His person to rule and defend the church. Thus also His being seated at the right hand of the Father is explained by Paul to mean that "he is the head over all things to the Church, which is his body" (Ephesians 1:20, 22). Nor is this different in purport from what He elsewhere teaches, that God has "given him a name which is above every name; that at the name of Jesus every knee shall bow, of things in heaven, and things in earth, and things under the earth, and that every tongue should confess that Jesus Christ is Lord, to the glory of God the Father" (Philippians 2:9–11).

JOHN CALVIN

THE GIFT OF GOD

What do you have that you did not receive?

1 CORINTHIANS 4:7

Those that are redeemed by Jesus Christ do, in all these respects, very directly and entirely depend on God for their all. First, the redeemed have all their good of God; God is the great Author of it: He is the First Cause of it, and not only so, but He is the only proper cause.

'Tis of God that we have our Redeemer: it is God that has provided a Saviour for us. Jesus Christ is not only of God in His person, as He is the only begotten Son of God, but He is from God, as we are concerned in Him and in His office of Mediator. He is the gift of God to us: God chose and anointed Him, appointed Him His work, and sent Him into the world.

And as it is God that gives, so 'tis God that accepts the Saviour. As it is God that provides and gives the Redeemer to buy salvation for us, so it is of God that salvation is bought: He gives the Purchaser, and He affords the thing purchased.

JONATHAN EDWARDS

CHRIST DRAWS NEAR

Come near to God and he will come near to you.

JAMES 4:8

Scripture throughout calls Him Lord, the Father having appointed Him over us for the express purpose of exercising His government through Him. For though many lordships are celebrated in the world, yet Paul says, "To us there is but one God, the Father, of whom are all things, and we in him; and one Lord Jesus Christ, by whom are all things, and we by him" (1 Corinthians 8:6).

Whence it is justly inferred that He is the same God who, by the mouth of Isaiah, declared, "The Lord is our Judge, the Lord is our Lawgiver, the Lord is our King: he will save us" (Isaiah 33:22). For though He everywhere describes all the power which He possesses as the benefit and gift of the Father, the meaning simply is that He reigns by divine authority, because His reason for assuming the office of Mediator was that descending from the bosom and incomprehensible glory of the Father, He might draw near to us.

JOHN CALVIN

THE PREEMINENCE OF CHRIST

He is the beginning and the firstborn
among the dead, so that in everything
he might have the supremacy.

COLOSSIANS 1:18

We may see by what has been said, how Christ has in all things the preeminence. For He is the great Redeemer, and therefore the work of redemption being the sum of God's works of providence shows the glory of our Lord Jesus Christ as being above all, and through all, and in all. That God intended the world for His Son's use in the affair of redemption is one reason why He created the world by Him (Ephesians 3:9–12).

What has been said shows how all the purposes of God are purposed in Christ; and how He is before all, and above all. All things consist in Him, are governed by Him, and are for Him (Colossians 1:15–18). God makes him His firstborn, higher than the kings of the earth, and sets His throne above their thrones. God has always upheld His kingdom, when others have come to an end; that appears at last above all, however greatly opposed for so many ages. All other kingdoms fall, but His kingdom is the last, and never gives place to any other.

JONATHAN EDWARDS

CHRIST THE MEDIATOR

There is one God and one mediator between
God and mankind, the man Christ Jesus.

1 TIMOTHY 2:5

This Son of God Himself took on human nature in such manner that His divine nature was not lost or changed into human nature, but each nature is in Him so truly, properly, and naturally that nothing has been diminished of His divine nature, so that He should not be truly, properly, and naturally God. Moreover, His human nature has not passed over into divine nature so that He should not be truly, properly, and naturally man, save only as far as inclination to sin is concerned.

None of His divine attributes has suffered because of the assumption of human feebleness, and, insofar as He is man, He is thus man that He has whatever belongs to true and literal human nature, so that nothing has been taken from it on account of the union with the divine nature, save the disposition to sin. Hence it is that both natures so reflect their own character in all their words and deeds that the religious mind sees without trouble what is to be credited to either nature, however rightly the whole is said to belong to the one Christ.

ULRICH ZWINGLI

OBEDIENCE REMOVED ENMITY

Since we have now been justified by his blood, how much more shall we be saved from God's wrath through him!

ROMANS 5:9

When it is asked then how Christ, by abolishing sin, removed the enmity between God and us, and purchased a righteousness which made Him favorable and kind to us, it may be answered generally that He accomplished this by the whole course of His obedience. This is proved by the testimony of Paul: "As by one man's disobedience many were made sinners, so by the obedience of one shall many be made righteous" (Romans 5:19).

And indeed He elsewhere extends the ground of pardon, which exempts from the curse of the Law, to the whole life of Christ: "When the fullness of the time was come, God sent forth his Son, made of a woman, made under the law, to redeem them that were under the law" (Galatians 4:4–5). Thus even at His baptism He declared that a part of righteousness was fulfilled by His yielding obedience to the command of the Father. In short, from the moment when He assumed the form of a servant, He began, in order to redeem us, to pay the price of deliverance.

JOHN CALVIN

A CONSTANT TENOR OF OBEDIENCE

Being found in appearance as a man, he humbled himself by becoming obedient to death—even death on a cross!

PHILIPPIANS 2:8

The obedience of Christ is said to have been even to death, in which not only its intensity as to degree is expressed, an intensity the greatest which can be rendered by anyone; but also its extension and duration, from the beginning of His life to its end. This appears from His obedience being referred to the whole of His humiliation, which appeared not in His death only, but in His whole life.

In other portions of Scripture, the obedience of Christ is described by the writing of the Law in His heart (Psalm 40), and His active observance of it (Hebrews 10:5). Again, it is spoken of as a race which Christ had to run (Hebrews 12:1–2), and as a work which He had to perform (John 17:4). These were not to be consummated by one act, but to be a constant tenor of obedience through His whole life.

FRANCIS TURRETIN

VOLUNTARY SUBJECTION

*"The reason my Father loves me is that I lay down
my life—only to take it up again. No one takes it
from me, but I lay it down of my own accord."*

JOHN 10:17–18

In the Confession of Faith, called the Apostles' Creed, the transition is admirably made from the birth of Christ to His death and resurrection, in which the completion of a perfect salvation consists. Still there is no exclusion of the other part of obedience which He performed in life. Thus Paul comprehends, from the beginning even to the end, His having assumed the form of a servant, humbled himself, and become obedient to death, even the death of the cross (Philippians 2:7).

And indeed, the first step in obedience was His voluntary subjection; for the sacrifice would have been unavailing to justification if not offered spontaneously. Hence our Lord, after testifying, "I lay down my life for the sheep," distinctly adds, "No man taketh it from me" (John 10:15, 18). In the same sense Isaiah says, "Like a sheep before her shearers is dumb, so he opened not his mouth" (Isaiah 53:7).

JOHN CALVIN

INCOMPARABLE LOVE

Here I am, I have come—it is
written about me in the scroll.

PSALM 40:7

The Gospel history relates that He came forth to meet the soldiers; and in the presence of Pilate, instead of defending Himself, stood to receive judgment. This, indeed, He did not without a struggle, for He had assumed our infirmities also, and in this way it behooved Him to prove that He was yielding obedience to His Father. It was no ordinary example of incomparable love toward us to struggle with dire terrors, and amid fearful tortures to cast away all care of Himself that He might provide for us. We must bear in mind that Christ could not duly propitiate God without renouncing His own feelings and subjecting Himself entirely to His Father's will.

To this effect the apostle appositely quotes a passage from the Psalms: "Lo, I come (in the volume of the book it is written of me) to do thy will, O God" (Hebrews 10:5; Psalm 40:7–8). Thus, as trembling consciences find no rest without sacrifice and ablution by which sins are expiated, we are properly directed thither, the source of our life being placed in the death of Christ.

JOHN CALVIN

WEAK LAW, POWERFUL GOD

What the law was powerless to do because it was
weakened by the flesh, God did by sending his
own Son in the likeness of sinful flesh to be a sin
offering. And so he condemned sin in the flesh.

ROMANS 8:3

It behooved Christ to be made in the likeness of sinful flesh, that He might supply what the Law could not do, in that it was weak, and fulfill the claims of the Law in us (Romans 8:3–4). This weakness of the Law is not to be understood subjectively, as if it were in the Law, but objectively, in the sinner in relation to the Law, on account of his inability to perform any one of the duties which it commands. This Law is said to be weak, not in relation to the infliction of punishment, but as to the observation of its precepts.

Christ, therefore, by supplying what the Law could not do in us, must fulfill all the Law demanded of us and work out what the apostle calls "righteousness" or the rights of the Law, without doubt a right to life obtained by doing what the Law commands. This required not only a passive but also an active obedience.

FRANCIS TURRETIN

SON AND MAN

To be sure, he was crucified in weakness, yet
he lives by God's power. Likewise, we are
weak in him, yet by God's power we will
live with him in our dealing with you.

2 CORINTHIANS 13:4

We acknowledge, indeed, that Christ in human nature is called a Son, not like believers by gratuitous adoption merely, but the true, natural, and therefore only Son, this being the mark which distinguishes Him from all others. The Scripture gives Him both names, calling Him at one time the Son of God, at another the Son of Man.

As to the latter, there can be no question that He is called a Son in accordance with the phraseology of the Hebrew language, because He is of the offspring of Adam. On the other hand, I maintain that He is called a Son on account of His Godhead and eternal essence, because it is no less congruous to refer to His divine nature, His being called the Son of God, than to refer to His human nature, His being called the Son of Man.

JOHN CALVIN

THE PERFECTION OF CHRIST'S ATONEMENT

*Through the Spirit of holiness [He] was appointed
the Son of God in power by his resurrection
from the dead: Jesus Christ our Lord.*

ROMANS 1:4

The perfection of the Atonement is confirmed by the approbation of God as Judge. If God declares that He is perfectly satisfied, let no one dare to say that the satisfaction is imperfect. The question is whether the Supreme Judge, who demands the satisfaction, approves of and receives it as altogether sufficient. That the Atonement has been approved and accepted by God is established, not only by the appointment of Christ to the mediatorial office, of whom the Father often declares that He is his beloved Son, in whom He is well pleased; but especially by His resurrection from the dead, which is irresistible evidence both of His divinity and of the perfection of the Atonement (Romans 1:4).

Unless Christ had satisfied to the uttermost, can we believe that God the Judge, whose inexorable justice demands full payment, would have freed Him and have exalted Him to that supreme glory which was the reward of His sufferings? (Philippians 2:9).

There is no room left for doubt respecting the perfection of the satisfaction, the full payment of the price of redemption.

FRANCIS TURRETIN

THE ETERNAL GODHEAD

*"I lay in Zion a stone that causes people to stumble
and a rock that makes them fall, and the one who
believes in him will never be put to shame."*

ROMANS 9:33

Though the apostles spoke of Him after His appearance in the flesh as Mediator, every passage which I adduce will be sufficient to prove His eternal Godhead. And the first thing deserving of special observation is that predictions concerning the eternal God are applied to Christ. Isaiah prophesies that "the Lord of Hosts" shall be "for a stone of stumbling, and for a rock of offence" (Isaiah 8:14). Paul asserts that this prophecy was fulfilled in Christ (Romans 9:33) and, therefore, declares that Christ is that Lord of Hosts.

In like manner, he says in another passage, "We shall all stand before the Judgment-seat of Christ. For it is written, As I live, saith the Lord, every knee shall bow to me, and every tongue shall confess to God." Since in Isaiah God predicts this of Himself (Isaiah 45:23), and Christ exhibits the reality fulfilled in himself, it follows that He is the very God, whose glory cannot be given to another.

JOHN CALVIN

CHRIST GOVERNS ALL THINGS

To us a son is given, and the government
will be on his shoulders.

ISAIAH 9:6

Ye have heard, then, that our Lord Christ, after His crucifixion and death, arose from the dead, and ascended on high, and was translated into an immortal state—not that He sits idly in heaven above in self-sufficient happiness; rather He takes the kingdom in His hands, governs it, and is a King of whom all the prophets and the whole Scriptures testify.

Wherefore, let us believe that He is continually with us, and sitting in judgment; and let us not imagine that He sits idly on high, but that He, from above, observes and governs all things, as Paul saith to the Ephesians, and especially the things of His kingdom, which is the Christian faith. Wherefore, the kingdom of Christ must go on here among us upon earth. Concerning this kingdom, we have said that it is so appointed that we all must increase and become purer from day to day, and that it is not administered by force but by the preaching of the mouth, that is, by the Gospel.

MARTIN LUTHER

OUR PARDON WRITTEN IN BLOOD

By this gospel you are saved.

1 CORINTHIANS 15:2

If you will have Jesus, He has you already. If you believe on Him, I tell you you cannot go to hell, for that were to make the sacrifice of Christ of none effect. It cannot be that a sacrifice should be accepted and yet the soul should die for whom that sacrifice has been received. If the believing soul could be condemned, then why a sacrifice? If Jesus died in my stead, why should I die also? Every believer can claim that the sacrifice was actually made for him: by faith he has laid his hands on it and made it his own, and therefore he may rest assured that he can never perish.

The Lord would not receive this offering on our behalf and then condemn us to die. The Lord cannot read our pardon written in the blood of His own Son and then smite us. That were impossible. Oh that you may have grace given you at once to look away to Jesus and to begin at the beginning, even at Jesus, who is the Fountainhead of mercy to guilty man!

CHARLES SPURGEON

YES AND AMEN

No matter how many promises God has made,
they are "Yes" in Christ. And so through him the
"Amen" is spoken by us to the glory of God.

2 CORINTHIANS 1:20

Mark, in his preface to the Gospel, calls it "The beginning of the Gospel of Jesus Christ." There is no use of collecting passages to prove what is already perfectly known. Christ at His advent "brought life and immortality to light through the Gospel" (2 Timothy 1:10). Paul does not mean by these words that the Fathers were plunged in the darkness of death before the Son of God became incarnate; but He claims for the Gospel the honorable distinction of being a new and extraordinary kind of embassy, by which God fulfilled what He had promised, these promises being realised in the person of the Son.

For though believers have at all times experienced the truth of Paul's declaration that "all the promises of God in him are yea and amen," inasmuch as these promises were sealed upon their hearts; yet because He has in His flesh completed all the parts of our salvation, this vivid manifestation of realities was justly entitled to this new and special distinction.

JOHN CALVIN

KEEP GROWING

As the deer pants for streams of water,
so my soul pants for you, my God.

PSALM 42:1

Grow in that root-grace, faith. Believe the promises more firmly than you have done. Let faith increase in fulness, constancy, simplicity. Grow also in love. Ask that your love may become extended, more intense, more practical, influencing every thought, word, and deed. Grow likewise in humility. Seek to lie very low, and know more of your own nothingness. As you grow downward in humility, seek also to grow upward—having nearer approaches to God in prayer and more intimate fellowship with Jesus.

May God the Holy Spirit enable you to "grow in the knowledge of our Lord and Saviour." He who grows not in the knowledge of Jesus refuses to be blessed. To know Him is "life eternal," and to advance in the knowledge of Him is to increase in happiness. He who does not long to know more of Christ knows nothing of Him yet. Whoever hath sipped this wine will thirst for more. If you know the love of Jesus, as the hart panteth for the waterbrooks, so will you pant after deeper draughts of His love.

CHARLES SPURGEON

THE PERFECT ATONEMENT

*We have been made holy through the sacrifice
of the body of Jesus Christ once for all.*

HEBREWS 10:10

The doctrine for which we contend is that Christ hath so perfectly satisfied divine justice for all our sins, by one offering of Himself; and not only for our guilt, but also for both temporal and eternal punishment, that henceforth there are no more propitiatory offerings to be made for sin; and that though, for the promotion of their penitence and sanctification, God often chastises His people, yet no satisfaction is to be made by them either in this or a future state of existence.

Such is the perfection of the Atonement that it corresponds to the justice of God revealed in the Word, to the demands of the Law, and to the miseries and necessities of those for whom it was made. Had it been in its own nature deficient, and derived its sufficiency only from God's acceptance of it through mere grace, then the victims under the Law might have possessed equal efficacy in making atonement for sin. Its perfection is derived from its own intrinsic fullness of merit.

FRANCIS TURRETIN

A LIVING HOPE

*Praise be to the God and Father of our Lord
Jesus Christ! In his great mercy he has given
us new birth into a living hope through the
resurrection of Jesus Christ from the dead.*

1 PETER 1:3

Seeing that in the cross, death, and burial of Christ, nothing but weakness appears, faith must go beyond all these in order that it may be provided with full strength. Hence, although in His death we have an effectual completion of salvation, because by it we are reconciled to God, satisfaction is given to His justice, the curse is removed, and the penalty paid; still it is not by His death, but by His resurrection, that we are said to be begotten again to a living hope (1 Peter 1:3).

He, by rising again, became victorious over death, so the victory of our faith consists only in His resurrection. The nature of it is better expressed in the words of Paul: "Who [Christ] was delivered for our offences, and was raised again for our justification" (Romans 4:25); as if he had said, *By His death sin was taken away, by His resurrection righteousness was renewed and restored.*

JOHN CALVIN

THE INFINITE LOVE OF CHRIST

We love because he first loved us.

1 JOHN 4:19

There is no light in the planet but that which proceedeth from the sun; and there is no true love to Jesus in the heart but that which cometh from the Lord Jesus Himself. From this overflowing fountain of the infinite love of God, all our love to God must spring. This must ever be a great and certain truth, that we love Him for no other reason than because He first loved us. Our love to Him is the fair offspring of His love to us.

Cold admiration, when studying the works of God, anyone may have, but the warmth of love can only be kindled in the heart by God's Spirit. How great the wonder that such as we should ever have been brought to love Jesus at all! How marvellous that when we had rebelled against Him, He should, by a display of such amazing love, seek to draw us back. No! Never should we have had a grain of love toward God unless it had been sown in us by the sweet seed of His love to us.

CHARLES SPURGEON

DEPENDENT ON CHRIST

He is before all things, and in him
all things hold together.

COLOSSIANS 1:17

There is an absolute and universal dependence of the redeemed on God. The nature and contrivance of our redemption is such that the redeemed are in everything directly, immediately, and entirely dependent on God: they are dependent on Him for all, and are dependent on Him every way.

The several ways wherein the dependence of one being may be upon another for its good, and wherein the redeemed of Jesus Christ depend on God for all their good, are these, namely, that they have all their good of Him, and that they have all through Him, and that they have all in Him. That He is the cause and original whence all their good comes, therein it is of Him; and that He is the medium by which it is obtained and conveyed, therein they have it through Him; and that He is that good itself that is given and conveyed, therein it is in Him.

JONATHAN EDWARDS

THE MESSIAH

You are the Messiah, the Son of the living God.

MATTHEW 16.16

The celebrated name of *Messiah* was given to the promised Mediator. But although I admit that He was so called from a view to the nature of the kingly office, still the prophetical and sacerdotal unctions have their proper place, and must not be overlooked. The former is expressly mentioned by Isaiah in these words: "The Spirit of the Lord God is upon me: because the Lord has anointed me to preach good tidings unto the meek; he has sent me to bind up the broken-hearted, to proclaim liberty to the captive, and the opening of the prison to them that are bound; to proclaim the acceptable year of the Lord" (Isaiah 60:1–2).

We see that He was anointed by the Spirit to be a herald and witness of His Father's grace, and not in the usual way; for He is distinguished from other teachers who had a similar office. And here, again, it is to be observed, that the unction which He received in order to perform the office of teacher was not for Himself, but for His whole body, that a corresponding efficacy of the Spirit might always accompany the preaching of the Gospel.

JOHN CALVIN

CHRIST IS ALL-SUFFICIENT

God was pleased to have all his fullness dwell in him.

COLOSSIANS 1:19

In Christ's person there is a fullness of divinity, a fullness of office, a fullness of merit and graces. Who, then, can doubt but that the satisfaction which He has made is one of infinite value and efficacy, and therefore of such fullness and all-sufficiency that nothing can be added to it? For though Christ's human nature, which was the instrument in the obedience and sufferings, was finite, yet this does not lessen the value of the satisfaction, because it derives its perfection from the divine person of Christ.

Our view is also established by the oneness of Christ's offering. Why does the apostle Paul assert that Christ has once offered Himself for us (Hebrews 7:9–10), and that by one offering of Himself He hath forever perfected them that are sanctified? Why does he always set before us the obedience of Christ alone as the ground of our justification, unless this obedience is full and complete? An offering's having been but once made necessarily imports its plenitude and the full accomplishment of its object.

FRANCIS TURRETIN

RECONCILED IN CHRIST

God presented Christ as a sacrifice of
atonement, through the shedding of his
blood—to be received by faith.

ROMANS 3:25

God the Father, by His love, prevents and anticipates our reconciliation in Christ. Nay, it is because He first loves us that He afterwards reconciles us to Himself. But because the iniquity, which deserves the indignation of God, remains in us until the death of Christ comes to our aid, and that iniquity is in His sight accursed and condemned, we are not admitted to full and sure communion with God unless, insofar as Christ unites us.

And, therefore, if we would indulge the hope of having God placable and propitious to us, we must fix our eyes and minds on Christ alone, as it is to Him alone it is owing that our sins, which necessarily provoked the wrath of God, are not imputed to us. For this reason Paul says that God "has blessed us with all spiritual blessings in heavenly places in Christ: according as he has chosen us in him before the foundation of the world" (Ephesians 1:3–4).

JOHN CALVIN

CHILDREN OF GOD

In Christ Jesus you are all children
of God through faith.

GALATIANS 3:26

The sum and substance of the Gospel is that our Lord Jesus Christ, the true Son of God, has made known to us the will of his heavenly Father, and has with His innocence released us from death and reconciled God. Hence Christ is the only way to salvation for all who ever were, are, and shall be. Who seeks or points out another door errs, yea, he is a murderer of souls and a thief.

Hence all who consider other teachings equal to or higher than the Gospel err, and do not know what the Gospel is. For Jesus Christ is the Guide and Leader, promised by God to all human beings, which promise was fulfilled. That He is an eternal salvation and Head of all believers, who are His body, but which is dead and can do nothing without Him. From this follows first that all who dwell in the Head are members and children of God, and that is the church or communion of the saints, the bride of Christ.

ULRICH ZWINGLI

EQUAL WITH GOD

The Son is the radiance of God's glory
and the exact representation of his being,
sustaining all things by his powerful word.

HEBREWS 1:3

The divinity of Christ, if judged by the works which are ascribed to Him in Scripture, becomes still more evident. When He said of Himself, "My Father worketh hitherto, and I work," the Jews perceived that He was laying claim to divine power. And therefore, as John relates (John 5:18), they sought the more to kill Him, because He not only broke the Sabbath, but also said that God was His Father, making Himself equal with God.

What, then, will be our stupidity if we do not perceive from the same passage that His divinity is plainly instructed? To govern the world by His power and providence, and regulate all things by an energy inherent in Himself (this an apostle ascribes to Him, Hebrews 1:3), surely belongs to none but the Creator. Nor does He merely share the government of the world with the Father, but also each of the other offices, which cannot be communicated to creatures.

JOHN CALVIN

LIVING WATER

*"If you knew the gift of God and who it is that
asks you for a drink, you would have asked him
and he would have given you living water."*

JOHN 4:10

The saints have both their spiritual excellency and blessedness by the gift of the Holy Ghost, or Spirit of God, and His dwelling in them. The Holy Spirit becoming an inhabitant is a vital principle in the soul: He, acting in, upon, and with the soul becomes a fountain of true holiness and joy, as a spring is of water, by the exertion and diffusion of itself, John 4:14: "But whosoever drinketh of the water that I shall give him, shall never thirst; but the water that I shall give him, shall be in him a well of water springing up into everlasting life."

Compare with John 7:38–39: "He that believeth on me, as the Scripture hath said, out of his belly shall flow rivers of living water; but this spake he of the Spirit, which they that believe on him should receive." The sum of what Christ has purchased for us is that spring of water spoken of in the former of those places, and those rivers of living water spoken of in the latter.

JONATHAN EDWARDS

HIS PRESENCE AND POWER

"Do not fear, for I am with you; do not be dismayed, for I am your God. I will strengthen you and help you; I will uphold you with my righteous right hand."

ISAIAH 41:10

We shall do well to stand toward Christ as those who are conscious of His power and presence. Brethren, our Lord is with us. The best of all is that He is with us indeed and of a truth. If we are with Jesus, and preach His truth, Jesus is assuredly with us; for He said, "Lo, I am with you alway, even unto the end of the world." That promise was not a pretty piece of romance; it is true that He is with us at this hour. Let us believe it, and act accordingly.

If we do not always feel His brightness, let us, like the flowers, turn toward the Sun. When the sun is not shining, the flowers know where there is most of light, and their faces turn that way. Let us be true heliotropes, or turners to the Sun.

CHARLES SPURGEON

REVIVED TO LIFE

Through him you believe in God, who raised
him from the dead and glorified him, and
so your faith and hope are in God.

1 PETER 1:21

Our salvation may be thus divided between the death and the resurrection of Christ: by the former sin was abolished and death annihilated; by the latter righteousness was restored and life revived, the power and efficacy of the former being still bestowed upon us by means of the latter. Paul accordingly affirms that He was declared to be the Son of God by His resurrection (Romans 1:4), because He then fully displayed that heavenly power which is both a bright mirror of His divinity, and a sure support of our faith; as he also elsewhere teaches that "though he was crucified through weakness, yet he liveth by the power of God" (2 Corinthians 13:4).

In perfect accordance with this is the passage in Peter, that God "raised him up from the dead, and gave him glory, that your faith and hope might be in God" (1 Peter 1:21). Not that faith founded merely on His death is vacillating, but that the divine power by which He maintains our faith is most conspicuous in His resurrection.

JOHN CALVIN

WHAT KIND OF MAN IS THIS?

The men were amazed and asked, "What kind of man is this? Even the winds and the waves obey him!"

MATTHEW 8:27

Soon after the world was created, and from age to age, He has been doing great things, bringing mighty events to pass, accomplishing wonders without number, often overturning the world in order to do it. He has been causing everything in the state of mankind, and all revolutions and changes in the habitable world, from generation to generation, to be subservient to this great design. Surely this must be some great and extraordinary person, and a great work indeed it must needs be, about which He is coming.

We read (Matthew 21:8–10) when Christ was coming into Jerusalem, and multitudes ran before Him, having cut down branches of palm trees, and strewed them in the way; and others spread their garments in the way, crying, "Hosanna to the Son of David," that the whole city was moved, saying, "Who is this?" They wondered who that extraordinary person should be, that there should be such preparation made on occasion of His coming into the city.

JONATHAN EDWARDS

WHOLLY TO CHRIST

We know, brothers and sisters loved
by God, that he has chosen you.

1 THESSALONIANS 1:4

Many persons want to know their election before they look to Christ, but they cannot learn it thus; it is only to be discovered by "looking unto Jesus." If you desire to ascertain your own election, after the following manner shall you assure your heart before God. Do you feel yourself to be a lost, guilty sinner? Go straightway to the cross of Christ, and tell Jesus so, and tell Him that you have read in the Bible, "Him that cometh unto me, I will in no wise cast out." Tell Him that He has said, "This is a faithful saying, and worthy of all acceptation, that Christ Jesus came into the world to save sinners."

Look to Jesus and believe on Him, and you shall make proof of your election directly, for so surely as thou believest, thou art elect. If you will give yourself wholly up to Christ and trust Him, then you are one of God's chosen ones; but if you stop and say, "I want to know first whether I am elect," you ask you know not what. Go to Jesus, be you never so guilty, just as you are.

CHARLES SPURGEON

THE NEW COVENANT

The entire law is fulfilled in keeping this one
command: "Love your neighbor as yourself."

GALATIANS 5:14

Though the apostle Paul attributes the blessedness of the saints to the remission of sin which flows from the blood of Christ (Romans 4:7), yet it does not follow from this that all our righteousness, and the whole of the satisfaction made by Christ, are founded in His Passion. For the apostle does not argue from the pardon of sins being precisely equivalent to the imputation of righteousness and its proceeding precisely from the same thing in the Atonement; but from the indissoluble connection among the blessings of the new covenant, a connection so intimate that everyone who obtains pardon of sin, necessarily and immediately obtains a right to life and becomes an heir of the kingdom of heaven.

In the same way Paul treats of love to our neighbour, and the fulfilling of the whole Law, as the same thing (Galatians 5:14); because, when love to our neighbour exists, all the other duties of the law will necessarily be performed.

FRANCIS TURRETIN

A DEBT WE COULDN'T PAY

He forgave us all our sins, having canceled
the charge of our legal indebtedness, which
stood against us and condemned us.

COLOSSIANS 2:13-14

What one person owes for himself, he cannot pay for another, if he be a private person. But nothing prevents such a payment, when the person is a public character, who may act both in his own name and in the name of those whom he represents. He who pays what he owes for himself, cannot by the same thing make a payment for others, unless he has voluntarily made himself a debtor for them, in which case he can. For, although he may be a debtor, yet this character arises from his own voluntary act—the debt which he has to pay for himself is a debt which, were it not for his own voluntary deed, he is not bound to pay, and hence, while he is paying for himself, he may, by the same act, pay for another.

So Christ, who became man, not for His own sake, but for our sakes, was under obligation to fulfill the Law in order to merit life, not for Himself, but for us.

FRANCIS TURRETIN

TO THE GLORY
OF GOD ALONE

THE CREATOR OF ALL THINGS

In the beginning God created the
heavens and the earth.

GENESIS 1:1

This is the fountainhead of my religion, to recognize God as the uncreated Creator of all things, who solely and alone has all things in His power and freely giveth us all things. They therefore overthrow this first foundation of faith who attribute to the creature what is the Creator's alone. For we confess in the creed that it is the Creator in whom we believe. It cannot, therefore, be the creature in whom we should put our trust.

Since we know that God is the Source and Creator of all things, it cannot be that we should understand that there is anything either before Him or along with Him that is not from Him. For if there could be anything which was not from Him, He would not be infinite, for He would not extend to where that other was that was outside of Him. Hence, though we see that in the Scriptures God is called Father, Son, and Holy Ghost, these are not different creatures or gods, but these three are one; the persons are three, but they are all and each one and the same God.

ULRICH ZWINGLI

WALK HUMBLY

Ascribe to the LORD the glory due his name;
worship the LORD in the splendor of his holiness.

PSALM 29:2

God's glory is the result of His nature and acts. He is glorious in His character, for there is such a store of everything that is holy, and good, and lovely in God that He must be glorious. The actions which flow from His character are also glorious; but while He intends that they should manifest to His creatures His goodness, and mercy, and justice, He is equally concerned that the glory associated with them should be given only to Himself. Nor is there aught in ourselves in which we may glory; for who maketh us to differ from another? And what have we that we did not receive from the God of all grace?

Then how careful ought we to be to walk humbly before the Lord! The moment we glorify ourselves, since there is room for one glory only in the universe, we set ourselves up as rivals to the Most High. Shall the insect of an hour glorify itself against the Sun which warmed it into life? Shall the potsherd exalt itself above the Man who fashioned it upon the wheel?

CHARLES SPURGEON

OCTOBER 23

A LOVELY HOLINESS

Who among the gods is like you, LORD?
Who is like you—majestic in holiness,
awesome in glory, working wonders?

EXODUS 15:11

A true sense of the divine and superlative excellency of the things of religion; a real sense of the excellency of God and Jesus Christ, and of the work of redemption, and the ways and works of God revealed in the Gospel: there is a divine and superlative glory in these things; an excellency that is of a vastly higher kind, and more sublime nature, than in other things, a glory greatly distinguishing them from all that is earthly and temporal. He that is spiritually enlightened truly apprehends and sees it, or has a sense of it.

He does not merely rationally believe that God is glorious, but he has a sense of the gloriousness of God in his heart. There is not only a rational belief that God is holy, and that holiness is a good thing, but there is a sense of the loveliness of God's holiness. There is not only a speculatively judging that God is gracious, but a sense how amiable God is on account of the beauty of this divine attribute.

JONATHAN EDWARDS

HIS GLORY CELEBRATED

In him we were also chosen . . . in order that
we, who were the first to put our hope in
Christ, might be for the praise of his glory.

EPHESIANS 1:11-12

The glory of God may sometimes be concealed, or imperfectly exhibited. But in the Ephesians God had given proofs of His goodness, that His glory might be celebrated and openly proclaimed.

The frequent mention of the glory of God ought not to be regarded as superfluous, for what is infinite cannot be too strongly expressed. This is particularly true in commendations of the divine mercy, for which every godly person will always feel himself unable to find adequate language. He will be more ready to utter, than other men will be to hear, the expression of praise; for the eloquence both of men and angels, after being strained to the utmost, falls immeasurably below the vastness of this subject. We may likewise observe that there is not a more effectual method of shutting the mouths of wicked men than by shewing that our views tend to illustrate, and theirs to obscure, the glory of God.

JOHN CALVIN

TRUE VIRTUE

*Glorify the LORD with me; let us
exalt his name together.*

PSALM 34:3

It appears that the truly virtuous mind, being as it were under the sovereign dominion of love to God, above all things seeks the glory of God, and makes this his supreme, governing, and ultimate end. This consists in the expression of God's perfections in their proper effects; the manifestation of God's glory to created understandings; the communications of the infinite fulness of God to the creature; the creature's highest esteem of God, love to, and joy in Him; and in the proper exercises and expressions of these.

And so far as a virtuous mind exercises true virtue in benevolence to created beings, it chiefly seeks the good of the creature; consisting in its knowledge or view of God's glory and beauty, its union with God, conformity and love to Him, and joy in Him. And that disposition of heart, that consent, union, or propensity of mind to being in general, which appears chiefly in such exercises, is virtue, truly so called; or in other words, true grace and real holiness. And no other disposition or affection but this is of the nature of true virtue.

JONATHAN EDWARDS

WHOLLY THE LORD'S

Better is one day in your courts than a thousand elsewhere; I would rather be a doorkeeper in the house of my God than dwell in the tents of the wicked.

PSALM 84:10

We have a choice between these two: to be eaten up by our corruptions, or by the zeal of God's house. It needs no hesitation; the choice of every man among us is to be wholly the Lord's—ardently, passionately, vehemently the Lord's servants, let the divine fervour cost us what it may of brain, and heart, and life. Our only hope of honour, and glory, and immortality lies in the fulfillment of our dedication unto God; as devoted things, we must be consumed with fire, or else be rejected.

For us to turn aside from our life-work and to seek distinction elsewhere is absolute folly; a blight will be upon us, and we shall not succeed in anything but the pursuit of God's glory through the teaching of the Word. "This people have I formed for Myself," saith God; "they shall shew forth My praise"; and if we will not do this, we shall do less than nothing. For this one thing we are created; and if we miss this, we shall live in vain.

CHARLES SPURGEON

GOD'S GLORY SHOULD BE KNOWN

Great is the LORD and most worthy of
praise; his greatness no one can fathom.

PSALM 145:3

It seems to be a thing in itself fit and desirable that the glorious perfections of God should be known, and the operations and expressions of them seen, by other beings besides Himself. If it be fit that God's power and wisdom, etc., should be exercised and expressed in some effects, then it seems proper that these exercises should appear.

God as perfectly knew Himself and His perfections, had as perfect an idea of the exercises and effects they were sufficient for, antecedently to any such actual operations of them. If, therefore, it be nevertheless a thing in itself valuable and worthy to be desired, that these glorious perfections be actually exhibited in their correspondent effects, then it seems also that the knowledge of these perfections and discoveries is valuable in itself absolutely considered; and that it is desirable that this knowledge should exist. It is a thing infinitely good in itself, that God's glory should be known by a glorious society of created beings.

JONATHAN EDWARDS

A SINGLE PURPOSE

"You are my witnesses," declares the LORD,
"and my servant whom I have chosen, so
that you may know and believe me and
understand that I am he. Before me no god was
formed, nor will there be one after me."

ISAIAH 43:10

When we misuse our Master's property, we are false to our trust. We are entrusted with a certain amount of talent, and strength, and influence, and we have to use this trust-money with a single purpose. Our purpose is to promote the Master's honour and glory. We are to seek God's glory, and nothing else.

By all means, let every man use his best influence on the right side in politics; but no minister has liberty to use his position in the church to promote party ends. I do not censure workers for temperance, but even this admirable movement must not push out the gospel: I trust it never does. I hold that no minister has a right to use his ability or office to cater for the mere amusement of the multitude.

The Master has sent us to win souls: all is within the compass of our commission which tends toward that end; but that is chiefly our work which drives directly and distinctly at that end.

CHARLES SPURGEON

EMANATION OF PERFECTION

With you is the fountain of life;
in your light we see light.

PSALM 36:9

As there is an infinite fulness of all possible good in God—a fulness of every perfection, of all excellency and beauty, and of infinite happiness—and as this fulness is capable of communication, or emanation outward; so it seems a thing amiable and valuable in itself that this infinite fountain of good should send forth abundant streams.

And as this is in itself excellent, so a disposition to this in the divine Being must be looked upon as an excellent disposition. Such an emanation of good is, in some sense, a multiplication of it. And if the fulness of good that is in the fountain is in itself excellent, then the emanation is excellent.

Thus it is fit, since there is an infinite fountain of light and knowledge, that this light should shine forth in beams of communicated knowledge and understanding; and, as there is an infinite fountain of holiness, moral excellence, and beauty, that so it should flow out in communicated holiness. And that, as there is an infinite fulness of joy and happiness, so these should have an emanation, and become a fountain flowing out in abundant streams, as beams from the sun.

JONATHAN EDWARDS

HOLY WONDER

LORD my God, you are very great; you are
clothed with splendor and majesty.

PSALM 104:1

We must not cease to wonder at the great marvels of our God. It would be very difficult to draw a line between holy wonder and real worship, for when the soul is overwhelmed with the majesty of God's glory, though it may not express itself in song or even utter its voice with bowed head in humble prayer, yet it silently adores. Our incarnate God is to be worshiped as "the Wonderful."

That God should consider His fallen creature, man, and instead of sweeping Him away with the besom of destruction, should Himself undertake to be man's Redeemer and to pay his ransom price, is indeed marvellous! But to each believer redemption is most marvellous as he views it in relation to himself. It is a miracle of grace indeed that Jesus should forsake the thrones and royalties above to suffer ignominiously below for you. Let your soul lose itself in wonder, for wonder is in this way a very practical emotion. Holy wonder will lead you to grateful worship and heartfelt thanksgiving.

CHARLES SPURGEON

THE GLORY OF HAPPINESS

*Rejoice in the Lord always. I
will say it again: Rejoice!*

PHILIPPIANS 4:4

Part of God's fulness which He communicates is His happiness. This happiness consists in enjoying and rejoicing in Himself, and so does also the creature's happiness. It is a participation of what is in God, and God and His glory are the objective ground of it. The happiness of the creature consists in rejoicing in God, by which also God is magnified and exalted.

Joy, or the exulting of the heart in God's glory, is one thing that belongs to praise. So that God is all in all, with respect to each part of that communication of the divine fulness which is made to the creature. What is communicated is divine, or something of God; and each communication is of that nature that the creature to whom it is made is thereby conformed to God and united to Him, and that in proportion as the communication is greater or less. And the communication itself is no other, in the very nature of it, than that wherein the very honour, exaltation, and praise of God consists.

JONATHAN EDWARDS

GLITTER IN THE KING'S CROWN

The God of all grace, who called you to his
eternal glory in Christ, after you have suffered
a little while, will himself restore you and
make you strong, firm and steadfast.

1 PETER 5:10

Our prolonged stay here is doubtless for God's glory. A tried saint, like a well-cut diamond, glitters much in the King's crown. Nothing reflects so much honour on a workman as a protracted and severe trial of his work, and its triumphant endurance of the ordeal without giving way in any part.

We are God's workmanship, in whom He will be glorified by our afflictions. It is for the honour of Jesus that we endure the trial of our faith with sacred joy. Let each man surrender his own longings to the glory of Jesus and feel, *If my lying in the dust would elevate my Lord by so much as an inch, let me still lie among the pots of earth. If to live on earth forever would make my Lord more glorious, it should be my heaven to be shut out of heaven.* Our time is fixed and settled by eternal decree. Let us not be anxious about it, but wait with patience till the gates of pearl shall open.

CHARLES SPURGEON

GOD'S GLORY IN THE SCRIPTURES

Glorious and majestic are his deeds, and
his righteousness endures forever.

PSALM 111:3

The Scripture speaks of God's glory as His ultimate end of the goodness of the moral part of the creation, and that end, in relation to which chiefly the value of their virtue consists. As in Philippians 1:10–11: "That ye may approve things that are excellent, that ye may be sincere, and without offence, till the day of Christ: being filled with the fruits of righteousness, which are by Jesus Christ, unto the glory and praise of God."

Here the apostle shows how the fruits of righteousness in them are valuable, and how they answer their end, namely in being "by Jesus Christ to the praise and glory of God." John 15:8 [says,] "Herein is my Father glorified, that ye bear much fruit." Signifying that by this means it is that the great end of religion is to be answered. And in 1 Peter 5:11, the apostle directs the Christians to regulate all their religious performances with reference to that one end. "If any man speak, let him speak as the oracles of God. If any man minister, let him do it as of the ability which God giveth, that God in all things may be glorified; to whom be praise and dominion forever and ever. Amen."

JONATHAN EDWARDS

A MOMENTARY AFFLICTION

Our light affliction, which is but for a moment, is working for us a far more exceeding and eternal weight of glory.

2 CORINTHIANS 4:17 NKJV

Suffering which God accepts must have God's glory as its end. If I suffer that I may earn a name or win applause, I shall get no other reward than that of the Pharisee. It is requisite also that love to Jesus, and love to His elect, be ever the mainspring of all our patience. We must manifest the Spirit of Christ in meekness, gentleness, and forgiveness. Let us search and see if we truly suffer with Jesus. And if we do thus suffer, what is our "light affliction" compared with reigning with Him?

Oh it is so blessed to be in the furnace with Christ, and such an honour to stand in the pillory with Him, that if there were no future reward, we might count ourselves happy in present honour; but when the recompense is so eternal, so infinitely more than we had any right to expect, shall we not take up the cross with alacrity, and go on our way rejoicing?

CHARLES SPURGEON

OUR HIGHEST END

"Our Father in heaven, hallowed be your name."

MATTHEW 6:9

There are some things in the Word of God which lead us to suppose that it requires of men that they should desire and seek God's glory as their highest and last end in what they do. As particularly from 1 Corinthians 10:30: "Whether therefore ye eat or drink, or whatsoever ye do, do all to the glory of God." And 1 Peter 4:11: "That God in all things may be glorified." And this may be argued, that Christ requires His followers should desire and seek God's glory in the first place, and above all things else, from that prayer which He gave His disciples as the pattern and rule, for the first petition of which is, "Hallowed be thy name." Which in Scripture language is the same with *Glorified be Thy name*; as is manifest from Leviticus 10:3, Ezekiel 28:22, and many other places.

Now our last and highest end is doubtless what should be first in our desires and consequently first in our prayers; and therefore we may argue that since Christ directs that God's glory should be first in our prayers, and therefore, we may argue, that since Christ directs that God's glory should be first in our prayers, that therefore this is our last end.

JONATHAN EDWARDS

AMBITION THAT FIRES YOUR SOUL

*From him and through him and for him are all
things. To him be the glory forever! Amen.*

ROMANS 11:36

Let nothing ever set your heart beating so mightily as love to Him. Let this ambition fire your soul; be this the foundation of every enterprise upon which you enter, and this your sustaining motive whenever your zeal would grow chill; make God your only object. Depend upon it, where self begins sorrow begins; but if God be my supreme delight and only object, Let your desire for God's glory be a growing desire. Has God prospered you in business? Give Him more as He has given you more. Has God given you experience? Praise Him by stronger faith than you exercised at first. Does your knowledge grow? Then sing more sweetly. Do you enjoy happier times than you once had? Then give Him more music; put more coals and more sweet frankincense into the censer of your praise. Practically in your life give Him honour, putting the "Amen" to this doxology to your great and gracious Lord, by your own individual service and increasing holiness.

CHARLES SPURGEON

VIRTUOUS AFFECTION

To him be glory in the church and in Christ Jesus
throughout all generations, forever and ever! Amen.

EPHESIANS 3:21

The glory of God appears, by the account given in Scripture, to be that event in the earnest desires of which, and in their delight in which, the best part of the moral world, and when in their best frames, most naturally express the direct tendency of the Spirit of true goodness, the virtuous and pious affections of their heart. This is the way in which the holy apostles, from time to time, gave vent to the ardent exercises of their piety and breathed forth their regard to the Supreme Being: Romans 11:36: "To whom be glory forever and ever. Amen." Romans 16:27: "To God only wise, be glory, through Jesus Christ, forever. Amen." Galatians 1:4–5: "Who gave himself for our sins, that he might deliver us from this present evil world, according to the will of God and our Father, to whom be glory forever and ever. Amen." 2 Timothy 4:18: "And the Lord shall deliver me from every evil work, and will preserve me to his heavenly kingdom: to whom be glory forever and ever. Amen."

JONATHAN EDWARDS

CHRIST'S ULTIMATE AIM

"Whoever speaks on their own does so to gain personal glory, but he who seeks the glory of the one who sent him is a man of truth."

JOHN 7:18

The Scripture leads us to suppose that Christ sought God's glory as His highest and last end. John 7:18 [says,] "He that speaketh of himself, seeketh his own glory; but he that seeketh his glory that sent him, the same is true, and no unrighteousness is in him." When Christ says He did not seek His own glory, we cannot reasonably understand that He had no regard to His own glory, even the glory of the human nature; for the glory of that nature was part of the reward promised Him and of the joy set before Him.

But we must understand that this was not His ultimate aim; it was not the end that chiefly governed His conduct, and therefore, when in opposition to this, in the latter part of the sentence, He says, "But he that seeketh his glory that sent him, the same is true." It is natural from the antithesis to understand that this was His ultimate aim, His supreme governing end.

JONATHAN EDWARDS

ALL TO GOD'S GLORY

Conduct yourselves in a manner
worthy of the gospel of Christ.
PHILIPPIANS 1:27

The Christian, while in the world, is not to be of the world. He should be distinguished from it in the great object of his life. To him, "to live" should be "Christ." Whether he eats, or drinks, or whatever he does, he should do all to God's glory. You may lay up treasure, but lay it up in heaven, where neither moth nor rust doth corrupt, where thieves break not through nor steal. You may strive to be rich, but be it your ambition to be "rich in faith" and good works. You may have pleasure, but when you are merry, sing psalms and make melody in your hearts to the Lord. In your spirit as well as in your aim, you should differ from the world.

Waiting humbly before God, delighting in communion with Him, and seeking to know His will, you will prove that you are of the heavenly race. And be separate from the world in your actions. If a thing be right, though you lose by it, it must be done; if it be wrong, though you would gain by it, you must scorn the sin for your Master's sake.

CHARLES SPURGEON

GOD'S MORAL GOVERNMENT

Ascribe to the LORD the glory due his name.

1 CHRONICLES 16:29

The Scripture leads us to suppose that God's glory is His last end in His moral government of the world in general. This has been already shown concerning several things that belong to God's moral government of the world, as particularly in the work of redemption, the chief of all His dispensations in His moral government of the world.

And I have also observed it, with respect to the duty which God requires of the subjects of His moral government, in requiring them to seek His glory as their last end. And this is actually the last end of the moral goodness required of them, the end which gives their moral goodness its chief value. And also that it is what that person which God has set at the head of the moral world, as its chief Governor, even Jesus Christ, seeks as His chief end. And it has been shown, that it is the chief end for which that part of the moral world which are good are made, or have their existence as good. I now further observe that this is the end of the establishment of the public worship and ordinances of God among mankind.

JONATHAN EDWARDS

FAITH BRINGS GLORY

God opposes the proud but shows
favor to the humble.

1 PETER 5:5

Faith gives all the glory to God. It is of faith that it might be by grace, and it is of grace that there might be no boasting; for God cannot endure pride. "The proud he knoweth afar off," and He has no wish to come nearer to them. He will not give salvation in a way which will suggest or foster pride. Paul saith, "Not of works, lest any man should boast." Now, faith excludes all boasting. The hand which receives charity does not say, "I am to be thanked for accepting the gift"; that would be absurd. When the hand conveys bread to the mouth it does not say to the body, "Thank me, for I feed you." It is a very simple thing that the hand does though a very necessary thing; and it never arrogates glory to itself for what it does.

So God has selected faith to receive the unspeakable gift of His grace because it cannot take to itself any credit, but must adore the gracious God who is the Giver of all good.

CHARLES SPURGEON

CONSEQUENCE OF CREATION

I will sing to the LORD all my life; I will
sing praise to my God as long as I live.

PSALM 104:33

In the 104th Psalm, after a very particular, orderly, and magnificent representation of God's works of creation and common providence, it is said in the 31st verse, "The glory of the Lord shall endure forever: the Lord shall rejoice in his works." Here God's glory is spoken of as the grand result and blessed consequence, on account of which he rejoices in these works. And this is one thing doubtless implied in the song of the seraphim, Isaiah 6:3: "Holy, holy, holy is the Lord of hosts, the whole earth is full of his glory."

The glory of God, in being the result and consequence of those works of Providence that have been mentioned, is in fact the consequence of the creation. The good attained in the use of a thing made for use is the result of the making of that thing, as signifying the time of day, when actually attained by the use of a watch, is the consequence of making the watch. So it is apparent that the glory of God is actually the result and consequence of the creation of the world.

JONATHAN EDWARDS

THE EMINENCE OF GLORY

We were therefore buried with him through
baptism into death in order that, just as Christ
was raised from the dead through the glory
of the Father, we too may live a new life.

ROMANS 6:4

Come and try this living Savior, if you have never done so before. This living Jesus is also raised to an eminence of glory and power. He does not now sorrow as "a humble man before his foes," nor labor as "the carpenter's son," but He is exalted far above principalities and power and every name that is named.

The Father has given Him all power in heaven and in earth, and He exercises this high endowment in carrying out His work of grace. Hear what Peter and the other apostles testified concerning Him before the high priest and the council: "The God of our fathers raised up Jesus, whom ye slew and hanged on a tree. Him hath God exalted with his right hand to be a Prince and a Saviour, for to give repentance to Israel, and forgiveness of sins" (Acts 5:30–31). The glory which surrounds the ascended Lord should breathe hope into every believer's breast.

CHARLES SPURGEON

ONE CREATOR

Is not he your father, who created you,
who made you and established you?

DEUTERONOMY 32:6 ESV

All the things that are, are either created or uncreated. The one and only uncreated thing is God, for there can be but one uncreated thing. If there were several uncreated things, there would be several eternals, for the uncreated and the eternal are so closely allied that as one is, so is also the other. For if there were several eternals, there would be several infinites, for these are so like unto and allied with each other that whatever is eternal is also infinite and whatever is infinite is also eternal.

Now, since there can be only one infinite (for as soon as we admit two infinite substances, each becomes finite), it is certain that the one and only uncreated thing is God. On this depends also the origin, source, and foundation of the first article of our faith, that is, when we say, "I believe in one God, the Father Almighty, Creator of heaven and earth," we confess and declare that we have an infallible faith, since it is one resting securely upon one only Creator.

ULRICH ZWINGLI

THE HILLS OF GLORY

I lift up my eyes to the mountains—
where does my help come from?

PSALM 121:1

Jesus endured great humiliation, and therefore there was room for Him to be exalted. By that humiliation He accomplished and endured all the Father's will, and therefore He was rewarded by being raised to glory. He uses that exaltation on behalf of His people.

Let my reader raise his eyes to these hills of glory, whence his help must come. Let him contemplate the high glories of the Prince and Savior. Is it not most hopeful for men that a Man is now on the throne of the universe? Is it not glorious that the Lord of all is the Savior of sinners? We have a Friend at court; yea, a Friend on the throne. He will use all His influence for those who entrust their affairs in His hands.

Come, friend, and commit your cause and your case to those once-pierced hands, which are now glorified with the signet rings of royal power and honor. No suit ever failed which was left with this great Advocate.

CHARLES SPURGEON

OUR CHIEF GOOD

I say to the LORD, "You are my Lord; apart
from you I have no good thing."

PSALM 16:2

Because He infinitely values His own glory, consisting in the knowledge of Himself, love to Himself, and joyfully sufficient in Himself, He therefore valued the image, communication, or participation of these in the creature. And it is because He values Himself that He delights in the knowledge, and love, and joy of the creature as being Himself the object of this knowledge, love, and self-sufficient. For it is the necessary consequence of true esteem and love that we value others' esteem of the same object, and dislike the contrary.

For the same reason, God approves of others' esteem and love of Himself. Thus it is easy to conceive how God should seek the good of the creature, consisting in the creature's knowledge and holiness, and even his happiness, from a supreme regard to Himself; as His happiness arises from that which is an image and participation of God's own beauty, and consists in the creature's exercising a supreme regard to God, and self-sufficiency in Him.

JONATHAN EDWARDS

THE EARTH SPEAKS OF HIS GLORY

The earth is the LORD's, and all its fullness,
the world and those who dwell therein.

PSALM 24:1 NKJV

We believe that "the earth is the Lord's, and the fulness thereof," and we go forth into it, not as into the domains of Satan where light comes not, nor into a chaos where rule is unknown, nor into a boiling sea where fate's resistless billows shipwreck mortals at their will; but we walk boldly on, having God within us and around us, living and moving and having our being in Him, and so, by faith, we dwell in a temple of providence and grace wherein everything doth speak of His glory.

We believe in a present God wherever we may be, and a working and operating God accomplishing His own purposes steadfastly and surely in all matters, places, and times; working out His designs as much in what seemeth evil as in that which is manifestly good; in all things driving on in His eternal chariot toward the goal which infinite wisdom has chosen. We believe in this God as being faithful to everything that He has spoken. The God of Abraham is the God and Father of our Lord Jesus Christ, and He is our God this day.

CHARLES SPURGEON

THE GLORY OF GOD'S DESIGN

Who can proclaim the mighty acts of the
LORD or fully declare his praise?

PSALM 106:2

Reason shows that it is fit and requisite that the intelligent and rational beings of the world should know something of God's scheme and design in His works, for they doubtless are principally concerned. God's great design in His works is doubtless concerning His reasonable creatures rather than brute beasts and lifeless things. The revolutions by which God's great design is brought to pass are doubtless chiefly among them and concern their state, and not the state of things without life or reason.

And therefore surely it is requisite that they should know something of it; especially since reason teaches that God has given His rational creatures a capacity of seeing Him in His works, for this end: that they may see God's glory in them, and give Him that glory. But how can they see God's glory in His works if they do not know what His design in them is, and what He aims at by what He is doing in the world?

JONATHAN EDWARDS

CROWNED WITH GLORY

We do see Jesus, who was made lower than the
angels for a little while, now crowned with glory
and honor because he suffered death, so that by the
grace of God he might taste death for everyone.

HEBREWS 2:9

Our faith in Jesus is most real. We believe in those dear wounds of His as we believe in nothing else; there is no fact so sure to us as that He was slain, and He has redeemed us to God by His blood. We believe in the brightness of His glory; for nothing seems to us so necessarily true as that He who was obedient unto death should, as His due reward, be crowned with glory and honor.

For this reason also we believe in a real Christ yet to come, a second time, in like manner as He went up into heaven; and though we may not enquire minutely into times and seasons, yet we are "looking for and hasting unto the coming of the day of God" at which time we expect the manifestation of the sons of God, and the rising of their bodies from the tomb. Christ Jesus is no fiction to us.

CHARLES SPURGEON

HEAVENLY HAPPINESS

"Take off your sandals, for the place where
you are standing is holy ground."

EXODUS 3:5

It is evident by the Scripture that discoveries of God's glory, when given in a great degree, have a tendency, by affecting the mind, to overbear the body. The Scripture teaches us that if these views should be given to such a degree as they are given in heaven, the weak frame of the body could not subsist under it, and that no man can, in that manner, see God and live.

The knowledge which the saints have of God's beauty and glory in this world, and those holy affections that arise from it, are of the same nature and kind with what the saints are the subjects of in heaven, differing only in degree and circumstances. What God gives them here is a foretaste of heavenly happiness, and an earnest of their future inheritance. And who shall limit God in His giving this earnest, or say He shall give so much of the inheritance, such a part of the future reward, as an earnest of the whole, and no more?

JONATHAN EDWARDS

TO HIS GLORY

For to me, to live is Christ and to die is gain.

PHILIPPIANS 1:21

The believer did not always live to Christ. He began to do so when God the Holy Spirit convinced him of sin, and when by grace he was brought to see the dying Saviour making a propitiation for his guilt. From the moment of the new and celestial birth the man begins to live to Christ. Jesus is to believers the one pearl of great price, for whom we are willing to part with all that we have. He has so completely won our love, that it beats alone for him; to His glory we would live, and in defence of His Gospel we would die; He is the pattern of our life, and the model after which we would sculpture our character. Paul's words mean more than most men think; they imply that the aim and end of his life was Christ—nay, his life itself was Jesus. In the words of an ancient saint, he did eat, and drink, and sleep eternal life. Jesus was his very breath, the soul of his soul, the heart of his heart, the life of his life.

CHARLES SPURGEON

CONTEMPLATE GOD'S GLORY

You are great and do marvelous deeds; you alone are God.

PSALM 86:10

The contemplation of God's glory in His works is the true way of acquiring genuine godliness. The pride of the flesh would always lead it to wing its way into heaven; but, as our understandings fail us in such an extended investigation, our most profitable course is, according to the small measure of our feeble capacity, to seek God in His works, which bear witness of Him. Let us therefore learn to awaken our understandings to contemplate the divine works, and let us leave the presumptuous to wander in their own intricate mazes.

To incline our hearts to exercise this modesty, David magnificently extols the works of God, calling them wondrous things, although to the blind, and those who have no taste for them, they are destitute of attraction. In the meantime, we ought carefully to attend to this truth, that the glory of the Godhead belongs exclusively to the one true God; for in no other being is it possible to find the wisdom, or the power, or the righteousness, or any of the numerous marks of divinity which shine forth in His wonderful works.

JOHN CALVIN

GAZE ON GOD'S GLORY

It is the Lord Christ you are serving.

COLOSSIANS 3:24

Persons cannot be said to forsake Christ and live on their experiences merely because they use them as evidences of grace, for there are no other evidences that they can take. But then may persons be said to live upon their experiences when they make a righteousness of them, and when, instead of keeping their eye on God's glory and Christ's excellency, they turn it on themselves. They entertain their minds by viewing their own attainments, their high experiences, and the great things they have met with, which are bright and beautiful in their own eyes. They are rich and increased with goods in their own apprehensions, and think that God has as admiring an esteem of them, on the same account, as they have of themselves.

This is living on experiences, and not on Christ, and is more abominable in the sight of God than the gross immoralities of those who make no pretences to religion. But this is a far different thing from improving experiences as evidences of an interest in a glorious Redeemer.

JONATHAN EDWARDS

UNRESTRAINED ZEAL

Zeal for your house consumes me.

PSALM 69:9

How is it with you, dear brother? Do you say, "Well, I am not the warmest of all, but then I am not the coldest of all"? Then I have a suspicion as to your temperature; but I leave the matter to your own judgment, only remarking that I have never yet met with fire that is moderately hot. Should any of you discover such an article, you will be wise to patent it, for it might be of service in many ways.

The fire with which I have been acquainted has been such that I have never given it my hand without remembering its warm embrace. Fire has never yet learned moderation. I am told that it is wrong to go to extremes, and upon that ground fire is certainly guilty; for it is not only intensely hot, but it has a tendency to consume and destroy without limit. When it once commenced with this city, in the olden time, it left little of it but ashes; there was no keeping it within bounds. May God grant us grace to go to extremes in His service! May we be filled with an unrestrainable zeal for His glory!

CHARLES SPURGEON

DELIGHT IN OUR SALVATION

"My food," said Jesus, "is to do the will of
him who sent me and to finish his work."

JOHN 4:34

Those who carry the message of the Gospel should follow their Master in His zeal, so wonderfully mixed and tempered with gentleness and condescension in His dealing with souls, preaching the gospel to the poor, and taking a gracious notice from time to time of little children. And they should imitate their Lord in His following the work of the ministry, not from mercenary views, or for the sake of worldly advantages, but for God's glory and men's salvation; and in having His heart engaged in His work; it being His great delight, and His meat, to do the will of His Father, and finish His work (John 4:34).

And having His heart set on the success of His great undertaking in the salvation of souls, this being the joy that was set before Him, for which He ran His race, endured the cross, and despised the shame; His delight in the prospect of the eternal salvation of souls more than countervailing the dread He had of His extreme sufferings. Many waters could not quench His love, neither could the floods drown it, for His love was stronger than death; yea, than the mighty pains and torments of such a death.

JONATHAN EDWARDS

STRUGGLE AGAINST OUR FOE

*"The thief comes only to steal and kill
and destroy; I have come that they may
have life, and have it to the full."*

JOHN 10:10

One thing which ought to animate us to perpetual contest with the devil is that he is everywhere called both our adversary and the adversary of God. For if the glory of God is dear to us, as it ought to be, we ought to struggle with all our might against him who aims at the extinction of that glory. If we are animated with proper zeal to maintain the kingdom of Christ, we must wage irreconcilable war with him who conspires its ruin.

Again, if we have any anxiety about our own salvation, we ought to make no peace nor truce with him who is continually laying schemes for its destruction. But such is the character given to Satan in the third chapter of Genesis, where he is seen seducing man from his allegiance to God, that he may both deprive God of His due honor, and plunge man headlong in destruction.

JOHN CALVIN

DILIGENTLY SERVE ALL

*Always give yourself fully to the work of
the Lord, because you know that your
labor in the Lord is not in vain.*

1 CORINTHIANS 15:58

Every young man should, from early youth, strive after steadiness, faithfulness, truth, faith, righteousness, and piety; and he should diligently practice these things. With these he can serve, with fruitful results, the cause of Christianity, society around him, and his country, for he will be useful to the body politic as well as to the individual citizen. Those are weak-minded persons who are concerned only about living a quiet life. They are not so godlike as those who, to their own detriment, diligently serve all men.

We ought to be very careful, at the same time, that those things which we undertake to the glory of God, to the honor of our country, and for the common welfare be not defiled by self and Satan, so that we do not at last turn to our own advantage what we wish to be regarded as having been done for the good of others. There are many who begin well and go in the right direction, but they soon become corrupted by vain ambition, which poisons and destroys every good resolution, and as a result they are led away from all that is good and noble. The Christian will regard a community as a household, yea, as one body in which all members enjoy pleasure or suffer pain.

ULRICH ZWINGLI

OWL OR FALCON?

We have different gifts, according to
the grace given to each of us.

ROMANS 12:6

Some men never can do much for God in the way which they would prefer, for they were never cut out for the work. Owls will never rival falcons by daylight, but then falcons would be lost in the enterprise of hunting barns at night for rats and mice. Each creature is not only good, but "very good" in its own place, fulfilling its own office; out of that place, it may become a nuisance.

Friend, be true to your own destiny! One man would make a splendid preacher of downright hard-hitting Saxon; why must he ruin himself by cultivating an ornate style? Another attempting to be extremely simple would throw himself away, for he is florid by nature; why should he not follow his bent? Apollos has the gift of eloquence; why must he copy blunt Cephas? Every man in his own order. It seems to me that nowadays, every man prefers his own disorder. Let each man find out what God wants him to do, and then let him do it, or die in the attempt.

CHARLES SPURGEON

TO SPREAD HIS GLORY

"Go and make disciples of all nations,
baptizing them in the name of the Father
and of the Son and of the Holy Spirit."

MATTHEW 28:19

The whole world knows that His glory has not been spread by force and weapons, but by poor fishermen. O wise man, do you think the poor fishermen were not clever enough for this? Where they worked, there they made hearts better; where they could not work, there men remained bad; and therefore was the faith true and from God. The signs which the Lord had promised followed their teaching: in His name they drove out the devil; they spoke in new tongues; if they drank any deadly drink, they received therefrom no harm.

Even if these wonders had not occurred, there would have been the wonder of wonders, that poor fishermen without any miracle could accomplish so great a work as the faith. It came from God, and so is Christ true and Christ is thy God, who is in heaven and awaits thee. You say you believe the Gospel, but you do not believe me. But the purer anything is, so much the nearer it stands to its end and purpose. The Christian life purifies the heart, and places it very near to the truth.

MARTIN LUTHER

HIS PROVIDENCE

Who is like the LORD our God, the One who
sits enthroned on high, who stoops down
to look on the heavens and the earth?

PSALM 113:5-6

Though God's glory is far above all heavens, the distance at which He is placed does not prevent His governing the world by His providence. God is highly exalted, but He sees after off, so that He needs not change place when He would condescend to take care of us. We on our part are poor and lowly, but our wretched condition is no reason why God will not concern Himself about us.

While we view with admiration the immensity of His glory as raised above all heavens, we must not disbelieve His willingness to foster us under His fatherly care. The two things are, with great propriety, conjoined here by [the psalmist], that, on the one hand, when we think of God's majesty we should not be terrified into a forgetfulness of His goodness and benignity, nor, on the other, lose our reverence for His majesty in contemplating the condescension of His mercy.

JOHN CALVIN

GRACE BRINGS GLORY

Out of his fullness we have all received
grace in place of grace already given.

JOHN 1:16

One thing is past all question: we shall bring our Lord most glory if we get from Him much grace. If I have much faith, so that I can take God at His word; much love, so that the zeal of His house eats me up; much hope, so that I am assured of fruit from my labor; much patience, so that I can endure hardness for Jesus' sake; then I shall greatly honor my Lord and King. Oh, to have much consecration, my whole nature being absorbed in His service; then, even though my talents may be slender, I shall make my life to burn and glow with the glory of the Lord!

This way of grace is open to us all. To be saintly is within each Christian's reach, and this is the surest method of honoring God. Though the preacher may not collect more than a hundred in a village chapel to hear him speak, he may be such a man of God that his little church will be choice seed-corn, each individual worthy to be weighed against gold.

CHARLES SPURGEON

DECLARE THE GLORY

*The heavens declare the glory of God; the
skies proclaim the work of his hands.*

PSALM 19:1

The beauty of the heavens and the firmament invite men to admire the greatness of God and preach His wonderful works. [In the same psalm] David says that the days and nights commit to each other the duty of telling the glory of God. For who imagines that when we regard the beauty of the sky on a night that is serene, we are not in the least excited to admire and adore Him who made so many beautiful stars, or that when we see a fine day in the clear light of the sun, or even when our Lord sends us the showers to fertilize the earth so that it may bring forth plants, we are not likewise affected?

What conclusion ought we to draw from this, my dear friends, if not that we who are much more than the heavens and all else that has been created, because all else has been made for us and not for themselves, that we, by the good example which we give our neighbor, are much more capable of proclaiming the glory of God than are the heavens and the stars?

MARTIN LUTHER

DIVINE BIDDING

Humble yourself before the Lord,
and he will lift you up.

JAMES 4:10

The world does not revolve, the sun does not blaze, the moon does not wax and wane, the stars do not shine entirely for the especial benefit of any one brother here; neither does Christendom exist for the purpose of finding us pulpits, nor our own particular church that it may furnish us with a congregation and an income; nay, nor does even so much as one believer exist that he may lay himself out for our sole comfort and honour. We are too insignificant to be of any great importance in God's vast universe; He can do either with us or without us, and our presence or absence will not disarrange His plans.

Yet, for all that, our subject is individuality, and we hope that each man will recognize and honorably maintain his personality. The proper recognition of the ego is a theme worthy of our attention. I will make a word if I may: let egotism stand for proud, vainglorious, intrusive selfhood, and let egoism stand for the humble, responsible, and honest selfhood which, finding itself in being, resolves to be at the divine bidding, and to be at its best to the glory of God.

CHARLES SPURGEON

A TREASURE OF GLORY

I will glory in the LORD; let the
afflicted hear and rejoice.

PSALM 34:2

One is not able to find one thing that is not fading and perishable. "All flesh is as grass, and the glory of the flesh is like the flower of the grass, the grass is withered, its flower is fallen." But it is not the same with God. He is the true good who has no part in the vanity of creatures, because He is truth itself, bearing for that reason the name Jehovah, signifying Him who is in and of Himself. He is an infinite and universal good, for He is the Shaddai, who possesses the fullness of all kinds of good things, in whom we find abundant provision.

Are we in darkness? He is a light without shadow to dissipate it. Are we soiled? He is perfect holiness to purify us. Are we in misery? He is a treasure of glory and happiness to enrich us. Are we in death? He is the Prince of life to deliver us from it. So then that for which society searches in vain in the variety of creation is that which we find perfectly in the unity of the Creator, who reinforces in His bosom all the good things for which we could wish.

FRANCIS TURRETIN

SPEAK OUT CHRIST'S GLORY

For Christ's sake, I delight in
weaknesses, in insults, in hardships.

2 CORINTHIANS 12:10

The Gospel is not there for us to aggrandize ourselves. The Gospel is to aggrandize Christ and the mercy of God. It holds out to men eternal gifts that are not gifts of our own manufacture. What right have we to receive praise and glory for gifts that are not of our own making? No wonder that God in His special grace subjects the ministers of the Gospel to all kinds of afflictions; otherwise they could not cope with this ugly beast called *vainglory*.

Paul had the Spirit of Christ. Nevertheless there was given unto him the messenger of Satan to buffet him in order that he should not come to exalt himself, because of the grandeur of his revelations. Saint Augustine's opinion is well taken: "If a minister of the Gospel is praised, he is in danger; if he is despised, he is also in danger." The ministers of the Gospel should be men who are not too easily affected by praise or criticism, but who simply speak out the benefit and the glory of Christ and seek the salvation of souls.

MARTIN LUTHER

ALL GLORY TO CHRIST

Be exalted, O God, above the heavens;
let your glory be over all the earth.

PSALM 57:5

To whom shall the glory be given? Oh! to Jesus, to Jesus; for the text says it is all by Jesus. It is not because I am a Christian that I get joy in my trouble—not necessarily so; it is not always the fact that troubles bring their consolations; but it is Christ who comes to me. I am sick in my chamber; Christ cometh upstairs, He sitteth by my bedside, and He talketh sweet words to me. I am dying; the chilly cold waters of Jordan have touched my foot, I feel my blood stagnate and freeze. I must die; Christ puts His arms around me and says, "Fear not, beloved; to die is to be blessed, the waters of death have their fountainhead in heaven, they are not bitter, they are sweet as nectar, for they flow from the throne of God." I wade in the stream, the billows gather around me, I feel that my heart and my flesh fail; but there is the same voice in my ears, "Fear not; I am with thee! be not dismayed; I am thy God."

Ah! ye who know not that matchless name, Jesus, ye have lost the sweetest note which e'er can give melody.

CHARLES SPURGEON

GLORY IN TRIALS

Praise be to the God of Shadrach,
Meshach and Abednego, who has sent
his angel and rescued his servants!

DANIEL 3:28

A tried saint brings more glory to God than an untried one. A believer in a dungeon reflects more glory on his Master than a believer in paradise, that a child of God in the burning fiery furnace displays more the glory of Godhead than even he who stands with a crown upon his head, perpetually singing praises before the eternal throne. Nothing reflects so much honor on a workman as a trial of his work, and its endurance of it.

So with God. It honors Him when His saints preserve their integrity. It is then for the glory of Jesus that we yet tarry. If my lying in the dust would elevate Christ one inch higher, I would say, "O let me remain, for it is sweet! to be here for the Lord." And if to live here forever would make Christ more glorious, I would prefer to live here eternally. If we could but add more jewels to the crown of Christ by remaining here, why should we wish to be taken out of the world? We should say, "It is blessed to be anywhere, where we can glorify Him."

CHARLES SPURGEON

ETERNAL KING OF GLORY

"You, Bethlehem Ephrathah, though you are little among the thousands of Judah, yet out of you shall come forth to Me the One to be Ruler in Israel."

MICAH 5:2 NKJV

If Christ was to be a ruler over His own people, then His government could be neither temporal nor corporeal, but He must rule over the entire people, past, present, and future. Therefore He must be an eternal King. And this He can only be spiritually. But as God bestows on Christ His own government, He could not be a human being only. For it is not possible for God to bestow His glory, government, property, or people on one who is not true God, as He Himself declares: "And my glory will I not give to another" (Isaiah 42:8).

Therefore Micah continues: "Whose goings forth are from of old, from everlasting," as if he would say: *I proclaim the Ruler that shall come out of Bethlehem, but He does not there begin to be; He has been already from the beginning before the world began, in that no day or beginning can be named in which He did not already have His being. Now from all eternity and before the creation of the world there existed nothing but God alone.*

MARTIN LUTHER

A CLEAR REVELATION

At that moment the curtain of the temple
was torn in two from top to bottom.
The earth shook, the rocks split.

MATTHEW 27:51

No mean miracle was wrought in the rending of so strong and thick a veil; but it was not intended merely as a display of power—many lessons were herein taught us. The old law of ordinances was put away, and like a worn-out vesture, rent and laid aside. When Jesus died, the sacrifices were all finished, because all fulfilled in Him, and therefore the place of their presentation was marked with an evident token of decay. That rent also revealed all the hidden things of the old dispensation: the mercy seat could now be seen, and the glory of God gleamed forth above it.

By the death of our Lord Jesus we have a clear revelation of God, for He was "not as Moses, who put a veil over his face." Life and immortality are now brought to light, and things which have been hidden since the foundation of the world are manifest in Him.

CHARLES SPURGEON

SON OF GOD

The Word became flesh and dwelt among us,
and we beheld His glory, the glory as of the only
begotten of the Father, full of grace and truth.

JOHN 1:14 NKJV

Here [John] expresses who the Word is, namely, the only begotten Son of God, who has all the glory of the Father. He calls Him the *only begotten* so as to distinguish Him from all the children of God, who are not natural children as this one is. With these words is shown His true divinity; for if He were not God, He could not in preference to others be called the *only begotten Son*, which is to say that He and no other is the Son of God.

This cannot be said of angels and pious men. For not one of them is the Son of God, but are all brethren and creatures of a like creation, children elected by grace, and not children born out of God's nature. But the expression "We beheld his glory" does not refer only to bodily sight; for the Jews also saw His glory, but did not regard it as the glory of the only begotten Son of God: it refers to the sight of the faithful, who believe it in their hearts.

MARTIN LUTHER

THE ESSENTIAL LIGHT

God saw that the light was good, and he
separated the light from the darkness.

GENESIS 1:4

Light might well be good since it sprang from that fiat of goodness, "Let there be light." We who enjoy it should be more grateful for it than we are, and see more of God in it and by it. Light physical is said by Solomon to be sweet, but Gospel light is infinitely more precious, for it reveals eternal things and ministers to our immortal natures.

When the Holy Spirit gives us spiritual light, and opens our eyes to behold the glory of God in the face of Jesus Christ, we behold sin in its true colours, and ourselves in our real position; we see the Most Holy God as He reveals Himself, the plan of mercy as He propounds it, and the world to come as the Word describes it. Spiritual light has many beams and prismatic colours, but whether they be knowledge, joy, holiness, or life, all are divinely good. If the light received be thus good, what must the essential Light be, and how glorious must be the place where He reveals Himself.

CHARLES SPURGEON

GOD'S POWER AND WISDOM

The wisdom of this world is foolishness in God's sight.

1 CORINTHIANS 3:19

It is indeed true that the brightest manifestation of divine glory finds not one genuine spectator among a hundred. Still, neither His power nor His wisdom is shrouded in darkness. His power is strikingly displayed when the rage of the wicked, to all appearance irresistible, is crushed in a single moment; their arrogance subdued, their strongest bulwarks overthrown, their armour dashed to pieces, their strength broken, their schemes defeated without an effort, and audacity which set itself above the heavens is precipitated to the lowest depths of the earth.

On the other hand, the poor are raised up out of the dust, and the needy lifted out of the dung hill (Psalm 113:7), the oppressed and afflicted are rescued in extremity, the despairing animated with hope, the unarmed defeat the armed, the few the many, the weak the strong. The excellence of the divine wisdom is manifested in distributing everything in due season, confounding the wisdom of the world, and taking the wise in their own craftiness (1 Corinthians 3:19); in short, conducting all things in perfect accordance with reason.

JOHN CALVIN

DO I LOVE HIM ENOUGH?

Though you have not seen him, you love him.

1 PETER 1:8

If we are to be robed in the power of the Lord, we must feel an intense longing for the glory of God and the salvation of the sons of men. Even when we are most successful, we must long for more success. If God has given us many souls, we must pine for a thousand times as many. Satisfaction with results will be the knell of progress. No man is good who thinks that he cannot be better. He has no holiness who thinks that he is holy enough, and he is not useful who thinks that he is useful enough. Desire to honour God grows as we grow.

Can you not sympathize with Mr. Welch, a Suffolk minister, who was noticed to sit and weep; and one said to him, "My dear Mr. Welch, why are you weeping?" "Well," he replied, "I cannot tell you"; but when they pressed him very hard, he answered, "I am weeping because I cannot love Christ more." That was worth weeping for, was it not? That man was noted everywhere for his intense love to his Master; and therefore he wept because he could not love Him more.

CHARLES SPURGEON

FRUIT UNTO HIS GLORY

The LORD gives strength to his people; the
LORD blesses his people with peace.

PSALM 29:11

It is probable that on His declaring Himself to be that King under whom the highest blessing of God was to be expected, they had in derision asked Him to produce His insignia. He bids them enter into their consciences, for "the kingdom of God" is "righteousness, and peace, and joy in the Holy Ghost" (Romans 14:17). Not being earthly or carnal, and so subject to corruption, but spiritual, [the kingdom] raises us even to eternal life, so that we can patiently live at present under toil, hunger, cold, contempt, disgrace, and other annoyances; contented with this, that our King will never abandon us, but will supply our necessities until our warfare is ended, and we are called to triumph: such being the nature of His kingdom, that He communicates to us whatever He received of his Father.

Since then He arms and equips us by His power, adorns us with splendor and magnificence, [and] enriches us with wealth, we here find the most abundant cause of glorying. We can bravely surmount all the insults of the world, and as He replenishes us liberally with His gifts, so we can in our turn bring forth fruit unto His glory.

JOHN CALVIN

GLORY ASCRIBED TO GOD

No flesh should glory in his presence.

1 CORINTHIANS 1:29 KJV

'Tis God's declared design that others should not "glory in his presence," which implies that 'tis His design to advance His own comparative glory. So much the more man "glories in God's presence," so much the less glory is ascribed to God. By its being thus ordered, that the creature should have so absolute and universal a dependence on God, provision is made that God should have our whole souls, and should be the object of our undivided respect.

If we had our dependence partly on God and partly on something else, man's respect would be divided to those different things on which he had dependence. Thus it would be if we depended on God only for a part of our good, and on ourselves or some other being for another part; or if we had our good only from God, and through another that was not God, and in something else distinct from both, our hearts would be divided. But now there is no occasion for this, God being not only He from or of whom we have all good, but also through whom, and one that is that good itself, that we have from Him and through Him.

JONATHAN EDWARDS

THE REST JESUS GIVES

"Come to me, all you who are weary and
burdened, and I will give you rest."

MATTHEW 11:28

L et us yield ourselves wholly to the Great Burden-Bearer, who says, "Come unto Me, and I will give you rest." Possessing this rest, all our faculties will be centred and focused upon one object, and with undivided hearts we shall seek God's glory. When I first began to teach in a Sunday school, I was speaking one day upon the words, "He that believeth on Me hath everlasting life." I was rather taken by surprise when one of the boys said to me, "Teacher, have you got everlasting life?" I replied, "I hope so." The scholar was not satisfied with my answer, so he asked another question, "But, teacher, don't you know?"

The boy was right; there can be no true testimony except that which springs from assured conviction of our own safety and joy in the Lord. We speak that we do know; we believe, and therefore speak. Rest of heart, through coming to Christ, enables us to invite others to Him with great confidence, for we can tell them what heavenly peace He has given to us.

CHARLES SPURGEON

HONOR, PRAISE, AND GLORY

To him who sits on the throne and to
the Lamb be praise and honor and glory
and power, for ever and ever!

REVELATION 5:13

He will surround us with His protection every day like a wall of fire. He will crown us with His free gifts and His compassion. He will dissolve our fears. He will sweeten our bitterness. He will comfort us in all our afflictions, and He will gloriously make us to triumph over all our enemies.

And instead of the way He cried over Jerusalem because of its unbelief and its impenitence, seeing our repentance and our faith He will rejoice in us, taking His great pleasure in us. His saving presence will always remain with us until, when we have passed blessedly through this valley of tears, He will receive us in His heavenly Jerusalem, the true vision of peace, where all our tears will be wiped away and all our mourning will have come to an end.

He will turn our tears into joy, our sighs into thanksgiving, and our wailing into triumphal song, as together with all the saints we take up the chorus of eternal "Hallelujah to him who is on the throne, and to the Lamb, be honor, praise, and glory, forever and ever." So be it.

FRANCIS TURRETIN

LABOR FOR THE LORD

*Whatever you do, work at it with all your
heart, as working for the Lord.*

COLOSSIANS 3:23

Among the toiling multitudes, the journeymen, the day
labourers, the domestic servants, the drudges of the kitchen,
the apostle found, as we find still, some of the Lord's chosen, and
to them he says, "Whatsoever ye do, do it heartily, as to the Lord,
and not unto men; knowing that of the Lord ye shall receive the
reward of the inheritance: for ye serve the Lord Christ." This
saying ennobles the weary routine of earthly employments, and
sheds a halo around the most humble occupations.

To wash feet may be servile, but to wash His feet is royal
work. To unloose the shoe-latchet is poor employ, but to unloose
the great Master's shoe is a princely privilege. The shop, the
barn, the scullery, and the smithy become temples when men
and women do all to the glory of God! Then "divine service" is
not a thing of a few hours and a few places, but all life becomes
holiness unto the Lord, and every place and thing, as conse-
crated as the tabernacle and its golden candlestick.

CHARLES SPURGEON

GOD'S GLORY BRINGS PEACE

Bring an end to the violence of the wicked
and make the righteous secure.

PSALM 7:9

Just as strife must exist where God's glory is not found, as Solomon says [in] Proverbs 13:10, "By pride cometh only contention," so also where God's glory is there must be peace. Why should they quarrel when they know that nothing is their own, but that all they are, have, and can desire is from God? They leave everything in His hands and are content that they have such a gracious God.

From this it follows that where there are true Christians, there is no strife, contention, or discord; as Isaiah says in Isaiah 2:4, "And they shall beat their swords into plowshears, and their spears into pruning hooks; nation shall not lift up sword against nation, neither shall they learn war any more!" Therefore our Lord Christ is called a King of peace, and is represented by King Solomon, whose name implies *rich in peace*, that inwardly He may give us peace in our conscience toward God through faith; and outwardly, that we may exercise love to our fellow men, so that through Him there may be everywhere peace on earth.

MARTIN LUTHER

DUE GLORY

Ascribe to the LORD the glory due his name.

PSALM 29:2

Certainly we will be obliged to recognize and confess it, when we will remember, that everything that He has done, all that was nothing but a pure act of mercy for which we never gave Him any cause. Yes, believers, let us give Him all the glory for it. Let us never sacrifice to our own snares and our own spinning, as if it had been by our merits that we had acquired this advantage. What? Would we dare to pretend to something of God's majesty? Would we dare to flatter ourselves with this thought, that we preceded it, and that He saw something in us more than in the others which obliged Him to choose us for His heritage?

May the doctors of error and of the lie, may the partisans of nature and the enemies of grace say of it what they will: for us, believers who are instructed in a better school, admit frankly that it is He who has preceded in His mercy, who chose us of His pure good pleasure, and that it is only to Him that all of the glory is due for it.

FRANCIS TURRETIN

GLORY DISPLAYED

*For a full 180 days he displayed the vast wealth of his
kingdom and the splendor and glory of his majesty.*

ESTHER 1:4

We speak of a ruler or a great man having achieved an accomplishment with great glory, and that everything passed off gloriously when it has passed off well, successfully, and bravely. Glory does not only mean a great repute, or far-famed honor, but it means also the things which give occasion for the fame, such as costly houses, vessels, clothes, servants, and the like, as Christ says of Solomon: "Consider the lilies of the field, how they grow; they toil not, neither do they spin; yet I say unto you, that even Solomon in all his glory was not arrayed like one of these" (Matthew 6:28–29).

In the book of Esther we read, "King Ahasuerus made a great feast . . . when he showed the riches of his glorious kingdom" (1:3–4). Thus we say: this is a glorious thing, a glorious manner, a glorious deed, *gloriosa res*. This is also what the Evangelist means when he says, "We have seen his glory," to wit, His glorious being and deeds, which are not an insignificant, common glory, but the glory as of the only begotten of the Father.

MARTIN LUTHER

HOW SHALL GLORY BE MANIFEST?

The LORD our God has shown us his glory and his majesty, and we have heard his voice from the fire.

DEUTERONOMY 5:24

God's great design in all His works is the manifestation of His own glory. Any aim less than this were unworthy of Himself. But how shall the glory of God be manifested to such fallen creatures as we are? Man's eye is not single; he has ever a side glance toward his own honour, has too high an estimate of his own powers, and so is not qualified to behold the glory of the Lord. It is clear, then, that self must stand out of the way, that there may be room for God to be exalted; and this is the reason why He bringeth His people ofttimes into straits and difficulties, that, being made conscious of their own folly and weakness, they may be fitted to behold the majesty of God when He comes forth to work their deliverance.

He whose life is one even and smooth path, will see but little of the glory of the Lord, for he has few occasions of self-emptying, and hence, but little fitness for being filled with the revelation of God.

CHARLES SPURGEON

THE GOSPEL EXALTS HIS GLORY

*Glory to God in the highest heaven, and on
earth peace to those on whom his favor rests.*

LUKE 2:14

While the Gospel is a heavenly light that teaches nothing
more than Christ, in whom God's grace is given to us
and all human merit is entirely cast aside, it exalts only the glory
of God, so that henceforth no one may be able to boast of his
own power, but must give God the glory, that it is of His love
and goodness alone that we are saved through Christ. See, the
divine honor, the divine glory, is the light in the Gospel, which
shines around us from heaven through the apostles and their
followers who preach the Gospel. The angel here [in Luke 2]
was in the place of all the preachers of the Gospel, and the shepherds in the place of all the hearers, as we shall see.

For this reason the Gospel can tolerate no other teaching
besides its own. The teaching of men is earthly light and human
glory; it exalts the honor and praise of men, and makes souls to
glory in their own works. The Gospel glories in Christ, in God's
grace and goodness, and teaches us to boast of and confide in
Christ.

MARTIN LUTHER

A DESIRE FOR HIS GLORY

*"I have brought you glory on earth by
finishing the work you gave me to do."*

JOHN 17:4

When we were united by faith to Christ, we were brought into such complete fellowship with Him that we were made one with Him, and His interests and ours became mutual and identical. We have fellowship with Christ in His love. What He loves we love. He loves the saints—so do we. He loves sinners—so do we. He loves the poor perishing race of man, and pants to see earth's deserts transformed into the garden of the Lord—so do we.

We have fellowship with Him in His desires. He desires the glory of God—we also labour for the same. He desires that the saints may be with Him where He is—we desire to be with Him there too. He desires to drive out sin—behold, we fight under His banner. He desires that His Father's name may be loved and adored by all His creatures—we pray daily, "Let thy kingdom come. Thy will be done on earth, even as it is in heaven."

We have fellowship with Christ in His sufferings. In our measure we commune with Him in his labours, ministering to men by the Word of truth and by deeds of love.

CHARLES SPURGEON

DECEMBER 24

MARY GIVES GOD GLORY

My soul glorifies the Lord and my
spirit rejoices in God my Savior.

LUKE 1:46-47

See what a great work the almighty God begins with the humble Mary. Think not that if the Spirit of God had not enlightened her understanding and faith, she would not have been able of her own soul's strength to have believed the angel. She would have regarded the speech of the angel rather as a deception or as a slander. For she, by no means, thought so of herself that she should be the mother of so great and excellent a Son, for the great promise was certainly far above her lowliness.

From this we learn, however, that the understanding of the Word of God and faith in it is not of any human reason or power, but cometh of the grace of God, which illuminates our minds and trains us.

Therefore Mary spoke with reason: "He that is mighty hath done to me great things, yea verily great things, for He hath so graciously spoken to me His lowly handmaiden, who never thought or imagined such a thing before He thus dealt with me."

MARTIN LUTHER

OUR EVERLASTING FEAST

I pray that the eyes of your heart may be
enlightened in order that you may know
the hope to which he has called you.

EPHESIANS 1:18

The redeemed have all their objective good in God. God Himself is the great good which they are brought to the possession and enjoyment of by redemption. He is the highest good and the sum of all that good which Christ purchased. God is the inheritance of the saints; He is the portion of their souls. God is their wealth and treasure, their food, their life, their dwelling place, their ornament and diadem, and their everlasting honor and glory.

They have none in heaven but God; He is the great good which the redeemed are received to at death, and which they are to rise to at the end of the world. The Lord God, He is the light of the heavenly Jerusalem; and is the "river of the water of life" that runs, and "the tree of life that grows, in the midst of the paradise of God." The glorious excellencies and beauty of God will be what will forever entertain the minds of the saints, and the love of God will be their everlasting feast.

JONATHAN EDWARDS

BEHOLD HIS PERFECTION

One thing I ask from the LORD . . . to
gaze on the beauty of the LORD.

PSALM 27:4

Since the perfection of blessedness consists in the knowledge of God, He has been pleased, in order that none might be excluded from the means of obtaining felicity, not only to deposit in our minds that seed of religion of which we have already spoken, but so to manifest His perfections in the whole structure of the universe, and daily place Himself in our view, that we cannot open our eyes without being compelled to behold Him. His essence, indeed, is incomprehensible, utterly transcending all human thought; but on each of His works His glory is engraven in characters so bright, so distinct, and so illustrious that none, however dull and illiterate, can plead ignorance as their excuse.

Hence, with perfect truth, the psalmist exclaims, "He covereth himself with light as with a garment" (Psalm 104:2), as if he had said that God for the first time was arrayed in visible attire when, in the creation of the world, He displayed those glorious banners, on which, to whatever side we turn, we behold His perfections visibly portrayed.

JOHN CALVIN

WINNING GLORY

Lord, all my desire is before thee.

PSALM 38:9 KJV

There is naught that can fill the heart of man except the Trinity. God has made man's heart a triangle. Men have been for centuries trying to make the globe fill the triangle, but they cannot do it; it is the Trinity alone that can fill a triangle, as old Quarles well says. There is no way of getting satisfaction but by gaining Christ, getting heaven, winning glory, getting the covenant, for the word *covenant* comprises all the other things.

"All my desire," says the psalmist. I nothing want on earth, happy in my Savior's love. I have not a desire, I have nothing to do but to live and be happy all my life in the company of Christ, and then to ascend to heaven, to be in His immediate presence, where "millions of years these wondering eyes shall o'er my Savior's beauties rove, and endless ages I'll adore the wonders of his love."

CHARLES SPURGEON

STAYING STAIN-FREE

Do not share in the sins of others. Keep yourself pure.

1 TIMOTHY 5:22

Ever since God exhibited Himself to us as a Father, we must be convicted of extreme ingratitude if we do not in turn exhibit ourselves as His sons. Ever since He ingrafted us into His body, we, who are His members, should anxiously beware of contracting any stain or taint. Ever since He who is our Head ascended to heaven, it is befitting in us to withdraw our affections from the earth, and with our whole soul aspire to heaven. Ever since the Holy Spirit dedicated us as temples to the Lord, we should make it our endeavor to show forth the glory of God, and guard against being profaned by the defilement of sin. Ever since our soul and body were destined to heavenly incorruptibility and an unfading crown, we should earnestly strive to keep them pure and uncorrupted against the day of the Lord.

These, I say, are the surest foundations of a well-regulated life, and you will search in vain for anything resembling them among philosophers, who, in their commendation of virtue, never rise higher than the natural dignity of man.

JOHN CALVIN

WE GLORY IN THE LORD

"This is to my Father's glory, that you bear much fruit, showing yourselves to be my disciples."

JOHN 15:8

The Christian's holiness becomes a tree of life. I suppose it means a living tree, a tree calculated to give life and sustain it in others. A fruit becomes a tree! A tree of life! Wonderful result this! Christ in the Christian produces a character which becomes a tree of life. The outward character is the fruit of the inner life; this outer life itself grows from a fruit into a tree, and as a tree it bears fruit in others to the praise and glory of God.

Dear brothers and sisters, I know some of God's saints who live very near to Him, and they are evidently a tree of life, for their very shadow is comforting, cooling, and refreshing to many weary souls. I have known the young, the tried, the downcast, go to them, sit beneath their shade, and pour out the tale of their troubles, and they have felt it a rich blessing to receive their sympathy, to be told of the faithfulness of the Lord, and to be guided in the way of wisdom.

CHARLES SPURGEON

GREAT HONOR AND PROFOUND RESPECT

*Yours, L ORD, is the greatness and the power and
the glory and the majesty and the splendor, for
everything in heaven and earth is yours.*

1 CHRONICLES 29:11

By the creature's being thus wholly and universally dependent on God, it appears that the creature is nothing and that
God is all. Hereby it appears that God is infinitely above us; that
God's strength and wisdom and holiness are infinitely greater
than ours. However great and glorious the creature apprehends
God to be, yet if he be not sensible of the difference between God
and him, so as to see that God's glory is great compared with
his own, he will not be disposed to give God the glory due to
His name.

If the creature, in any respect, sets himself upon a level with
God, or exalts himself to any competition with Him, however
he may apprehend that great honor and profound respect may
belong to God from those that are more inferior, and at a greater
distance, he will not be so sensible of its being due from him. So
much the more men exalt themselves, so much the less will they
surely be disposed to exalt God.

JONATHAN EDWARDS

PROCLAIMING GOD'S GLORY

By faith we understand that the universe was
formed at God's command, so that what is
seen was not made out of what was visible.

HEBREWS 11:3

We know God, who is Himself invisible, only through His works. This is the reason why the Lord, that He may invite us to the knowledge of Himself, places the fabric of heaven and earth before our eyes, rendering Himself, in a certain manner, manifest in them. For His eternal power and Godhead (as Paul says) are there exhibited (Romans 1:20).

And that declaration of David is most true, that the heavens, though without a tongue, are yet eloquent heralds of the glory of God, and that this most beautiful order of nature silently proclaims His admirable wisdom (Psalm 19:1). This is the more diligently to be observed, because so few pursue the right method of knowing God, while the greater part adhere to the creatures without any consideration of the Creator Himself.

For men are commonly subject to these two extremes; namely that some, forgetful of God, apply the whole force of their mind to the consideration of nature; and others, overlooking the works of God, aspire with a foolish and insane curiosity to inquire into his Essence. Both labor in vain.

JOHN CALVIN

BIBLIOGRAPHY

Beza, Theodore. *A Complete Summary of Christianity (summa totius christianismi).* Grand Rapids, MI: Reformed Reprints, 2012.

Beza, Theodore. *Faith and Justification.* New York, NY: Fig Books, 2012.

Beza, Theodore. *Select Works of Theodore Beza.* 1561.

Calvin, John. *Calvin's Complete Bible Commentaries.* Ada, MI: Baker Books, 2009.

Calvin, John. *Institutes of the Christian Religion.* Peabody, MA: Hendrickson Publishers, 2007.

Edwards, Jonathan. *The Complete Works of Jonathan Edwards: Christ Exalted, Sinners in the Hands of an Angry God, A Divine and Supernatural Light, Christian Knowledge, On. . . .* New Haven, CT: Yale University Press, 2015.

Edwards, Jonathan, *A History on the Work of Redemption.* New Haven, CT: Yale University Press, 1989.

Edwards, Jonathan. *Selected Sermons of Jonathan Edwards.* New Haven, CT: Yale University Press, 2015.

Luther, Martin. *Commentary on the Epistle to the Galatians.* Miami, FL: HardPress, 2017.

Luther, Martin. *The Complete Works of Martin Luther: Volume 1, Sermons 1–12.* Harrington, DE: Delmarva Publications, Inc., 2013.

Luther, Martin. *The Great Orators of the Reformation Era.* Shawnee, KS: Gideon House Books, 2017.

Needham, George C., ed. *The Life and Labors of Charles H. Spurgeon.* New York, NY: BiblioLife, 2009.

Spurgeon, Charles H. *All of Grace.* Nashville, TN: B&H Publishing Group, 2017.

Spurgeon, Charles H. *An All-Round Ministry: Addresses to Ministers and Students.* Canton, OH: Pinnacle Press, 2017.

Spurgeon, Charles H. *Christian Classics: Six Books by Charles Spurgeon in a Single Collection.* New York, NY: Niche Edition, 2011.

Spurgeon, Charles H. *The Complete Works of Charles Spurgeon: Volume 1, Sermons 1–53.* Harrington, DE: Delmarva Publications, Inc., 2013.

Spurgeon, Charles H. *Morning and Evening: A Devotional Daily Encouragement.* Peabody, MA: Hendrickson Publishers, 2010.

Spurgeon, Charles H. *The Soul–Winner: How to Lead Sinners to the Saviour.* London: Forgotten Books, 2018.

Spurgeon, Charles H. *Till He Come: Communion Meditations and Addresses.* Dallas, TX: Gideon House Books, 2016.

Turretin, Francis. *The Atonement of Christ.* London: Counted Faithful, 2017.

Turretin, Francis. *"The Happiness of the People of God" Sermon on Psalm 33:12.* San Diego, CA: Thaddeus Publications, 2010.

Turretin, Francis. *"Jesus' Tears for Jerusalem" Sermon on Luke 19:41, 42.* San Diego, CA: Thaddeus Publications, 2010.

Turretin, Francis. *The Substitutionary Atonement of Jesus Christ.* Crossville, TN: Puritan Publications, 2005, 2014.

Zwingli, Ulrich. *The Christian Education of Youth.* Shawnee, KS: Gideon House Books, 2011.

Zwingli, Ulrich. *On Providence: And Other Essays.* Durham, NC: Labyrinth Press, 1922.

Zwingli, Ulrich. *Selected Works.* Philadelphia: University of Pennsylvania, 1901.

SOURCES BY DATE

JANUARY

1. Spurgeon, 93.
2. *Orators*, 55.
3. *Sermons*, 206.
4. Spurgeon, 94.
5. *Institutes*, 609.
6. *Morning*, 5.
7. *Morning*, 178.
8. *Orators*, 55.
9. *Morning*, 218.
10. *Complete*, 188.
11. *Morning*, 203.
12. *Galatians*, 32–33.
13. *Classics*, 382.
14. *Galatians*, 112.
15. *All-Round*, 69.
16. *Orators*, 77.
17. *Morning*, 34.
18. *Galatians*, 65.
19. *History*, 291.
20. *Morning*, 42.
21. *Galatians*, 169–170.
22. *Morning*, 44.
23. *History*, 182.
24. *Happiness*, 12.
25. *Classics*, 292.
26. *Institutes*, 80.
27. *Morning*, 22.
28. Ibid., 179.
29. Turretin, 15.
30. *Morning*, 148.
31. *History*, 290.

FEBRUARY

1. *Galatians*, 147.
2. *Classic*, 294.
3. *Orators*, 60.
4. *Classics*, 127.

5. *Calvin*, Vol. 1, 62.
6. *Till,* 187.
7. *Happiness*, 13.
8. *Morning,* 135.
9. *Morning,* 184.
10. *Orators*, 53.
11. *Life, 582.*
12. *Complete*, 162.
13. Spurgeon, 316.
14. *Orators,* 79.
15. Edwards, 618.
16. *Classics*, 2.
17. *Till, 63.*

18. *Institutes*, 71.
19. *All-Round*, 26.
20. *Institutes*, 92.
21. *Morning*, 157.
22. *Galatians*, 149.
23. *Institutes*, 383.
24. *Complete*, 190.
25. *Morning*, 127.
26. *All-Round,* 20.
27. *Galatians*, 60.
28. *Classics*, 135.
29. *Galatians*, 21.

MARCH

1. *Morning,* 25.
2. *Select*, Kindle Locations, 488–490.
3. *Complete, 160.*
4. *Classics,* 113.
5. *Galatians*, 163.
6. *Institutes*, 171.
7. Spurgeon, 540.
8. *All-Round,* 119.
9. *Galatians*, 21–22.
10. *Morning,* 65.
11. *Morning,* 26.
12. *Galatians*, 140.

13. *Morning, 131.*
14. *Grace,* 44.
15. *Orators*, 80.
16. *Institutes*, 356.
17. Edwards, 44.
18. *Grace,* 57.
19. *Sermons*, 206.
20. *Galatians*, 84.
21. Spurgeon, 206.
22. *Orators*, 82.
23. *Institutes*, 357.
24. Spurgeon, 207.
25. *Galatians*, 30–31.

26. *Providence*, 268.
27. *Grace*, 80.
28. *Galatians*, 70.
29. *Classics*, 194.

30. *Institutes*, 366.
31. Spurgeon, Kindle Locations, 207.

APRIL

1. *Galatians*, 71.
2. *Classics*, 110.
3. *Institutes*, 284.
4. *Grace,* 65.
5. *Institutes*, 368.
6. Spurgeon, 206.
7. *Galatians*, 43.
8. *Institutes*, 369.
9. Spurgeon, 205.
10. *Institutes*, 373.
11. *Grace,* 76.
12. *Galatians*, 146.
13. *Grace,* 76.
14. *Institutes*, 358.
15. *Galatians*, 7.

16. *Grace,* 99.
17. Calvin, 14.
18. *Galatians*, 27.
19. Spurgeon, 208.
20. Calvin, 16.
21. Edwards, 412.
22. Calvin, 175.
23. Spurgeon, 208.
24. Edwards, 83.
25. Calvin, 195.
26. *Galatians*, 69.
27. Edwards, 579.
28. *Classics*, 112.
29. *Beza,* 64.
30. *Galatians*, 43.

MAY

1. *Institutes*, 359.
2. *Grace,* 66.
3. *Galatians*, 31.
4. *Select,* 69.
5. Spurgeon, 207.

6. *Galatians*, 42.
7. *Institutes*, 356.
8. *Grace,* 66.
9. *Select,* 10.
10. *Galatians*, 43–44.

11. *Classics*, 43.

12. *Sermons*, 206.

13. *Galatians*, 44.

14. *Classics*, 43.

15. *Select*, 29.

16. *Galatians*, 51.

17. Spurgeon, 206.

18. *Galatians*, 53.

19. *Select*, 231.

20. Spurgeon, 209.

21. *Galatians*, 78.

22. Edwards, 112.

23. *Classics*, 239.

24. *Galatians*, 68.

25. Spurgeon, 205.

26. Calvin, 407.

27. Spurgeon, 206.

28. *Grace,* 49.

29. *Zwingli,* 64.

30. Calvin, 227.

31. *Sermons*, 206.

JUNE

1. Calvin, 209.

2. *Zwingli,* 94.

3. *Orators*, 74.

4. *Grace,* 45.

5. *Orators*, 134.

6. *Institutes*, 341.

7. *Orators*, 134.

8. *Atonement*, 35.

9. *Sermons*, 206.

10. *Grace,* 19.

11. Calvin, 230.

12. *Grace,* 51.

13. *Sermons*, 206.

14. *Grace,* 145.

15. *Galatians*, 19.

16. Spurgeon, 242.

17. *Galatians*, 5.

18. *Sermons*, 206.

19. *Grace,* 19.

20. Calvin, 104.

21. *Grace,* 14.

22. Calvin, Vol. 7, 149.

23. *Grace,* 18.

24. Calvin, Vol. 7, 150.

25. *Grace,* 41.

26. Calvin, Vol. 7, 153.

27. *Grace,* 42.

28. *Galatians*, 93.

29. *Grace,* 123.

30. *Complete*, 71.

JULY

1. Calvin, 237.
2. *Classics*, 143.
3. *Complete*, 9.
4. Calvin, 188.
5. *Galatians*, 112.
6. *Atonement*, 57.
7. *Galatians*, 113.
8. *Summary*, 15.
9. *Spurgeon*, 132.
10. *Orators*, 58.
11. *Sermons*, 206.
12. Calvin, 322.
13. Spurgeon, 146.
14. *Orators*, 68.
15. Calvin, 311.
16. Spurgeon, 283.
17. *Sermons*, 206.
18. Spurgeon, 240.
19. Calvin, 300.
20. *Providence*, 243.
21. *Morning*, 324.
22. *Institutes*, 194.
23. *Morning*, 10.
24. *Complete*, 133.
25. Calvin, 400.
26. *Complete*, 252.
27. *Sermons*, 206.
28. Calvin, 246.
29. *Sermons*, 206.
30. Calvin, 295.
31. *Complete*, 100.

AUGUST

1. Calvin, 182.
2. *Grace*, 50.
3. Calvin, 208.
4. *Sermons*, 206.
5. Calvin, 209.
6. *Grace*, 51.
7. Calvin, 215.
8. *Institutes*, 270.
9. Edwards, 115.
10. *Morning*, 124.
11. *Institutes*, 86.
12. *Morning*, 215.
13. *Edwards*, 134.
14. *Grace*, 26.
15. *Atonement*, 91.
16. *Institutes*, 329.

17. *Complete*, 133.
18. *Classics*, 107.
19. *Institutes*, 269.
20. Edwards, 571.
21. *Institutes*, 311.
22. Edwards, 498.
23. Edwards, 243.
24. *Classics*, 177.

25. *Classics*, 119.
26. Edwards, 446.
27. *Complete,* 20.
28. *Classics*, 100.
29. *Complete*, 96.
30. Edwards, 266.
31. *Complete*, 79.

SEPTEMBER

1. Edwards, 552.
2. *Grace,* 59.
3. *Complete,* 257.
4. *Classics*, 122.
5. *Complete*, 15.
6. *Providence*, 241.
7. *Complete*, 74.
8. *Institutes*, 86.
9. Edwards, 232.
10. *Institutes*, 86.
11. *Grace,* 58.
12. *Institutes*, 275.
13. *Providence*, 242.
14. *Institutes*, 310.
15. *Classics*, 118.
16. *Institutes*, 313.
17. *Atonement*, 105.
18. *Institutes*, 321.

19. *Sermons*, 206.
20. *Institutes*, 321.
21. Edwards, 510.
22. *Providence*, 244.
23. *Institutes*, 327.
24. *Atonement*, 100–101.
25. *Institutes*, 327.
26. *Institutes*, 327.
27. *Atonement*, 101–102.
28. *Institutes*, 314.
29. *Atonement*, 70–71.
30. *Institutes*, 73.

OCTOBER

1. *Orators*, 54.
2. *Classics*, 99.
3. *Institutes*, 270.
4. *Morning, 7.*
5. *Atonement*, 68.
6. *Institutes,* 334.
7. *Classics*, Vol. 5, 11.
8. *Sermons*, 206.
9. *Institutes*, 319.
10. *Atonement,* 69–70.
11. *Institutes*, 326.
12. *Works,* 78.
13. *Institutes*, 74.
14. *Sermons*, 206.
15. *All-Round, 249.*
16. *Institutes*, 334.
17. Edwards, 169.
18. *Morning, 17.*
19. *Atonement*, 105–106.
20. *Atonement*, 106–107.
21. *Providence*, 241.
22. *Classics*, 16.
23. Edwards, 14.
24. Calvin, 210.
25. Edwards, 271.
26. *Classics*, 188.
27. Edwards, 205.
28. *All Round, 177.*
29. Edwards, 206.
30. *Classics*, 26.
31. Edwards, 210.

NOVEMBER

1. *Morning, 254.*
2. Edwards, 489.
3. *Morning, 370.*
4. Edwards, 230.
5. *Morning, 643.*
6. Edwards, 230.
7. Edwards, 231.
8. *Classics*, 9.
9. Edwards, 234.
10. *Grace, 74.*
11. Edwards, 236.
12. *Classics*, 209.
13. *Providence*, 239.
14. *Classics*, 133.
15. Edwards, 530.
16. *Classics*, 43.

17. Edwards, 352.
18. *All-Round, 7.*
19. Edwards, 26.
20. *Classics, 7.*
21. Calvin, 386.
22. Edwards, 260.
23. *All-Round, 9.*

24. Edwards, 456.
25. *Institutes*, 98.
26. *Zwingli,* 84.
27. *Classics,* 141.
28. *Orators,* 45.
29. *Calvin,* 205.
30. *Classics,* 152.

DECEMBER

1. *Orators,* 142.
2. *Classics,* 43.
3. *Happiness,* 13.
4. *Galatians,* 169.
5. Spurgeon, 84.
6. Spurgeon, 297.
7. *Complete,* 354.
8. *Morning, 19.*
9. *Complete,* 156.
10. *Classics,* 5.
11. *Institutes,* 21.
12. *All-Round, 227.*
13. *Institutes,* 320.
14. *Sermons,* 206.
15. *Till, 130.*
16. Turretin, 17.
17. *Morning, 692.*
18. *Complete,* 117.
19. *Happiness,* 14.

20. *Complete,* 156.
21. *Classics,* 19.
22. *Complete,* 107.
23. *Classics,* 23.
24. *Orators,* 70.
25. *Sermons,* 206.
26. *Institutes,* 16.
27. *Spurgeon,* 413.
28. *Institutes,* 446.
29. *Soul,* 131.
30. *Sermons,* 206.
31. Calvin, 20.

NOTES

JANUARY 1–MARCH 13

1. See Lombard, lib. 2 dist. 2, sqq.
2. Colossians 1:28; 2 Timothy 3:16–17.
3. John 15:15; 16:13.
4. John 20:30–31.
5. William Cowper, 1719.

MARCH 14–MAY 27

1. Source unknown.
2. Source unknown.
3. Romans 1:17; 3:21–27; 4:3; 5:1; 9:30–33; 11:6; Galatians 2:16–21; 3:9–10, 18; Philippians 3:9; 2 Timothy 1:9; Titus 3:5; Hebrews 11:7.
4. *De Civitate Dei*, lib. 11, ch. 2.
5. Romans 10:2–4; Mark 16:15–16; Romans 1:28; Galatians 1:8–9.
6. Romans 8:16, 38; Ephesians 3:12; Hebrews 10:22–23; 1 John 4:13, 5:19; Romans 3:27, 4:20; 1 Corinthians 4:4, 9:26–27.
7. Ephesians 1:17; Philippians 1:29; 2 Thessalonians 3:2.
8. Matthew 29:19–20; Acts 6:4; Romans 10:17; James 1:18; 1 Peter 1:23–25.